THE SIGN OF HIS COMING

THE SIGN OF HIS COMING

by

S<small>ID</small> L<small>EVETT</small> & G<small>EOFF</small> H<small>ENSTOCK</small>

The Christadelphian
404 Shaftmoor Lane
Hall Green
Birmingham B28 8SZ, UK

2013

First published 2013

ISBN 978-0-85189-246-7

Printed and bound in Malta by
GUTENBERG PRESS LIMITED

CONTENTS

PREFACE

PROPHECY is not simply historical facts and predictions of events yet to occur. Prophecy is integral to the Gospel message; it is not a 'sundry extra'. It is essential to a full appreciation of God. If the prophesied events of the future do not take place there is no salvation. An understanding of past events helps us to perceive the character of God and His workings with the nations and His people, both spiritual and natural.

Our aim has been to produce a relatively easy-to-read book on prophecy as we see no reason why this subject should be written in a complicated style. Some may wish that it were shorter, whilst others may have preferred more information on certain topics. We have, however, chosen a middle course which we hope will satisfy the majority of readers.

Those who want to pursue certain topics in greater detail can refer to the recommended reading material. Most chapters can be read independently of others but reading them consecutively will provide a 'flow' of the outworking of prophecy both in events that have occurred and those yet to take place, in particular as they relate to the promises made to the patriarchs which are at the heart of the Gospel message.

Much of the subject matter will be well known to those of a generation brought up on Sunday evening lectures and reading the works of respected brethren. We have, however, aimed to present our material in a different style from that commonly utilised in books on prophecy. We have also included information on a number of not so well known matters. Hopefully that will assist readers to see the broad spread of events that brought certain prophecies to a conclusion. The reader may also understand the excitement that gripped Bible students as they saw the beginnings of events that ultimately led to the restoration of God's people, albeit with some unexpected happenings along the way.

We also review matters that will occur prior to the establishment of God's kingdom. In so doing, we note that past events often occurred over time frames and in ways which differed considerably from those many Bible students had expected. It therefore follows that we should not expect precision about future events and we examine both long-held views and some options.

The all-important message we wish to convey is the sense of awe and privilege we should have in being members of God's household, holding an awareness of His dealings with the nations in the past, with a consequent confidence that prophesied future events will indeed occur. He inhabits eternity but is also a God who walks with those of a "humble and contrite heart" and His presence is with us.

Overall we hope that the book will provide the reader with a greater awareness of God's workings, especially over the past 120 years, as events relating to Israel's return began to become apparent. Those ongoing events point to the nearness of Christ's return. We must keep that in our minds as we continue to serve Him in an increasingly secular society.

The greatest sign God has given us is the restoration of His people to Israel and the ongoing world attention on that region. Other signs, such as those from the Olivet Prophecy, add to our understanding of events preceding the return of Christ, but the countdown began with Israel's return to the land.

May we continue to watch all the signs God has given us and perceive the greatness of the precious promises we have embraced as members of His household.

ACKNOWLEDGEMENTS

WE have appreciated the encouragement of brothers and sisters who expressed an interest in a new book on prophecy and provided suggestions on topics for inclusion. We apologise if some preferred topics have not been included and trust that the material provided will assist readers to perceive the vastness of God's activity in bringing many prophecies to a conclusion. In so doing may they be encouraged to watch for signs of great events to come. We thank those who provided observations on specific chapters and we express our indebtedness to Sister Anne Melles and Brother Ivan Woods for their careful review of all material and their advice on grammar, sentence structure and general clarity.

Finally, our thanks to our respective wives who have endured our pre-occupation with the project, have read and commented on the whole book and spent many hours absent from us having granted permission for us to spend much time at our desks immersed in papers and books.

SID LEVETT AND GEOFF HENSTOCK

1

AN AGREEMENT ABOVE ALL AGREEMENTS

THE future fascinates most people: a time not yet experienced but often debated. For those in previous eras what was the future is now the present or has passed, but our future still lies ahead; the future for all believers in God, past and present, remains to be revealed. Because of the enormous significance of what is to come upon the earth – for the planet and for each man and woman – it is important that we give the matter serious consideration.

Effective consideration of future events requires an understanding of past events. In planning for the future in any field of enterprise it is common practice to go back some period of time to set the scene. A relatively short period of time will often be sufficient. The God we worship, however, inhabits eternity, so when considering events that God has in store for the future we must go back thousands of years to find the background to what lies ahead.

By this we have already identified that we are dealing with a planning exercise that far exceeds any ever put in place by mankind. We are treading here on awesome ground. Man is time bound: things men and women set in place, whether physical or conceptual, have finite time periods. They generally either moulder away or fall out of vogue. Not so the things of God. A consideration of the future plan of God is not an academic exercise. It is instead a participation in a process restricted to those with a "mind of the spirit" capable of perceiving and believing that what God has said will occur, will indeed occur. Others might intellectually understand what has been revealed but cannot perceive its reality because they regard it as foolishness:

> "The natural person does not accept the things of the Spirit of God, for they are folly to him, and he is not able to understand them because they are spiritually discerned."
>
> (1 Corinthians 2:14)

To commence our consideration we need to go back some 4,000 years to the beginning of a chain of events that continues to play out and will reach a conclusion in time to come. Nothing in the history of mankind comes anywhere near a concept such as this. It is the believers' privilege to be aware of what has been, what is and what is yet to occur.

The Beginning

Around 2,000 years before the birth of Christ, events that would bring about that birth were set in train. In so doing we see a key development in that even earlier enigmatic event in the Garden of Eden in which God stated that there would be enmity between the seed of the woman and the seed of the serpent (Genesis 3:15). In the city of Ur in Mesopotamia, now Iraq, lived a man named Abram, later changed to Abraham, who stood out from the crowd by virtue of his faith and was noted by God. A method of worship not known to us but prescribed by God must have existed at the time. Abraham followed that way of worship. Furthermore he obviously followed it from the heart, not solely by outward observation.

1

Because of his faith God called him to a mighty purpose. The effect of this cannot be overstated for it underpins God's dealings with His people Israel, the Gospel message and what is yet to occur upon the earth. What is more, it underpins the calling of God's household and that affects each one of us.

God called upon Abraham to leave Ur and journey to a land that God would show him, saying:

> "I will make of you a great nation, and I will bless you and make your name great, so that you will be a blessing. I will bless those who bless you, and him who dishonours you I will curse, and in you all the families of the earth shall be blessed." (Genesis 12:2,3)

Abraham obeyed the command of God and shortly thereafter, when he reached the land to which God directed him, this promise was expanded with a very significant addition:

> "Abram passed through the land unto the place of Shechem, unto the oak of Moreh. And the Canaanite was then in the land. And the LORD appeared unto Abram, and said, Unto thy seed will I give this land." (verses 6,7, RV)

This is significant; it makes clear that the existing inhabitants of the land would be dispossessed and the land given to Abraham's seed in due course. And this promise was made at Shechem – a city today located in the West Bank, territory claimed by the Palestinians but occupied since 1967 by Israel.

The promises in Genesis 12 were further expanded in the next chapter:

> "The LORD said unto Abram ... Lift up now thine eyes, and look from the place where thou art, northward and southward and eastward and westward: for all the land which thou seest, to thee will I give it , and to thy seed for ever." (13:14,15, RV)

The boundaries are more fully defined in Genesis 15:18-21. It is interesting that after receiving this promise Abraham was invited to walk through the land he had been promised, and the first place he visited was Hebron – also today located in the West Bank and a centre of tension between Palestinian and Jewish residents.

There are three key issues from this record that continue to the present day:

- A great nation would descend from Abraham.
- A blessing would be available to all people (other than those who curse Abraham and his seed).
- The land of Canaan, then occupied by other peoples, would be given to Abraham and his seed for ever.

Still relevant today

For those who have been aware of the promises from an early age, the 'gloss' of their importance may have worn off. However, these are particularly significant matters of which most of mankind is unaware and which have even bypassed many of those who have some familiarity with the word of God. The continuing significance is brought home to us by the writings of the Apostle Paul:

> "You are all sons of God, through faith. For as many of you as were baptized into Christ have put on Christ. There is neither Jew nor Greek, there is neither slave nor free, there is neither male nor female, for you are all one in Christ Jesus. And if you are Christ's, then you are Abraham's offspring, heirs according to promise." (Galatians 3:26-29)

God's promise to Abraham is not a thing of the past. It is an ongoing, active agreement with all aspects of it remaining current. The continuing existence of the Jewish people as an identifiable race provides evidence of the "great nation" part. The "blessing" of salvation is available to all who believe the Gospel message and are baptised. The presence of Jews once again in the land known as Israel brings the third part of the promise into play. Even those who completely discount the Biblical record are aware that Israel claims a God-given right to the land. Of itself that does not prove that they must remain there for ever (the exiles who returned after the Babylonian captivity also believed that they had a God-given right to the land), but those who believe God's word have confidence that the promise will be completely fulfilled. We hope that the information contained in this book will help the reader to see the wonder of fulfilled prophecy and its relevance for events which are unfolding in the world today; more importantly, we hope that consideration of these matters will generate confidence about the certainty of future events that have been foretold.

Blessed with understanding

It is a privilege to know of the ongoing activity of these promises as generally the churches have for centuries contended that they relate to 'Christian' believers and not to Israel. Some evangelical groups, however, are an exception as, particularly since 1967, they have come to accept the prophecies relating to Israel, whilst retaining conventional church doctrine. The Catholic Church, in particular, rejects application to Israel and it is of interest that in recent times they have seen fit to reiterate that opinion. In October 2010, bishops from the Middle East met for two weeks at the Vatican and at the concluding session, chaired by Pope Benedict XVI, issued an official statement including the following:

- The concept of the Promised Land cannot be used as a basis to justify the return of the Jews to Israel and the displacement of the Palestinians.
- For Christians, one can no longer talk of the land promised to the Jewish people. There is no longer a chosen people. All men and women of all countries have become the chosen people – the 'promise' was abolished by the presence of Christ.[1]

The political bias behind this is quite apparent and clearly no credence has been given to Paul's statement:

"I ask, then, has God rejected his people? By no means! For I myself am an Israelite, a descendant of Abraham, a member of the tribe of Benjamin. God has not rejected his people whom he foreknew."   (Romans 11:1,2)

Lessons for today from Ur

In our current technological age it may seem inconceivable that someone from 4,000 years ago could be an example for life in our time. If we cannot perceive of a life without modern technology such as laptops, the internet or even electric hairdryers, depending on our preferences, we may particularly struggle to see the relevance.

The broad principles and challenges of life have remained unaltered throughout the centuries. Abraham lived in one of the most sophisticated cities of that era – a city in which the majority cared little about the God of the universe. Nothing has changed. By and large the interests of most people are limited to the daily affairs of business, the home, entertainment and personal comforts.

Styles may have changed but principles have not. We must be the 'Abrahams' of the cities and towns in which we live. By necessity we participate in many of the daily affairs of society, but we do so

1 *The Jerusalem Post*, October 23, 2010.

"as unto the Lord". Certain activities of the present world are clearly to be avoided completely and others to be restricted. The promises gave Abraham a basis from which he sought to serve God in his generation and they can do the same for us. God's revealed word contains examples of lifestyles and an understanding of what is to come upon this world. May our consideration of the people and the events help us to see more clearly the greatness of knowing God and the Lord Jesus Christ.

Further Reading

Brother Harry Whittaker, *Abraham – Father of the faithful*.

2

DISPERSED TO ALL CORNERS

SOME 2,000 years after the promises were given to him, a large nation had descended from Abraham but we find it at a very low point in its history. Defeated, demoralised and dejected, the people of Israel were dispersed in part from their land in AD 70 and essentially in full in AD 135, with just a few poor Jews remaining in their ancient homeland.

It is not the intention of this book to provide a history of the Jewish people, but an outline of the Biblical period and some information on their subsequent dispersal across the globe is called for. If history is not your preferred topic, may we suggest that you at least skim through the information in this chapter. A detailed knowledge of the dispersal and later growth of the Jews is not essential for perceiving the outcome of certain prophecies but it will assist in understanding the background to the prevailing circumstances.

Timeline of Jewish History
BC

2166	Abraham
1446	Exodus from Egypt
1406	Entry into Canaan
1375	Period of the Judges commences
1050	Saul
1010	David
971	Solomon
931	Divided into 2 Kingdoms
721	Israel (10 tribes) to Assyria
587	Judah (2 tribes) to Babylon
539	Persian Rule
538	Return from Babylon
332	Greek Rule
142	Hasmoneans (Jewish)
63	Roman Rule

AD

70	Destruction of Temple
135	Banishment from the land
330	Byzantium Rule
636	Commencement of Rule by various Muslim groups
1517	Ottoman (Turkish) Rule commences
1917	Balfour Declaration and the British remove the Turks from Palestine
1920	British Mandate of Palestine
1948	State of Israel proclaimed
1967	Israel captures Jerusalem

Turbulent times

A very turbulent four centuries preceded the birth of Christ and the fall of Jerusalem 75 years later. Alexander the Great, conqueror of Egypt, Persia and the area later called Palestine, entered Jerusalem in 332 BC after the city sensibly surrendered to him without a battle. Although Alexander died in 323 BC at the age of thirty-three, Greek occupation continued and introduced the Hellenistic era which had a marked influence on Jewish culture and religion. There was an increase in building activity, creation of works of art and the introduction of Greek language, theatres, stadiums and gymnasiums. Many Jews took to this with fervour to show that they were 'enlightened', and it was rich, aristocratic priestly families who led the way. The lesson for us in a world that prides itself in human achievements and 'sophistication' is apparent.

Inevitably the adoption of Greek ways led to conflict with those who wished to maintain the ways of their fathers. Various groupings were established, one being the group of the 'pious' (Hasidim) from which the party of the Pharisees later came. A group of radically pious Jews called the Essenes was also formed, some of whom went to live in the wilderness. A third group was the Hellenistic influenced Sadducees consisting mainly of the leading aristocratic families and priests.

Matters came to a head in 167 BC when Antiochus IV Epiphanes (a descendant of Seleucus, one of Alexander's four generals) banned adherence to the Law of Moses and built an altar to Zeus in the temple, thus fulfilling the primary application of the "abomination of desolation" (Daniel 11:31).

The time had come for an uprising by those committed to the Jewish way of life. It occurred three years later headed by Judas Maccabeus, of the priestly Hasmonean family, who led a successful series of battles against the Seleucid troops. The desecrated temple was rededicated, and the event is recognised to the present time by the Feast of Hanukkah (Purification). Success over the Greek Seleucids led to the establishment of the Hasmonean dynasty which, by a resolution of an assembly of priests and elders in 141 BC, provided the appointed "leader and high priest forever until there should arise a faithful prophet". The resolution was acknowledged by the Roman Senate, the Romans by this time having replaced the Greeks as the prevailing power in the region.

Continuing periods of dissension in the ruling family led to civil war, causing the Roman legions under Pompey to enter Jerusalem in 63 BC and take control of the region known as Judea (i.e., land of the Jews.) The Romans allowed the Jews to administer the region as a semi-independent state and appointed John Hyrcanus II of the Hasmonean family as High Priest, but restricted his previous secular authority by appointing Antipater as Procurator. Antipater's son, Herod, was appointed King of Judea by the Romans in 37 BC and was the infamous ruling monarch at the time of the birth of Christ. After Herod's death in 4 BC Judea came under direct Roman administration.

Jewish dissent

A Jewish uprising commenced in AD 66 and was finally crushed in AD 70 by the Roman army led by Titus. Fighting was intense. The historian Josephus estimates that 600,000 Jews died in the battles. Extensive damage was caused to the city, including the destruction of the temple constructed by Herod which fulfilled words of Jesus that "the days will come when there will not be left here one stone upon another that will not be thrown down" (Luke 21:6). Those who believed these and the other words of Jesus in what is known as the Olivet Prophecy fled to Pella on the east side of the Jordan before the Romans entered the city; those who remained faced the appalling time that was prophesied.

Despite this crushing defeat, a further Jewish uprising led by Bar Kochba took place in AD 135. This was likewise crushed by the Romans, resulting in Jerusalem being declared by the Emperor Hadrian to be a city in which no Jew was to live. The region was renamed Syria Palestina, from the word "Philistines", as an insult to the Jews who regarded it as their promised land. The land later became known as Palestine, a name which only came back into common use from the nineteenth century.

God's Punishment

The Jews were banished from their land, and approximately two thousand years would elapse before they returned in significant numbers. This final dispersion is the trigger point for many of the matters to be considered in the pages that follow; it brought to final fulfilment the many prophecies that spoke of banishment from the land as punishment for disregarding the way of life shown to them by God through his prophets. For example:

"I will lay your cities waste and will make your sanctuaries desolate, and I will not smell your pleasing aromas. And I myself will devastate the land, so that your enemies who settle in it shall be appalled at it. And I will scatter you among the nations, and I will unsheathe the sword after you, and your land shall be a desolation, and your cities shall be a waste."

(Leviticus 26:31-33)

"The LORD will bring a nation against you from far away, from the end of the earth, swooping down like the eagle, a nation whose

Detail from the Arch of Titus, Rome, showing the sack of Jerusalem

Photo: Sid Levett

Photo: Judy Levett

Stones from the temple, Jerusalem

language you do not understand, a hard-faced nation who shall not respect the old or show mercy to the young ... until they have caused you to perish. They shall besiege you in all your towns, until your high and fortified walls, in which you trusted, come down throughout all your land. And they shall besiege you in all your towns throughout all your land, which the LORD your God has given you."

(Deuteronomy 28:49-52)

To all corners of the earth

In common with much of history prior to AD 1000, there is limited written record of Jewish communities outside the Holy Land, but there is sufficient information to provide us with a good picture of the broad spread of locations in which Jews were present.

Extensive dispersion of Jews to all parts of the world, particularly Europe, commenced with those terrible events of AD 70 and 135. It is, however, of interest that prior to the commencement of this great Diaspora more Jews were voluntarily living outside of Palestine than in it. The acclaimed Jewish scholar, Salo Wittmayer Baron (1895-1989), estimated that in AD 70 two million Jews lived in Palestine, but four million in the Roman Empire outside Palestine and a million in Babylonia and other non-Roman countries. Not all of these had been banished to those lands and many were there by choice, including a community that had not returned from the exile to Babylon.

Conquest of other nations by the Greeks spread the Greek language across a large portion of the then known world. The Roman Empire provided a broad network of roads and an improvement in security, both of which aided travel across the region. All these outcomes of Greek and Roman occupation facilitated two significant events: the preaching of the Gospel and the dispersion of the Jews to many corners of the accessible world. Rome, by edict, directly brought about the major dispersion of the Jews and it was the Roman Empire that indirectly facilitated their spread to many nations. None of this was by coincidence for it was the hand of God at work. It was the "fullness of time" for bringing about the spread of the Gospel and the spread of a people who, by and large, rejected that message.

As trade expanded into areas made accessible by Roman roads, Jews moved into towns and villages that later became major centres for the Jewish community, both in numbers of inhabitants and in religious and secular learning. Jews arrived in some areas almost on the coat-tails of the Roman army.

The Middle East and Africa

Between the fourth and sixth centuries there were Jewish centres in Yemen and other parts of Arabia. A number of those settlements were destroyed in 525 by Christians from Ethiopia aided by the Roman emperor Justinian. Up to the seventh century Jews were living in central Arabia including Medina. They were initially accepted by Muhammad but were later exterminated or forced to migrate to Syria or Mesopotamia. For centuries following the exile to Babylon in 587 BC a Jewish community, comprising voluntary migrants from Judea and descendants of those who did not return to Jerusalem in 538 BC, existed in that city and was left in peace by the Islamic caliphs. However, after the Mongol onslaught of AD 1258, the community declined into insignificance. Jews forced to leave Judea went to various Middle East and African countries where small communities existed into the current era, with many migrating back to Israel since 1948.

Europe, England and Russia

By far the major growth and the influence of the Jews occurred in Europe and Russia where key events and major fulfilments of prophecy took place. We shall, therefore, direct our attention to these regions. There is evidence of a Jewish presence in southern France in the second century. Several centuries later a number of towns in that region had large Jewish communities sometimes confined to allocated areas, as in Avignon from the thirteenth century, and often with a flourishing Jewish culture. The first known printing of a book in Hebrew took place in Avignon in 1444.

Records exist of Jewish communities in southern Russia in the eighth century, some of whom were Khazars (a Turkish people) who converted to Judaism around 700. In 970 they were driven further south by the Russians into the Crimea. In 1016 a joint Russian-Byzantine force destroyed the Khazar kingdom and the Jews fled to other parts of Russia, the Byzantine Empire and to the Mediterranean. This virtually ended Jewish occupation in the southern parts but communities were developing elsewhere in Russia.

These communities are significant to our considerations for the privations they endured, in fulfilment of what had been prophesied, and for their influence in later centuries in developing the concept of a return to the Promised Land.

The first written record of Jews in England is of some arriving with the Normans in 1066, but they were probably present in small numbers from early Roman times. They generally had a peaceful existence in England until being banished by King Edward I in 1290. Debts owing to them were cancelled and their possessions became property of the crown. In 1656 they were re-admitted by Oliver Cromwell, but the major growth in the community was in the late nineteenth and early twentieth centuries as a result of persecution in Europe and Russia.

By 1000 significant Jewish communities existed in many central and northern European cities including Cologne, Frankfurt and Prague. After a period it became common practice to restrict Jews to specified parts of the towns and cities across Europe. Initially these were simply defined areas for Jewish occupation so that Christians did not have to live in the same vicinity. Amongst the earliest cities to establish defined Jewish quarters was Barcelona in 1350, followed by Frankfurt in 1460, Prague in

Jewish ghettos

IT is from the decision taken in Venice that 'ghetto' became the word universally used for an area in which people were confined. The Jews were moved to the foundry area, being the worst part of the city. The ancient Italian word for metal, *geto*, was utilised to describe the metal producing section of the city and over time became 'ghetto', an area for confining people, commonly Jews.

Entrance to Ghetto, Venice

Photo: Sid Levett

1473 and Madrid in 1480.[1] There is uncertainty about which city was the first to put Jews in walled areas with lockable gates. It is possibly Venice where, in 1517, the Doge's Palace and the Catholic Church moved all the Jews in the city to a defined area which was locked and guarded. The idea spread and cities that followed included Rome in 1556, Vienna in 1570 and Florence in 1571.

Occupations and population growth

Some Jews gained employment as financial advisers to rulers and people of authority but generally they eked out an existence as farmers, craftsmen and tailors. Others became moneylenders to the community at large which could be profitable but ran the risk of authorities confiscating funds or passing laws exempting Christians from repaying money borrowed from Jews. At certain times they lived in relative peace and prosperity, one such period being the eleventh and twelfth centuries in Spain where, despite paying heavy taxes, many Jews became wealthy landowners. Others had positions in the royal court and some became diplomats and tax advisers and collectors. It was, however, not to last as we shall see in later chapters. By and large their lot in Europe was to be confined to specified areas, restricted in the occupations open to them and often subject to punishments and forced migrations, sometimes in consequence of being blamed for plagues and other adverse events.

Despite challenges to existence, by the twentieth century there were approximately six million Jews in Europe, of which three-and-a-half million lived in Poland. The extremely high proportion in Poland arises from events centuries earlier. A benevolent attitude to Jews was displayed by various early

1 Full details are mapped by Sir Martin Gilbert, *The Routledge Atlas of Jewish History*, Eighth Edition, Map 44, "Jewish Ghettoes 1215-1870".

rulers commencing with King Boleslaus III (1102-1139) and particularly by King Casimir III (1333-1370) who encouraged Jews to move to Poland from Western European countries in which they were being persecuted.

The toleration began declining in the seventeenth century through the influence of the Catholic Church and the surrounding, sometimes conquering, nations including Germany and Russia. By the eighteenth century Jews in Poland, as in most European countries, were confined to specified areas of towns and restricted in the activities and occupations in which they could participate. At the beginning of World War Two around three million Jews lived in Russia. Again, Casimir III can be credited as a key factor because the descendants of many of those who migrated to Poland moved on to the then lightly populated areas of Ukraine and Lithuania and thence into Russia.

Emancipation and assimilation

In the 1790s Napoleon Bonaparte, initially commander of the French army and later emperor of France, burst upon the scene in Europe generating terror and causing much death and destruction in wars against several countries. Unlikely as it may seem, such circumstances brought about the release of the Jews from ghettoes and the abolishment of many constraining regulations, including those that restricted Jewish access to education and entry to many professions.

The hand of God is evident in all this as Napoleon was clearly used to bring about major changes. Several countries in the Holy Roman Empire, ruled from Vienna by the Habsburgs, were conquered, thereby severely reducing the Empire's influence. Papal power was thus significantly reduced and the Jews were liberated. This liberation set in train developments that, within a century, would markedly contribute to a despising of the increased Jewish influence across much of Europe.

Venice, possibly the first city to establish a defined ghetto, found itself the first city to have its Jews set free when Napoleon conquered the city in 1797 and broke down the gates of the ghetto. Napoleon moved on to Egypt and Palestine and in the siege of Acre in 1799 issued a proclamation declaring a Jewish state in Palestine, then occupied by the Ottoman Turks. Historians are divided on the reasons for the proclamation, with some contending it was not a serious intention but aimed at swaying the opinion of Jewish advisers to the Ottomans. Whatever the intention, it is an intriguing development and one that is most unlikely to have come from Napoleon's Catholic background. He was, however, a prodigious reader and may have come across Restoration Theory writings and been influenced by them.

The French Revolution greatly reduced the power of the Catholic Church in France and, based on ideals espoused by the Revolution, the Constitutional Assembly in 1789 issued the Declaration of the Rights of Man guaranteeing freedom of religion and various civil rights. As Napoleon's victories spread he transplanted these principles into the legislation of conquered countries, thus further weakening the influence of the Church and increasing the freedom of Jews and others. What was enshrined in law was not necessarily applied in practice but it was the beginning of a previously unknown level of freedom. In Portugal, Jews were given the same rights as other citizens and synagogues were opened for the first time in 300 years. In Italy, the Netherlands and Germany, Jews were allowed civil and religious freedom for the first time.

Napoleon's success helped to ensure that the forces unleashed by the French Revolution rippled across Europe and even into the realms of the Ottoman Empire. This helped to nourish a spirit of nationalism among many formerly downtrodden peoples, including the Jews, and was a major influence on the Zionist movement as it developed a century later. We shall come back to these themes in later chapters.

As with Pharaoh at the time of the Exodus, it can be said of Napoleon, "for this purpose I have raised you up, to show you my power, so that my name may be proclaimed in all the earth" (Exodus 9:16). Initially evident only to Bible students, the activity of God through men such as Napoleon, and others to be mentioned in following chapters, will be made manifest to the whole world as God's ultimate purpose with His people is revealed.

After the 1815 defeat of Napoleon by Wellington at Waterloo, many of the rights were restricted and, in some cases, the ghettoes reimposed; but the age of European Enlightenment had commenced and the previous restrictions were never fully to apply again. Interestingly the ghetto in Rome remained in place under the influence of the Catholic Church until the overthrow of the Papal States in 1870 as part of Italian unification. Even in Russia, where Napoleon in 1812 failed to conquer Moscow and retreated, reforms were introduced for a period of time under Czar Alexander II, the successor in 1855 to Nicholas I who had enforced restrictions against Jews.

The new-found freedom for Jews was particularly reflected in access to schools and universities. With a penchant for learning they entered willingly into secular education. This led to two pivotal outcomes over the course of the next century: one was an influx of Jews into the arts, sciences and many professions; the other was their desire to participate more fully in the society of their respective countries. The effect of the first was an increased despising of the Jews for their success by the very society in which they wished to participate more fully; the second led to a declining interest in displaying their 'Jewishness', both cultural and religious.

By the 1930s Jews across Europe dominated many of the professions. For example, in Hungary where Jews comprised five per cent of the population, they provided eighty per cent of stockbrokers, sixty per cent of doctors and fifty per cent of lawyers. In Germany with Jews accounting for one per cent of the population, twenty-six per cent of lawyers and fifteen per cent of doctors were Jewish (Jews had only been permitted to attend university in Germany since 1870). In Poland where Jews represented ten per cent of the population they were the majority in most professions with the result that there were significant manpower shortages in many professions after World War Two.

Chaim Potok in *Wanderings* states:

"German Jewry lived in feverish yearning for emancipation. Ghetto restrictions had loosened. Conversion was rife among the Jewish intellectual elite in the decades that closed out the eighteenth century ... They write books and plays and works on aesthetics. Their German style is exquisite ... Rabbis preach in flawless German; synagogues take on the hushed aura of the Lutheran service. Traditionalists cast about desperately for a means of stemming the assimilationist dance, the whirling of the German Jew in the arms of his new beloved ... They were astounded when they encountered violent anti-Semitism among German university students. In their aggressive hunger for German culture the Jews seemed not to notice the defensiveness of the Germans, the way they were recoiling from this overheated Jewish re-entry into creative culture confrontation after centuries of dormancy."

"Now in Russia too the dance began, in slow-motion at first, as the government removed the relentless pressures of the past and Jews began to participate in the culture of the land. They entered the arts. They became journalists, lawyers, dramatists, novelists, poets, critics, composers, painters, sculptors. They seemed suddenly everywhere in the economic, political and cultural life of the motherland. Some Russians recoiled. Even the liberal and revolutionary groups were not enthusiastic about this passionate Jewish participation in Russian life ... The dance came to an abrupt end in a bloodbath of government-inspired pogroms."[2]

Thus, as World War Two loomed, the scene was set for Hitler's Final Solution to the 'Jewish Problem' and for Russian atrocities against the Jews. Before moving on to that time frame we shall look at two other themes that significantly formed a background to the return of the Jews to the Promised Land.

Further Reading

Chaim Potok, *Wanderings*.
Hans Kung, *Judaism*.
Sir Martin Gilbert, *Atlas of Jewish History*.
Franz Kobler, *Napoleon and the Jews*.

2 Chaim Potok, *Wanderings*, pages 371, 376.

3

THE ZIONIST MOVEMENT

IN many human endeavours, whether a scientific discovery, a unique building, an ideology or a concept that motivates many, often a single individual is identified almost exclusively with the initiative. It is generally true that many people will have held similar ideas, or contributed to the concept over a period of time, but bringing it to fruition has required an individual with exceptional skill. That was certainly the case with the Zionist Movement with which Theodor Herzl was to become essentially synonymous.

Throughout the long centuries of Jewish dispersal, there had been little in the way of an organised concept of returning to the land of their fathers. This was partly because of a desire when persecution arose to move on, if feasible, to another country in search of acceptance and sometimes assimilation. Partly it was because a return was impractical with Palestine in the hands of the Turks.

Not surprisingly, development of the idea of an organised return had its origins where persecution was most severe. Early Zionists were inspired by the struggles for independence of various nationalities in Eastern Europe who were oppressed by imperial overlords based largely in Vienna and Constantinople. These groups in turn had been inspired by the ideals that emanated from the French Revolution which have proven to be such a destabilising force in the world since the end of the eighteenth century, as foreshadowed in the terms of the sixth vial in Revelation 16:12-16. As David ben Gurion wrote:

"Zionism derives from two sources. One is deep, irrational, lasting, independent of time and place, and as old as the Jewish people ... the Messianic hope. The second source was a source of renewal and action, the fruit of realistic political thought, born of the circumstances of time and place ... The charter of liberation enunciating the Rights of Man and Nation, which the French Revolution bequeathed on Europe, the national revival movements which developed among several European peoples ... the new means of transport ... the rise of the working class ... the mass migration from Europe to overseas countries all helped to bring about a new direction in Jewish thought ... The Messianic hope, which for scores of generations had worn a religious garb and had appealed to a force above Nature, now changed its religious and passive form and became political and national."[1]

For a period of time in the nineteenth century there was a glimmer of hope that Jewish assimilation and acceptance would occur as the notion of 'enlightenment' spread, and this happened to a degree in more liberal societies such as Britain. But in the less liberal societies of Eastern Europe this did not occur. In Russia, for instance, these hopes were extinguished in 1881 with escalating violence against Jews and the introduction of laws to drive them from the countryside into city slums. Restrictions on their access to education and

1 *Israel Government Year Book*, 5714, page 5.

entry to professions were also imposed. Similar persecution was seen in Romania and elsewhere.

Persecution of Jews stimulated the establishment of numerous Zionist clubs in Russia, many adopting the title Chovevei Zion – Lovers of Zion. Their common view was "that there is no salvation for the People of Israel unless they establish a government of their own in the Land of Israel". There is, however, in most concepts, a big step between holding an ideal and bringing it to a conclusion. This was particularly the case in Russia where the views of a largely impoverished group, lacking clout and influence, were unlikely to develop any traction.

A step forward occurred when the ideals of these groups were expressed by a Russian-Jewish doctor, Leon Pinsker, in *Selbstemanzipation* (*Auto-emancipation*), published in 1882. Initially a supporter of 'enlightenment' as an answer to the suffering of the Jews, Pinsker now espoused the view that assimilation was not viable and the only solution was for the Jews to establish a land of their own, although not necessarily in Palestine. The book generated much interest amongst Russian Jewry but had little influence elsewhere.

In 1884, Pinsker arranged a national conference of Zionist clubs and societies at which consensus was reached for establishing a fund to finance Jewish settlements in Palestine. Between 1882 and 1903, 25,000 Jews migrated to Palestine, many under the influence of Zionist societies, but some simply fleeing Russian oppression. A few of religious persuasion wanted to emigrate to spend time in study and prayer. The total number of emigrants was a small proportion of the Jews of Europe and Russia. Joining a Zionist society was one thing but migrating to Palestine was another. In Russia, where poverty may have prevented some from emigrating, there was substantial interest but

minimal outcome, whilst in Europe the concept fell essentially on deaf ears.

At the same time that small numbers of Jews migrated from Russia and other oppressive European states to Palestine, a substantially large number of Jews left these same nations for the United States. For many of them, the lure of a booming economy in a democratic nation keen to expand proved more appealing than the rigours of life in an impoverished, disease-ridden backwater like Palestine, ruled by an oppressive and autocratic regime hostile to Jewish endeavours.

A man for the times

Enter Theodor Herzl. Wealthy, urbane, sophisticated, well-educated and possessing considerable self-confidence, Herzl was ideally suited to the role of taking Zionism to rulers, statesmen, financiers and others of influence. He was the 'door-opener' the movement needed. Today he would be described as a man who could market the concept.

His coming upon the scene was no coincidence. A man who fitted so perfectly was surely appointed by God to take the message to those who could influence outcomes at national levels. He could also foster commercial initiatives in Palestine and motivate Jews to accept the opportunities that arose to emigrate from Europe and Russia. Clearly Herzl was a man chosen by God to fulfil a purpose. Interestingly, Herzl was the right man not because of his religious conviction, which was minimal, but because he had the credentials for the task.

Herzl was born in 1860 into a wealthy banking family in Budapest, then part of the Habsburg Empire with its emphasis on Germanic/Austrian culture. He was brought up in the Jewish community but the focus of his parents, and later of Herzl himself, was to succeed in the upper levels of society. Obtaining a law degree from the University of Vienna in 1884,

Theodor Herzl

army captain, Alfred Dreyfus, was falsely accused of espionage. Whilst covering the trial in his role as a journalist, Herzl was stunned by the intensity of the crowd shouting "Death to the Jew" as Dreyfus was publically stripped of his rank. Herzl was now convinced that enlightenment and assimilation were ephemeral concepts. (It was later proven that Dreyfus was innocent of the charges brought against him and that he was the victim of anti-Semitic forces in France.)

Der Judenstaat

Realising that Jews would continue to be oppressed by the nations in which they lived, Herzl came to the conclusion that the only solution was an independent Jewish state, endorsed by the world's great powers and, preferably, established in Israel. This concept was expressed in a lengthy written address that Herzl planned to deliver in front of the wealthy Rothschild family who he considered should be the financiers of the scheme.

Students of prophecy may be surprised that Israel was merely a preferred option, rather than an absolute requirement, and that the need to return there was not seen as being linked in any way with the Jewish prophets. What we have to appreciate is that Herzl's concept was essentially secular and political. Assimilation had not worked so an alternative was proposed, based largely on humanist thought. In fact, Herzl prided himself on having personally developed the concept of a return to the land. Conservative religious Jews who believed in a return to Israel considered it had to be directed by the Messiah. Consequently they shunned the Zionist movement, as many still do.

Herzl's address was expanded into a book, published in 1896, entitled *Der Judenstaat* (translated loosely as *The Jewish State,* but more specifically as *The Jew-State*). The choice of the

his main interest was writing plays and essays. His legal career was abandoned for journalism on a leading Austrian newspaper, where he became very popular for his elegant and stylish articles on social and cultural events.

Early in his adult life, Herzl accepted the fashionable view that religious and racial prejudice would pass away in the age of enlightenment. Confidence in that view began to be eroded by mounting anti-Semitism in Germany, France and Austria. His opinion was finally swayed, in 1895, by the Dreyfus case in France when a French Jewish word 'Jew' was deliberate and aimed at both anti-Semites and cultured Western Jews who at that time preferred to use expressions such as Hebrew or Israelite.

Much has been written about Herzl and the esteem in which he was held. The American-Jewish historian Howard Sachar wrote:

"It was Zionism articulated for the first time by a man of the world, a distinguished political observer and broadly travelled journalist. *The Judenstaat*, therefore, in its transfixing eloquence and orderly exposition, introduced Zionism to European readers, to editors, university men, statesmen, and other moulders of public opinion, in the kind of language they were accustomed to reading. More important yet, Herzl stood alone in his attempt to resolve the Jewish question not merely through the dramatic and far-reaching notion of a Jewish state but through the active collaboration of leading European powers. From the very outset, he projected Zionism into international statecraft".[2]

Another surprising aspect is that, although Herzl's proposal was widely spread throughout the Jewish community, and discussed at length, many Jews did not receive it favourably. Despite "next year in Jerusalem" being stated annually by Jews at their Passover celebrations, the reality was that very few in Western Europe seriously contemplated the idea.

Sachar writes about the response from individual Jews and Jewish organisations:

"An Austrian Jew, Stefan Zweig, recalled, 'I can still remember the general astonishment and annoyance of the middle class Jewish elements of Vienna. What has happened, they said angrily, to this otherwise intelligent, witty, and cultivated writer? What foolishness is this that he has thought up and writes about? Why should we go to Palestine? Our language is German and not Hebrew, and beautiful Austria is our homeland. Are we not well off under the good Emperor Franz Josef? Do we not make an adequate living, and is our position not secure?'"[3]

"Editorials in German Jewish newspapers denounced the proposed Zionist assembly as treason to the Fatherland and a danger to Judaism ... The Association of Rabbis in Germany issued a statement:

1. The efforts of so-called Zionists to found a Jewish national state in Palestine contradict the messianic promises of Judaism as contained in Holy Writ and in later religious sources.

2. Judaism obligates its adherents to serve with all devotion the Fatherland to which they belong, and to further its national interests with all their heart and with all their strength."[4]

In the light of subsequent events in Austria and Germany, this intense opposition to a return to Palestine is breathtaking for its failure to perceive how the so-called Fatherland viewed the Jewish community, and its misunderstanding of the return foretold by the prophets.

The largest Jewish community, outside Europe and Russia was in the United States. Over two-and-a-half million Eastern European Jews migrated there in the 1880s alone. Their interest was in developing a new life in the 'Promised Land' to which they had migrated, rather than moving on to the rigours of life in Palestine. Additionally, many considered that

---

2 Howard Sachar, *A History of Israel – From the Rise of Zionism to Our Time*, page 41.

3 *ibid*, page 42.
4 *ibid*, page 44.

showing support for Zionism would raise questions about their loyalty to the United States.

Zionist Congress

Undeterred, Herzl pressed on with plans to hold an international Zionist Congress. It took place in Basle, Switzerland in August 1897, with 204 delegates from fifteen countries, mainly European, but including a handful of delegates from the United States, Algeria and Palestine. As a consummate marketer, aware of image and prestige, Herzl insisted that all delegates wear formal attire. Through his connections, he arranged for all the leading newspapers of Europe to be represented. He wanted to present an image of an orderly and dignified group of people with a message, not only for their own community, but for the world powers. Herzl was aware that a return to the land could not be achieved by Jewish input alone.

The scene was set with the opening lines of Herzl's speech: "We are here to lay the foundation stone of the house which is to shelter the Jewish nation." The Congress went on to discuss methods of arousing a Jewish consciousness of the benefits of having their own land, and of applying diplomatic efforts to acquire a charter for Jewish settlement

Second Zionist, Congress, 1898

in the Holy Land. A decision was taken to form a company to raise the huge funds needed to encourage migration and develop the land. This, however, became a difficult task as the fabulously wealthy Rothschild and Montefiore families did not provide the hoped for generous donations.

As with his writings, this Congress and subsequent gatherings generated much publicity and discussion but major obstacles remained, including Turkish occupation of Palestine and relatively small interest in migrating there. Nevertheless, extensive publicity was obtained and numerous Zionist societies were formed across the world.

Meetings with dignitaries

Herzl's demeanour and connections at high diplomatic levels enabled him to meet with a broad range of dignitaries. His crowning achievements were meetings with the German Kaiser, the Turkish Sultan and the Pope.

In October 1898, Herzl, through connections with the German ambassador in Vienna, was granted an audience with Kaiser Wilhelm II. The meeting took place in Constantinople, where the Kaiser was visiting the Ottoman Sultan. Herzl proposed a German protectorate of Palestine, in which the Kaiser expressed interest, largely for the purpose of ridding Germany of radical Jews. Elated, Herzl thought that the Kaiser would proceed with his agreement to put the proposal to the Sultan. A second meeting with the Kaiser took place the following month, this time during the Kaiser's visit to Jerusalem. Herzl left that meeting bitterly disappointed on learning that the Kaiser's advisers had recommended against raising the matter with the Sultan and that no action would be taken.

In 1900, after extensive negotiations and many generous payments to Turkish officials, Herzl was granted a meeting with the Ottoman Sultan, Abdul Hamid, in Constantinople. Being aware of the serious debt problem of the Ottoman Empire, Herzl offered to arrange a Jewish syndicate to buy-out the debt, in exchange for a charter for a land settlement in Palestine. The Sultan expressed interest and, once more, Herzl returned to Vienna convinced that progress was at last being made. Again elation turned to despair when he learnt that the interest expressed was only for the purpose of improving the negotiating position of the Turks with French financiers.

A meeting with the Pope took place in January 1904, but to no effect. The Pope's opinion was "... that either the Jews will continue waiting for the Messiah who has already appeared. In that case they will be denying the divinity of Jesus and we cannot help them. Alternatively they will go there without any religion, and then we can be even less favourable to them".

Looking back we can see now that the probability of Germany, Turkey or the Vatican being providers of support to the Jews was remote indeed. Herzl, however, saw the whole process as one requiring input from the world powers and devoted his energies to that end. There is no indication he perceived that God would have any role in the outcome. These disappointments, coupled with the stress of bitter internal disputes and extensive negotiations with people in authority, affected Herzl's health, already weakened by a heart condition. He died in Austria on July 3, 1904, at the age of forty-four.

The outcome

On face value, Herzl's huge effort produced minimal results. The Jewish population in Palestine increased from 24,000 in 1882 to 60,000 in 1918. (The Jewish population in 1914 was actually 85,000 but many fled to Egypt after World War One broke out.

Most of these were to return after the war.) This was a very small proportion of the global Jewish population but it was a marked increase compared to the number of Jews who migrated to the land in prior periods.

The first wave of immigration occurred in 1881, when a number of agricultural colonies were established. Conditions were very harsh and the colonies struggled, maintaining their existence only by substantial donations from Baron Rothschild and smaller donations from others, including Christadelphians. A second wave of immigrants arrived from 1904, mainly as a result of persecution in Russia. A third wave occurred in the 1920s, the majority from Poland. Millions of Jews left Eastern Europe and Russia during this period but most migrated to the United States and Canada. Palestine was not high on their agenda, even to avoid persecution. The assimilated Jews of Western Europe barely raised a thought about migrating anywhere, let alone Palestine. It was to be a decision many would regret.

Despite the failure in its early years to achieve a recognised homeland in Palestine for the Jews, the Zionist movement commenced a thought process in Jewish communities that, three decades after Herzl's death, would be seized upon as they realised there was no future for them in Europe. It also influenced later actions by certain world leaders in facilitating the return of the Jews to their land. Overall it is an example of how God, at times, initiates events that develop over a period of many more years than expected, as one of the steps in the fulfilment of His plan for the earth. Under God's hand, the Zionist movement was a key contributor to the return to the land. Sir Ronald Storrs, who served as the British Governor of Jerusalem after its capture by Allenby in the First World War, made this observation about Zionism:

"The Return stood indeed for something more than a tradition, an ideal or a hope. It was The Hope – *Miqveh Yisroel*, the Hope of Israel, which had never deserted the Jews in their darkest hour – when indeed the Shechinah had shone all the brighter, 'a jewel hung in ghastly night'. In the triumph of the Peace [after the war] the wrongs of all the world would be righted; why not also the ancient of wrongs?"[5]

A prophecy which foreshadows the rise of Zionism and its limited impact on European Jewry, Jeremiah 16:16, speaks of God first sending fishers who would seek to lure His people back to the land as an angler tries to lure a fish to take his bait. It is implicit that the fishers have only limited success because the prophecy goes on to say that God would afterwards send hunters to harass the Jews and force them to move. The full horror of this prophecy only became evident in the events of the Holocaust of World War Two.

Although support for the Zionist movement was found mainly amongst the Jews of Eastern Europe, and did not initially gain a large number of supporters amongst those of the West, it had a big impact on many Christians. Bible students were thrilled to witness events contributing to the return of the Jews. Many saw this as a necessary prelude to the return of Christ and the establishment of God's kingdom on earth. In the early years of the twentieth century, inspired by the early stirrings of the Zionist movement, Brother Frank Jannaway wrote three books about these matters – *Palestine and the Jews*, *Palestine and the Powers* and *Palestine and the World* – one of which was published by a mainstream publisher, which suggests that interest in these developments was not limited to Christadelphians.

5 Sir Ronald Storrs, *Zionism and Palestine*, Penguin Books, 1940, page 48.

Theodor Herzl's opinion that world powers would need to become engaged in the formation of a recognised Jewish homeland in Palestine was quite correct. However, the support was not to come from Germany, Turkey or the Vatican despite Herzl's high level meetings seeking their input. Instead, the support for a Jewish homeland was to come from Britain for several reasons, not the least being the Bible-influenced opinions of some of the nation's leaders, who watched the growth of Zionism with interest. It was also Britain and her allies that would bring about the removal of the obstacle of Turkish occupation of Palestine. Some very dramatic events were about to occur.

"Fear not, for I am with you; I will bring your offspring from the east, and from the west I will gather you. I will say to the north, Give up, and to the south, Do not withhold; bring my sons from afar and my daughters from the end of the earth." (Isaiah 43:5,6)

Further Reading

Howard M Sachar, *A History of Israel – From the Rise of Zionism to Our Time.*

Brother John V Collyer, *Israel: Land of People and Destiny.*

Barbara Tuchman, *Bible and Sword.*

Brother Stephen Green, *God's Purpose with Israel.*

4

THE BALFOUR DECLARATION

CHRISTADELPHIANS of an older generation who regularly attended Sunday lectures will recall hearing many talks in which the Balfour Declaration was highlighted as a key component of God bringing about the restoration of Israel. The words, "His Majesty's Government view with favour the establishment in Palestine of a national home for the Jewish people ..." were etched in the minds of those listeners, and for good purpose. This is indeed a significant document.

Bible students, waiting for signs of the return of the Jews to the land of their origins, had been encouraged by the development of the Zionist Movement late in the nineteenth century. Just a few years later, in the latter stages of World War One, they were thrilled by the British Government's release of a document which became known as the Balfour Declaration, even though many more people than Lord Balfour were involved in its preparation. These two developments were seen, quite correctly, as significant steps towards the restoration of the nation of Israel as a forerunner to the return of Christ.

Much more than these two developments, however, would be needed to generate a desire in the hearts of many Jews to return and for world leaders to produce the political will to facilitate that return. Some thirty years were to pass before significant numbers of Jews were to migrate to the land and no one could have anticipated the events that would generate that migration. Furthermore, a longer period of time than many expected has elapsed since the establishment of the State of Israel until the return of Christ. This is not a failure of the prophecies but a reminder that, as in many other prophesied events, God's time frame often differs from the expectations of sincere Bible students.

The cost of waging World War One, the destruction of property and a death toll of approximately nine million military personnel and seven million civilians, had devastating economic and social consequences. The number of fatalities was beyond comprehension: barely a family in England and Europe was untouched. People felt that never again should this be allowed to happen, yet a mere twenty years later it did, and even more nations were involved.

World War One led to the dissolution of the German, Austro-Hungarian, Russian and Turkish Empires. In their place arose many new individual states: some other existing nations emerged from the war with redrawn borders. Ethnic groupings were often ignored when new borders were allocated, resulting in violent disputes that continue to the present, as we saw in the break up of the former Yugoslavia which led to new states in Croatia, Serbia, etc. These changes have had a significant impact on world affairs, in particular in the Middle East.

Dragon's teeth

Many historians acknowledge the Balfour Declaration as a key factor in bringing about the

British Mandate for Palestine and the continuing unrest in that region. Bible students, however, see in these events the progression of prophecies relating to the return of the Jews and the decline of the Turkish Empire.

The significance of the Balfour Declaration from a Biblical perspective was highlighted in public lectures. Its significance continues to the present, even if the passage of time means that some make the mistake of seeing it as past history. It may have happened many years back, but it is a key milestone in God's continuing plan. Even secular historians with no interest in or respect for Bible prophecy recognise the Balfour Declaration as central to an understanding of the tensions which are at the heart of the Arab-Israeli conflict. As one historian commented in 2010:

> "Because it was unpredictable and characterised by contradictions, deceptions, misinterpretations, and wishful thinking, the lead-up to the Balfour Declaration sowed dragon's teeth. It produced a murderous harvest, and we go on harvesting even today."[1]

Many who recognise the significance of the Balfour Declaration question why Britain would go to such lengths to acknowledge the rights of the Jews to a homeland of their own. Britain was one of the last countries in the 'old world' in which Jews settled and its Jewish population has always been a very small minority. It is an intriguing question. The answer lies partly in the political and military imperatives of the time and partly in the people involved in bringing about the issue of the declaration.

Reasons commonly listed by historians for the declaration include:

1 Jonathan Schneer, *The Balfour Declaration – The Origins of the Arab-Israeli Conflict*, page 370.

- to encourage Russian Jews to do what they could to keep Russia in the war, thus tying up part of the German army on the Eastern Front;
- to generate support among Jews in the United States for America to join in the war;
- as a reward to Chaim Weizmann for his contribution to the British war effort;
- to facilitate Britain gaining a Mandate to administer Palestine, thus enhancing the nation's interests in a region crucial to land and sea access to India.

The first two points were initial objectives, but by the time the declaration was released in 1917 Russia had withdrawn from the war and the United States had become a participant. It is also now considered that, even if the declaration had been issued earlier, Jewish influence on the Russian outcome would have been minimal. The third and fourth points are key factors, but in addition to all these – and often ignored by historians – were the religious beliefs of the major participants by which they were motivated to continue with discussions on the wording and to see the declaration issued. For this we need to consider the background of those who significantly contributed to the outcome.

Lord Balfour

Born in 1848, Arthur James Balfour entered parliament in 1874. He held several cabinet positions before becoming Prime Minister in 1902 but his Conservative government lost power in 1905, including the loss of Balfour's Manchester East seat. A by-election shortly thereafter secured for him the City of London seat and he became Leader of the Opposition until 1911. It was, however, his role as Foreign Secretary in the wartime coalition government of Lloyd George that was to give him lasting recognition. He is synonymous with the British Government's document that bears

Photo: George Grantham Bain – Wikimedia Commons

Arthur Balfour

suggested that Balfour may have had a nanny who was a Christadelphian[3] and it is known that Brother Robert Roberts had contact with him in 1890 when he sent him a copy of *Nazareth Revisited*. When he died, Brother C C Walker was invited to attend Lord Balfour's memorial service.[4]

David Lloyd George and Chaim Weizmann

Born in Wales in 1863, Lloyd George was of humble origins. From a religious perspective he was strongly influenced by his family's connection with Welsh chapels and the Temperance movement. Lloyd George's father died when he was two and he was brought up by his mother, with support from his uncle, Lloyd. In later life he added his uncle's name to his own to make a more impressive name for a parliamentarian, a practice adopted by others at the time.

His uncle was a shoemaker, well-read and a Baptist lay preacher. He had a major influence on Lloyd George, who excelled at school but left at fourteen to become an articled clerk to a solicitor. He went on to practice law, focusing on providing assistance to the working man. He was also an inspiring lay preacher in the local Welsh chapel. A man of considerable talent, he entered Parliament in 1890 and rapidly rose through the ranks. In 1915 under the coalition government of Prime Minister Asquith, he was appointed Minister of Munitions. Under his direction significant improvements in processes were made and the manufacturing rate of munitions increased markedly.

In this Ministerial role he met a man who was to make a major contribution to the war effort and, unconnected as it may seem, to the return of the Jews to Palestine. Despite the increase Lloyd

his signature and acknowledges the right of the Jews to a homeland of their own.

Balfour was a supporter of Zionist aspirations, but not necessarily as a consequence of holding the strong personal religious beliefs of many of his colleagues. It has been suggested that Balfour was motivated by a desire to discourage Jews from settling in Britain more than by a passion for Jewish nationhood[2]. Nonetheless, he would have had an awareness of Israel's place in the Bible. The Balfour family was known to be religious and Bible reading was a feature of their family life. It has been

2 *The Economist*, July 13, 2013, special report on the Arab Spring, page 5.

3 *The Testimony*, March 2008, page 11.
4 *The Christadelphian*, 1930, pages 220-221 and 222-223.

Photo: Harris & Ewing – Wikimedia Commons

David Lloyd George

University of Manchester in 1904. It is interesting that Weizmann's immigration to Britain was assisted by Herbert Samuel, the first British Cabinet Minister to advocate Zionism and later the first British High Commissioner under the Mandate of Palestine.

Weizmann isolated an organism capable of transforming the starch in maize and other cereals into acetone butyl alcohol, which is used for manufacturing explosive armaments. The quantity of acetone that was able to be produced, as a consequence of this discovery, markedly increased the output of munitions, particularly for the heavy armaments used on the Western Front and by the

Photo: Hugo Mendelson – Wikimedia Commons

Chaim Weizmann

George achieved in armament production, Britain was desperately short of munitions, to the extent that the war effort was in dire straits. An inability to source sufficient acetone, which traditionally had been imported from Germany, hampered the production of munitions. Chaim Weizmann, a Jewish immigrant from Russia, was a brilliant chemist and vice-president of the English Zionist Federation at the time of meeting Lloyd George.

Educated in Germany and Switzerland, Chaim Weizmann was appointed lecturer in chemistry at the University of Geneva in 1901 and moved to the

British Navy. Weizmann later moved to Palestine and, in 1949, became the first President of the State of Israel.

The meeting of these two men was surely not by coincidence, for their collective influences were pivotal to the return of the Jews to the land. Once again God utilised men with appropriate skills and beliefs to bring about, step by step, outcomes prophesied many centuries earlier.

In June 1916 Lloyd George was appointed Secretary for War. He became distressed at the loss of life and the direction the war was taking but found he could not change the views of the military chiefs. Frustrated with the situation he submitted his resignation in December 1916. Shortly after this Prime Minister Asquith also resigned.

King George V summoned a number of senior ministers to Buckingham Palace to determine a course of action. The outcome was that Lloyd George was appointed as Prime Minister and Balfour as Foreign Secretary. The Liberal / Conservative coalition government continued and a new war Cabinet of five members was appointed. The members met daily and were in constant contact with the War Office and the military chiefs in the hope of bringing the war to a conclusion, although the appalling loss of life was to continue for another two years. Instrumental in his endeavour to conclude the war, and also to assist the Jews in obtaining a homeland, was Lloyd George's religious conviction. Jill Hamilton in *God, Guns and Israel* quotes from Lloyd George's biographer, John Grigg:

"... he had been brought up on the Bible, and the story of the ancient Jews was as familiar to him as the history of England. He was a romantic nationalist ... the idea of reuniting the Jewish people with the land of their forefathers appealed to him."[5]

The War Cabinet

Membership of the War Cabinet changed at times; over the period of its existence ten men were participants, in addition to Balfour who attended regularly in his role as Foreign Secretary. They were from markedly different backgrounds. Some like Lloyd George were of humble origins and raised in the Nonconformist churches. Others were from aristocratic families, where membership of the Church of England was a given, although strong evangelical influences had entered the lives of many of these. The majority of members had an extensive knowledge of the Old Testament, including the events that took place at various locations. The Bible played a large part in their upbringing, to an extent difficult to appreciate in today's essentially secular world.

It was a world in which many people knew their Bible and could recite sections of it, but many of the War Cabinet members went beyond that. Several were firm believers in the 'Restoration Theory', whose adherents looked to the return of the Jews to Palestine and their conversion to Christianity as precursors to the return of Christ. Their strong conviction in this concept provided much of the impetus for persevering with issuing the declaration despite the tortuous negotiations about the wording.

• Andrew Bonar Law, who became Prime Minister in 1922, was initially simply called Andrew Law. His father, a minister in the Free Church of Scotland, named his son after Andrew Bonar, a Scottish missionary who founded the Hebrew Christian Testimony to Israel, a mission to convert Jews in Palestine to Christianity. In

---

5 Jill Hamilton, *God, Guns and Israel*, page 5.

acknowledgment of his namesake, Andrew Law added 'Bonar' to his surname in adult life.

- Arthur Henderson, leader of the Labour Party, born in a Glasgow tenement, was a lay preacher in the Wesleyan Methodist Church and a Temperance campaigner.
- Lord Curzon, an Oxford graduate and the sole Etonian in the group, was from an aristocratic family. He had a keen interest in the Bible and was the only War Cabinet member to have visited the Holy Land. When visiting the Church of the Holy Sepulchre in Jerusalem he voiced his disapproval of the inaccurate historical information provided by the attendants. His biographer, Kenneth Rose, said of Curzon's 1883 journey: "Brought up on the Bible, he filled notebook upon notebook with eloquent recollections of the Old Testament."[6]
- In 1917 Jan Christian Smuts, then the Defence Minister of South Africa, joined the War Cabinet as a representative of the Dominions. An ardent Zionist sympathiser, Smuts became a close friend of Chaim Weizmann and, in War Cabinet meetings, argued in favour of a Jewish homeland and for fighting the Turks in Palestine.

With members such as these, led by Lloyd George with his restorationist beliefs, the War Cabinet had a desire, additional to any potential military and political benefits, to support the establishment of a homeland for the Jews.

Three hundred years in the making

By the early twentieth century mainstream churches had long attributed Israel-based prophecies to the 'Church' and had essentially discarded belief in the return of Christ. There were, however, many

6 *ibid*, page 8.

A puzzling contradiction

AS an aside, it is worth considering a matter that has quite likely crossed the minds of many readers. From a Christadelphian perspective it may seem puzzling that people can hold a firm belief in the return of Christ, yet have no qualms about being involved in the deal-making of politics and participation in warfare.

There is no single, simple answer to this as many factors prevail. Primarily it seems that these apparently incongruous concepts are rationalised by a belief in a right to defend their nation from what are perceived as the forces of evil. This is what is known as the 'justifiable war' philosophy utilised by some politicians and church leaders. Secondly, it requires a belief that God needs the assistance of 'good' men and women in bringing about prophetical outcomes and defeating evil. Those who hold such views generally struggle to understand that God uses evil men to bring about events consistent with His plan for the earth, nor can they accept that killing others to defend a homeland is not the way for a follower of Christ. They assume that it is God's will for nations perceived as 'good' to engage in warfare with those defined as 'evil'. We shall see this is a key issue in other topics to be considered later.

Nonconformists, and some in the mainstream churches, who held to the Restoration Theory. That belief was a significant contributing factor to the Balfour Declaration. It was a belief extant in England and parts of Europe for many years, with its development arising from the availability of the Bible in English and other languages after centuries of darkness.

Barbara Tuchman in her book *Bible and Sword* traces the history of British interest in the Holy Land and the Jews. Expelled from England in 1290 by King Edward I, Jews were not readmitted until 1656 when Oliver Cromwell issued a decree allowing their return. Historians often relate the readmission to matters of trade and commerce but there was more to it than that. Puritan belief, which developed from the availability of the Bible in English, strongly opposed the formal rituals and hierarchical structure of the Church of England formed by King Henry VIII out of the Roman Catholic Church. The work of translators such as Tyndale and Coverdale in the sixteenth century bore fruit as the people gained greater access to the Bible.

Bible-based Nonconformist churches, by and large, held a strong belief in the prophesied return of the Jews to the Holy Land as a prelude to the return of Christ. It was, however, an opinion laid on top of traditional church doctrines rather than part of a broader alternative theology. Furthermore, it was coupled with a belief that the Jews had to be converted to Christianity before Christ could return. This generated much support for missionary work in Palestine and subsequently much frustration with the abject failure of most efforts. Members of the Nonconformist churches came mainly from middle and working class backgrounds. There were, however, some members of the aristocracy who accepted the Restoration Theory. Some were in positions of considerable influence and assisted in introducing reforming legislation and in setting moral standards.

Lord Palmerston, one of Queen Victoria's high-profile cabinet ministers, who held the post of Foreign Secretary intermittently between 1830 and 1851, was responsible for the initial considerations that would culminate in Britain declaring a Jewish homeland in Palestine. He engaged in extensive discussions with Egypt, France and Turkey, which at various times occupied parts of Palestine and Syria. He also endeavoured, but failed, to persuade the Turkish sultan that an increase in the number of Jews in Palestine would be advantageous to Turkey. Some of these discussions were precursors to the drawing up, by Britain and France after World War One, of the artificial borders and the appointment of so-called ruling dynasties of many countries that occupy the current map of the Middle East. These decisions are partly responsible for much of the unrest in the region.

Interestingly, although he helped create a climate in which Britain became enmeshed in the Middle East, Lord Palmerston was strongly opposed to Britain occupying territory in the region. In 1857, when Prime Minister, he wrote a letter to the Foreign Secretary, Lord Clarendon, about the Middle East in which he stated quite plainly, "We don't want to have Egypt. What we wish about Egypt is that it should continue attached to the Turkish Empire … We want to trade with Egypt, and to travel through Egypt, but we do not want the burden of governing Egypt …".[7] This sentiment is especially interesting in view of an observation made in *Elpis Israel* which was published just eight years before:

"I know not whether the men, who at present contrive the foreign policy of Britain, entertain the idea of assuming the sovereignty of the Holy Land, and of promoting its colonization by the Jews; their present intentions, however, are of no

7 Cited in *Studies in Diplomatic History*, Sir James Headlam-Morley, Methuen, 1930, page 55.

importance one way or the other; because they will be compelled, by events soon to happen, to do what, under existing circumstances, heaven and earth combined could not move them to attempt."[8]

At that time, as Lord Palmerston's letter confirmed, the British had little interest in occupying territory in the eastern Mediterranean. Construction of the Suez Canal in the 1860s and the opening of a more direct sea route to India and Australasia changed that. The United Kingdom purchased first a share in the Suez Canal and then, in 1882, occupied Egypt to ensure trade was not disrupted. Britain's move into the Middle East in the 1880s excited Bible students of the day who, on the strength of Brother Thomas' prognostication, had expected some such development.

It is curious that Brother Thomas had sent Lord Palmerston a copy of the first edition of *Elpis Israel* and received from the Viscount a courteous acknowledgement of the gift.[9] Given what we know of his interest in Middle Eastern affairs and the Jews he may well have given close consideration to Brother Thomas' writings, even if he did not subscribe to all of the propositions presented.

Lord Ashley, step-son-in-law of Lord Palmerston, was a traditional Tory parliamentarian but, unusually for his background, was actively engaged in the Evangelical movement. In Parliament he promoted factory reforms, anti-slavery legislation, temperance movements, support for orphanages and schooling. He supported Lord Palmerston in generating discussion in Britain on encouraging Jewish migration to Palestine, and in negotiating with the Turkish government to allow it. The source of his commitment was his nanny, Maria Mills, a member of the Evangelical movement. As was common at the time among the upper classes, she may have been the provider of practically all the love he experienced as a child.

In *God, Guns and Israel*, Jill Hamilton states of Lord Ashley:

"The inspiration to make Palestine a home for the Jewish people was part of his upbringing, his firm belief in the divine predictions in the Bible, and belief in the 'restoration' of the Jewish people to the Holy Land as a fulfilment of prophecy. Just like the Puritans of Cromwell's time, Ashley was then one of the many Protestants who believed that the Second Coming required the conversion of the Jews, and their restoration to Palestine. Conducting his own life according to a literal acceptance of the Bible, he styled the Jews 'God's ancient people' and like other keen Bible scholars, he had learned Hebrew at Oxford so that he could study the original texts of the Old Testament. Touchingly, he wore a gold ring inscribed with the words 'Pray for the peace of Jerusalem; they shall prosper that love thee.'"[10]

These are but a few examples of those who believed in the prophecies that the Jews would return to their land and worked, where they could, to facilitate it. By this we can see that God used for His purpose people who were in the right place at the right time and who adhered to opinions developed over many years as the word of God became available outside the constraints of the official church. While people have freewill to do as they wish, God utilises some for good and others for evil in conformity with their attitudes and opinions. The participants are not 'programmed' to act out their part but, having made their choice, some will be utilised for God's purpose.

8 Brother John Thomas, *Elpis Israel*, page 442, 14th ed.
9 Brother Robert Roberts, *Dr Thomas: His Life and Works*, page 182.

10 Jill Hamilton, *God, Guns and Israel*, page 67.

Consistency of the Christadelphian position

With so many at that time believing in the Second Coming, we may ask what is different about the Christadelphian position on that topic? Some of its unique features are:

- Belief in the Second Coming is not overlaid on traditional erroneous doctrines of the mainstream churches, such as the immortality of the soul, heaven-going and the existence of a supernatural devil.
- A definitive, scripturally-based opinion is held on the purpose of Christ's return and the establishment of God's kingdom. Those who mix the return with erroneous doctrine often have a very obscure understanding of how all the components link together.
- The conversion of the Jews to Christianity is not seen as a necessary pre-requisite to the return of Christ.
- Salvation is available to those who, through belief and baptism, become "heirs to the promises".

This is not the place for a treatise on the background to the Christadelphians. The subject matter in this chapter does, however, raise the question of why be different if there are others who look to the return of Christ. The following comment from Brother John Thomas is helpful in answering that question:

"'The truth' is set forth in the law and the prophets; but we must add to these the apostolic testimony contained in the New Testament if we would comprehend it '*as it is in Jesus*'. The kingdom is the subject matter of 'the truth'; but 'as it is in Jesus', is the truth concerning him as the king and supreme pontiff of the dominion; and *the things concerning his name*, as taught in the doctrine of the apostles. As a whole 'the truth' is defined as '*the things concerning the Kingdom of God and the Name of Jesus Christ*'. This phrase covers the entire ground upon which the '*one faith*', and the '*one hope*', of the Gospel are based; so that if a man believe only the '*things of the kingdom*', his faith is defective in the 'things of the name'; or, if his belief is confined to the '*the things of the name*', it is deficient in the 'things of the kingdom'. There can be no separation of them recognised in a 'like precious faith' to that of the apostles. They believed and taught all these things; God hath joined them together, and no man can expect His favour who separates them, or abolishes the necessity of believing the things He has revealed for faith".[1]

---

1 Brother John Thomas, *Elpis Israel*, page 189, 14th edition.

Formation during the First World War of a War Cabinet with so many members holding the Restoration Theory was a window of opportunity brought about by God. It was a belief virtually about to disappear from religious life. A major reason for this would appear to be the decline in religious thought after the appalling destruction and loss of life in World War One, and the despondency caused by the failure to convert the Jews. The latter was seen as an integral part of events that would precede the return of Christ. The spiritual opportunity for most of the Western world may now have passed. There has, however, been a resurgence of Restoration Theory in some circles and we consider the possible impact of that in a later chapter on the United States Presidents.

The wording

The Balfour Declaration is a classic example of British Foreign Office writing: succinctly worded, grammatically correct, offering something to one party (the Jews) without commitment to the timing of the outcome or the exactitude of boundaries, whilst endeavouring to convince the other party (the Arabs) that their interests would be protected.

In fact, many contributed to the wording over a period of months. Balfour was, of course, involved as was Lloyd George and officials of the Foreign Office. The wording was amended by input from the Zionist Organisation, particularly by Dr Chaim Weizmann (some historians contend that the initial draft was prepared by associates of Weizmann). Anti-Zionist Jews also participated and achieved a change from "<u>the</u> home for the Jews" to "<u>a</u> home for the Jews". President Woodrow Wilson of the United States (at the request of Britain) also had input, taking his advice from Justice Louis Brandeis, a Jewish lawyer appointed to the United States Supreme Court by Wilson.

Britain sought support from other Western Powers, particularly France and Italy, but the support of the United States was seen as essential for proceeding with the declaration. Progress stalled until Wilson finally cabled his support in October 1917, having rejected earlier drafts. Although not expressed in the wording, implicit in the support by other countries was the fact that Palestine was to become a British protectorate. The wording was not debated in the House of Commons or the House of Lords. Instead, the final decision was made solely by the War Cabinet and was issued on November 2, 1917, in the form of a letter from the Foreign Secretary, Lord Balfour, to Lord Rothschild, President of the British Zionist Federation:

"Dear Lord Rothschild,

I have much pleasure in conveying to you, on behalf of His Majesty's Government, the following declaration of sympathy with Jewish Zionist aspirations which has been submitted to, and approved by, the Cabinet:

'His Majesty's Government view with favour the establishment in Palestine of a national home for the Jewish people, and will use their best endeavours to facilitate the achievement of this object, it being clearly understood that nothing shall be done which may prejudice the civil and religious rights of existing non-Jewish communities in Palestine, or the rights and political status enjoyed by Jews in any other country.'

I should be grateful if you would bring this declaration to the knowledge of the Zionist Federation."

Foreign Office,
November 2nd, 1917.

Dear Lord Rothschild,

I have much pleasure in conveying to you, on behalf of His Majesty's Government, the following declaration of sympathy with Jewish Zionist aspirations which has been submitted to, and approved by, the Cabinet.

"His Majesty's Government view with favour the establishment in Palestine of a national home for the Jewish people, and will use their best endeavours to facilitate the achievement of this object, it being clearly understood that nothing shall be done which may prejudice the civil and religious rights of existing non-Jewish communities in Palestine, or the rights and political status enjoyed by Jews in any other country".

I should be grateful if you would bring this declaration to the knowledge of the Zionist Federation.

The Balfour Declaration

Diplomatic intrigue

Even as the Declaration was being issued, the British Government was engaged in secret negotiations with Turkey for a bilateral peace treaty under which Turkey would be guaranteed her possessions in the Middle East, including Palestine. A bribe was even paid to Turkish leader Enver Pasha in December 1917 which he graciously repaid when negotiations broke down the following month. It might be speculated that these negotiations were doomed to failure because prophecy required that the Euphratean power of the Ottoman Empire had to be dried up (Revelation 16:12) and therefore Turkey could not come out of the war with her territory intact.

At about this same time, in the Sykes-Picot negotiations between Britain and France, the British proposed that, after the war, Palestine should come under international administration. Earlier in World War One the British, through intermediaries such as T E Lawrence (Lawrence of Arabia), had persuaded certain Arab leaders in the Middle East to rise up against their Turkish overlords by promising them control of vast territories including Palestine. By the end of 1917, therefore, Britain was in the invidious position of having promised Palestine to the Arabs, the Turks, the Jews and an international consortium! Having conquered the land, Britain is said to have considered giving the territory to Belgium.[11] No wonder Britain's policy machinations in relation to Palestine's future have been described as sowing dragon's teeth.

The impact

Although the Balfour Declaration did not deliver the strategic outcomes the British Government hoped it would in terms of support for the war effort, in particular coming too late to have any influence over developments in Russia, its impact was huge. The Jewish community in England was extremely grateful. Public meetings were held throughout the country and many resolutions of thanks were relayed to the government. Hearkening back to Biblical times, British Jews displayed pictures of King George V alongside images of Cyrus as they celebrated the issue of the Declaration. In the United States, the Jewish community was equally thrilled with the outcome. Large parades took place in many cities and much gratitude was expressed.

Millions of leaflets were dropped by aircraft over Germany and Austria to inform the Jews, and others, of the decision. The news travelled to Russia where the Jewish community rejoiced greatly, even though the Bolsheviks had just seized power and decided to discontinue the war with Germany. The British Government had succeeded in its aim to secure the support of world Jewry, even if this made no material difference to the war effort. Less effusively, many Bible students rejoiced at this further step in the fulfilment of prophecies that God's people would one day be back in the land.

When the Balfour Declaration was made public it captured the imagination of Christadelphians around the world. More than six pages of the December 1917 issue of the *The Christadelphian* were devoted to discussion about the document and its implications; several further articles were published in the magazine during 1918.

Christadelphians and others who looked beyond political and military outcomes were thrilled to see these beginnings of a restoration. They already knew their Bibles but turned again, individually and in groups, to read with heightened interest words such as:

"And he said to me, 'Son of man, can these bones live?' And I answered, 'O Lord GOD, you know.' Then he said to me, 'Prophesy over these bones, and say to them, O dry bones, hear the word of the LORD. Thus says the Lord GOD to these bones: Behold, I will cause breath to enter you, and you shall live. And I will lay sinews upon you, and will cause flesh to come upon you, and cover you with skin, and put breath in you, and you shall live, and you shall know that I am the LORD.'" (Ezekiel 37:3-6)

The complete fulfilment of Ezekiel 37 appeared near. God's time frame, however, operates on a different scale from man's expectations. Events that would further shake the earth were yet to occur and, although the scale of them was unexpected, Bible students saw in them further evidence of the fulfilment of prophecy.

---

11 *The Economist*, July 13, 2013, special report on the Arab Spring, page 5.

Further Reading

Jill Hamilton, *God, Guns and Israel*.
Jonathan Schneer, *The Balfour Declaration – The Origins of the Arab-Israeli Conflict*.
Barbara Tuchman, *Bible and Sword*.

5

THE EUPHRATES DRIES UP

RELEASE of the Balfour Declaration in November 1917 was an exciting event for Bible students of that time as it provided hope that the long expected regathering of God's people might occur in their lifetime. Barely had they absorbed that prospect when another event of considerable significance occurred. In December 1917 the Turks were removed from Palestine after the defeat of their army, thereby removing a major impediment to the return of the Jews to their homeland.

Almost a century later these events may seem like 'dry-as-dust' historical facts, but the announcement that troops from Britain and her Allies had defeated the Turks and were occupying Jerusalem was an event of momentous significance to keen Bible students. The fulfilment of a prophecy that many were convinced applied to Turkey, and was a necessary step in facilitating the return of the Jews, was like the voice of God from Mount Sinai. Here, before believers' eyes, was evidence that God's plan for the earth was moving forward and confidence could be placed in the prophetic word. We too can thrill to this evidence and place similar confidence in the outworking of prophecies yet to be fulfilled.

Think of the time when these events transpired. The world was reeling from the death and destruction of war and scriptural teaching was being challenged by scepticism on various fronts, particularly the theories contained in Charles Darwin's book *On the Origin of Species,* published in 1859. In this context we can only imagine the encouragement this series of events – the Zionist Congresses, the Balfour Declaration, the ousting of the Turks from Palestine – provided to Bible believers.

The prophecy

"The sixth angel poured out his bowl [vial, KJV] on the great river Euphrates, and its water was dried up, to prepare the way for the kings from the east." (Revelation 16:12)

This prophecy has long been seen as having application to Turkey. As early as the seventeenth century Joseph Mede interpreted the 'drying up of the Euphrates' as the 'drying up' or contraction of the Ottoman Empire. This took place from the eighteenth to the twentieth century. Brother John Thomas endorsed this view in *Eureka,* written in the 1860s:

"The effect of the outpouring of the vial is to dry up '*the water*' of the political Euphrates … The Euphrates represents a power of the apocalyptic Babylon; and as the name is indicative of water flowing in a certain channel, '*water*' must signify *the power* of the Euphratean empire, expressed, as governments ordinarily express it, *by force and arms.*

There is one other place, and one only, in the apocalypse, where *water* is used in the singular; as, in chapter 12:15, in the words, 'the Serpent cast out of his mouth *water* as a flood after the Woman, that he might cause her to be carried

AN ASIDE ABOUT OTHER SYMBOLS

Kings of the East

God needed to shrink the Ottoman Empire so that "the way of the kings of the east might be prepared" (Revelation 16:12, KJV). Who are these kings of the east? J B Rotherham in his 'emphatic idiom' translation renders this phrase as "the kings who were from the rising of the sun". Young's Literal Translation renders it as "the kings who are from the rising of the sun". These translations help us to see that the kings to whom the passage refers are Christ and the saints when Christ returns to establish God's kingdom. The imagery links us to Christ, the sun of righteousness who shall arise with healing in his wings when he returns to the earth (Malachi 4:2).

Several symbols – one vial

Each component of the sixth vial is significant, as is the placing of the various symbols within the one vial. There must be a link between the drying up of the power represented by the River Euphrates in verse 12 and the frog-like spirits of verse 13. History confirms that this is the case. The frog-like spirits of militant national self-determination had a particular relationship with the break up of the Ottoman Empire. In fact, as conflicts in the Balkans in the 1990s and more recent events in the Middle East testify, they continue to have an impact on the territory formerly occupied by that empire.

The Ottoman power had to be dried up so that the events ushering in the return of Christ could proceed. This is the subject matter of verses 13 and 14. Without going into the imagery in too much detail, this picture of the frog-like spirits bringing instability into the world refers to the explosion of nationalism in the last two centuries, in particular in the Middle East, which has resulted in a flourishing of new nations, especially since World War Two.[1] This spirit was unleashed by the French Revolution, and the frogs suggest that connection with France. The frogs also have a secondary relevance to the vision; they seem to be emblematic of people asserting their rights and refusing to be downtrodden, such as occurred in the French Revolution.

---

1 Section 10 of *The Apocalypse and History,* by W H Barker and W H Boulton, provides an overview of how the Ottoman Empire dried up before the forces of nationalism.

away of the flood.' In this place 'water' signifies power incorporated in armies, sent forth from government to sweep away, as by a flood, the objects of its displeasure. Hence, the water of the Great River Euphrates, in like manner, represents *the military power* of the Ottoman empire; which is dissipated by a process of evaporation, a drying up; a gradual exhaustion, so as at last to leave the channel of the river in the heart of the Great City, empty; and devoid of all power to impede or interfere with operations developing in the southeastern recesses of the empire."[1]

The popular Revivalist preacher and writer, Grattan Guinness, provided a similar interpretation in *The Approaching End of the Age,* published in 1878:

"The rise and fall of the Ottoman Empire are symbolized in the Apocalypse, by the overflow and drying up of the great river Euphrates ... Sir Edward Creasy's *History of the Ottoman Turks* opens with the following sentence. 'Six centuries ago a pastoral band of four hundred Turkish families was journeying westward, *from the upper streams of the river Euphrates*: their armed force consisted of four hundred and forty-four horsemen, and their leader's name was Ertoghrul.' This little band of Euphratean horsemen were the ancestors of that terrible host or 'army of horsemen two hundred thousand thousand' strong, whom the Seer of Patmos beheld, loosed *from the Euphrates*, and overflowing the Roman earth, carrying distress and death wherever they went – the 'second woe' sent by God as a judgement on Christendom for its depravity and apostasy."[2]

1 Brother John Thomas, *Eureka*, Volume 3, pages 534,535.
2 Grattan Guinness, *The Approaching End Of The Age*, page 280.

Both these writings are in a style unfamiliar to modern readers, but they clearly establish that serious Bible students were convinced that Revelation 16:12 was a prophecy of the impending decline of the Ottoman Empire. In this regard they saw in the drying up of the Euphrates the reversal of the events described in the prophecy of the sixth seal or second woe trumpet (9:13-21). It was a conclusion they reached long before 1917 and consequently many were thrilled by the news of Allenby's defeat of the Turks in Palestine.

The Desert Campaign

After the monumental failure of the Gallipoli campaign in 1915, British and Allied troops were sent to Egypt for recovery. The majority were subsequently sent to battlegrounds in France but others remained in Egypt to defend the Suez Canal from Turkish attack. This force comprising mainly British and Anzac (Australian and New Zealand) troops was called the Egyptian Expeditionary Force (EEF) and was under the command of General Sir Archibald Murray. Some Bible students at the time perceived this combined force as an example or precursor of 'Tarshish and the young lions' of Ezekiel 38.

The defence lines were initially close to the Canal but in February 1916 a new defensive position was established at El Arish, eighty kilometres to the east. This was also to become the springboard for a push further east to Palestine and thence Syria. Moving the troops together with the necessary armaments, food and water, was a logistical nightmare. Maintaining supply lines is a key issue in all warfare, but with hundreds of thousands of men and thousands of horses to feed and water in a desert region, the challenge was huge. The horses were mainly used for pulling artillery and supplies but at this time some were still utilised in warfare by cavalry regiments. Cavalry was of limited use in the trench warfare of the Western Front but became a critical part of the desert theatre of war.

The move eastwards was conducted along the Mediterranean coast, north of Sinai, where there was a series of oases. Remaining near the coast also meant that the troops could come under artillery protection from the Royal Navy in the event of attack by the Turks. Eventually the EEF crossed the border into Palestine but continuing on to Jerusalem was no easy task.

This is not the place to explain the Desert Campaign in detail but some understanding of it assists in perceiving the difficulty of the task and the privations endured. It was part of God's plan, although not recognised by those involved, that the Turks would be removed from Palestine but it is human beings that commence wars and they have to endure the consequent effects, even when the prophetic word is being fulfilled. It was not a simple matter to move all the men and equipment across the desert and take Jerusalem. In addition to enduring heat, sandstorms and limited supplies, it was necessary to remove Turkish forces from cities to the west of Jerusalem for military reasons and to guarantee access to sufficient water to continue the advance to Jerusalem. Major battles took place at Gaza and Beersheba to achieve these outcomes.

Gaza

The first attack on Gaza in March 1917 ended in failure due to the incompetence of senior command. The EEF attacked Gaza with a preconceived plan to withdraw to water the horses if the city had not been captured by nightfall. The Welsh Division suffered huge losses on the outskirts, but the British and Anzac forces approaching from different directions joined up after entering the city despite losing many men. The Turkish commander, envisaging defeat,

was about to commence destroying the wells when British command, unaware of the success, issued a withdrawal.

The death toll and injuries were extensive but it all had to be done again. In April Gaza was attacked after a massive bombardment of the city by the British and French navies. Despite the bombardment and the use of tanks in addition to the infantry regiments, the Turks held the city and again the British and Anzac forces withdrew.

This was all too much for the British Government. General Allenby was appointed to replace General Murray, who had been exaggerating his battle reports to the War Cabinet. Allenby was despatched with instructions from Prime Minister Lloyd George to capture Jerusalem as a Christmas present for the British people to offset the gloom over the failures at Gaza and the huge death toll on the Western Front.

Beersheba

The two failures at Gaza caused a major change in strategy. A decision was taken to attack the Turkish garrison at Beersheba and to do so from the south which would be unexpected because of the difficult terrain and lack of water. Supplies were essential and the railway line from the Suez Canal, initiated by Murray, was extended to Shellal[3] just south of Gaza. Constructing a railway across the desert in such a short time is amazing and demonstrates the amount of effort required to maintain an army at war.

3 During the second battle for Gaza Australian troops discovered a Byzantine era mosaic, now known as the Shellal Mosaic. On display in the Australian War Memorial, Canberra, it is the subject of debate on whether it is a legitimate 'spoil of war' or should be returned (see: www.awm.gov.au/blog/2008/01/09/the-shellal-mosaic/).

A recent joint Israeli-Australian postage stamp issue commemorating the capture of Beersheba by the Australian Light Horse Brigade in 1917.

To create a diversion a heavy artillery bombardment of Gaza took place during late October 1917, while the major force moved to Beersheba. On October 31, British artillery commenced a barrage attack on Beersheba followed by an infantry attack. Speed was of paramount importance as the town and its supplies, particularly the water wells, had to be taken intact to support an advance towards Jerusalem. Two brigades of the Australian Mounted Division had been kept in reserve for this purpose and on the order they commenced what has become the legendary charge of the Australian Light Horse Brigade. Some military historians regard it as the last successful cavalry charge in history. The religious writer, Kelvin Crombie, describes the event and the significance of the outcome:

"At 4.30 pm on October 31, 1917 about 800 bayonet-wielding Australian horsemen set off in three columns at a canter across the five kilometre plain to Beersheba, on what would not only become an epic 'cavalry' charge, but on a venture which was to change the destiny of the former Ottoman Empire, and the course of world history ...

The horsemen rode about three kilometres before reaching the first Turkish trenches ... Many of the troops dismounted and fought the entrenched Turks in fierce hand to hand fighting ... A number of horsemen continued towards the town itself, where explosives set around the water wells were about to be detonated. Fortunately the rapid Australian advance hindered their complete destruction. By a stroke of luck [perhaps by divine arrangement] the German engineer responsible for the destruction of the wells was in Jerusalem at the time, and his replacement was in the process of detonating the explosives at random in the switchboard of a central building, when the Light Horsemen rode in. He was hindered from accomplishing his task. Had he succeeded then he would have turned a British-Anzac victory into defeat – and changed the destiny of the campaign. Had those valuable water wells been destroyed, Allenby's strategy of a quick and decisive victory and movement northwards towards Jaffa and Jerusalem would have been thwarted."[4]

If at this point readers think they have previously heard of Beersheba and wells in the same context they are correct, for there is a scriptural account:

"When Abraham reproved Abimelech about a well of water that Abimelech's servants had

4 Kelvin Crombie, *Anzacs, Empires and Israel's Restoration*, page 178.

seized, Abimelech said, 'I do not know who has done this thing; you did not tell me, and I have not heard of it until today.' So Abraham took sheep and oxen and gave them to Abimelech, and the two men made a covenant. Abraham set seven ewe lambs of the flock apart. And Abimelech said to Abraham, 'What is the meaning of these seven ewe lambs that you have set apart?' He said,'These seven ewe lambs you will take from my hand, that this may be a witness for me that I dug this well.' Therefore that place was called Beersheba, because there both of them swore an oath. So they made a covenant at Beersheba. Then Abimelech and Phicol the commander of his army rose up and returned to the land of the Philistines. Abraham planted a tamarisk tree in Beersheba and called there on the name of the LORD, the Everlasting God." (Genesis 21:25-33)

How amazing that some 4,000 years later the water wells of Beersheba were once again a central issue. More than that, how remarkable it was that those wells would be connected to the outworking of God's covenant with Abraham, in particular to events opening the way for his descendants to return to the land. The word of God is active in events in the nations and in the lives of those who through belief and baptism are connected to that same covenant of promise.

Jewish assistance

There was little that most Jews living under the oppressive Ottoman rule could do to support the British-led Anzac military action and any attempt to do so would have dire consequences. There was, however, a Jew in a unique position to provide support and he took the opportunity to do so. Aaron Aaronsohn was an internationally recognised agronomist who had developed a weather-resistant strain of wheat. He also conducted extensive research into dry-farming techniques from which he developed methods for reviving Palestinian soil, an important feature for Zionist farmers attempting to produce better crops. Aware that Zionist ambitions could not proceed under Turkish rule, Aaronsohn formed a spy network, comprising family members and associates, which was entitled NILI, an acronym from the Hebrew words for 'The Eternal One of Israel Will Not Lie'. Because of their renowned agricultural work, members of the group could move freely throughout Palestine and in 1916 two of them, travelling on an anti-locust campaign, crossed the border into Egypt. They made contact with British officials who displayed little interest in dealing with Jewish spies. Aware that Turkey was planning a second attempt to secure the Suez Canal and concerned also about the plight of Jews in Palestine, Aaronsohn obtained permission to travel to Germany for research purposes. From Germany he travelled to the United States and from there was secretly taken by a naval vessel to England.

He met with senior officials in England who were enthusiastic about the information he could provide and sent him to meet with military leaders in Egypt. Aaronsohn remained in Cairo to liaise with the military whilst his sister Sarah and associates supplied information on Turkish military bases and army movements. When Allenby assumed control of the EEF in 1917 he sought specific information to assist in an attack on Beersheba. Sarah and her associates provided data on weather, water sources, malarial swamps and every route in the area, all of which was invaluable to the attacking forces.

Just like a fictional spy story, the group was exposed when one of their carrier pigeons was caught by the Turks – but this was real life. The members of the spy network were captured and killed after being tortured. It was only the taking of Jerusalem that saved the Jews of Palestine from savage Turkish retribution. Ironically, Aaronsohn, who had escaped capture, died in a plane crash in 1919 en route from London to the Paris Peace Conference.

There is clearly no specific prophecy that relates to incidents such as these but they make up the myriad steps, sometimes small, that bring about the completion of a prophesied event. This is an example of God utilising the abilities of certain people and their position in the community to assist in achieving prophesied outcomes. The people involved must, however, have the commitment and the courage to complete the task. Jewish historian Martin Gilbert contends that Britain's indebtedness to the Jewish spy group for their contribution to the success of the Palestinian campaign was a contributing factor to the issue of the Balfour Declaration.[5]

Taking Jerusalem

Within two weeks of capturing Beersheba, Allenby's troops moved north to engage the Turkish forces and take Jerusalem. Allenby's strategy was to avoid fighting in the city of Jerusalem by defeating the Turks in the Judean-Samarian hills and then to cut road access to the city. The fighting commenced on November 18, 1917 and continued for three weeks with extensive losses on both sides. The final offensive began on the morning of December 8; British regiments moved towards Jerusalem from Jaffa, the Welsh moved north from Hebron and the Australians fought their way into and captured Bethlehem by that evening. With losses in the hills and armies moving towards them, the Turks admitted defeat and fled, including those

remaining in Jerusalem. It was more than Allenby could have expected and his official report stated:

"Towards dusk the British troops were reported to have passed Lifta, and to be within sight of the city. On this news being received, a sudden panic fell on the Turks west and south-west of the town, and at 5 o'clock civilians were surprised to see a Turkish column galloping furiously cityward along the Jaffa road. In passing they alarmed all units within sight or hearing, and the weary infantry arose and fled, bootless and without rifles, never pausing to think or fight. After four centuries of conquest the Turk was ridding the land of his presence in bitterness of defeat, and a great enthusiasm arose among the Jews."[6]

The official entry

On December 9, the mayor of Jerusalem and other officials came out of the city to meet the victors. They encountered two soldiers searching for food, who hurriedly located senior officers. Brigadier-General Watson, much to his surprise, became the recipient of the keys of the city handed over by civilian officials.

The ceremony to mark the capture of Jerusalem and the end of four hundred years of Ottoman Turk rule took place on December 11. The official entry is graphically portrayed in the iconic photograph of Allenby and his senior officers entering the city on foot through the Jaffa Gate. It was a carefully staged event with Allenby following the strict instructions of the British Government to enter, not as a conquering hero, but in humility, reflecting the significance of the occasion and the importance of the Holy City. The official party with a guard of honour comprising troops from all participating nations continued to the Tower of David for a

5 Sir Martin Gilbert, *The Story of Israel*, page 10.

6 Crombie, op. cit., page 195.

Allenby entering Jerusalem

ceremony, including the reading of a proclamation of martial law.

An awkward moment

After the ceremony the official party proceeded to lunch at the former General Staff Headquarters of the Turkish army. During lunch an awkward diplomatic incident occurred. The incident had its origins in an agreement negotiated in 1916 by Sir Mark Sykes of Britain and François George Picot of France, acting on behalf of their respective governments. Known as the Sykes-Picot Agreement, and subsequently endorsed by Russia, it specified the allocation of territories should Britain be successful in defeating the Ottoman Turks. Britain was to control Jordan, southern Iraq and a coastal area of Palestine near Haifa mainly for accessing the other two regions. France was allocated south-east Turkey, northern Iraq, Syria and Lebanon, while Russia was granted Istanbul, the Dardanelles and Armenia. Palestine was to be jointly administered by the three countries.

As noted in Chapter four, this was one of several agreements made by Britain around this time with conflicting allocations of regions. The agreement which ultimately had the greatest effect was the Balfour Declaration of November 1917, acknowledging the right of the Jews to a homeland in Palestine. Interestingly, Sykes did not argue against this variance to his agreement with Picot as he had by that time become sympathetic to Zionist ideals. It also negated promises made to the Arabs by Colonel T E Lawrence (Lawrence of Arabia) that they could possess Syria in recognition of the support they provide to the British by opposing the Turks. In addition, it ran counter to an agreement that the Cairo office of the Foreign Service made with Hussein bin Ali for him to become ruler of Jordan. The agreement was entered into when the war was going badly for Britain and France was bearing the brunt of German attacks on the Western Front. As circumstances improved for Britain, further consideration was given to what had been agreed and the concept of joint administration of Palestine was becoming increasingly unacceptable. Francois Picot was about to discover just how far British interest in shared control of Palestine had fallen.

French troops had been refused participation in the battles for Palestine but Picot was invited, albeit reluctantly, to join the official party for the entry to Jerusalem. During lunch he informed the assembled group that on the following day he would commence setting up civil government in Jerusalem. Colonel T E Lawrence, one of Allenby's senior officers, participated in the official entry and in *Seven Pillars of Wisdom* he expressed, in his inimitable style, the effect of Picot's statement on those in attendance at the lunch:

"Salad, chicken mayonnaise and foie gras sandwiches hung in our wet mouths unmunched, while we turned to Allenby and gaped. Even he seemed for the moment at a loss. We began to fear that the idol might betray a frailty. But his face grew red: he swallowed, his chin coming forward (in the way we loved), whilst he said, grimly, 'In the military zone the only authority is that of the Commander-in-Chief – myself'."[7]

And thus ended France's quest for involvement in the administration of Palestine.

Some parts of the Sykes-Picot Agreement were, however, subsequently met when a mandate for France to administer Syria and Lebanon was granted in 1920 by the Supreme Council of the Paris Peace Conference.

A 'drying up' indeed

The contraction of the Turkish Empire took place over a period of over two hundred years, being indeed a 'drying up' as stated in Revelation. The Turks were defeated in the battle of Vienna in 1689 preventing them moving into Western Europe and resulting by 1699 in the Hungarian section of their empire being ceded to the Habsburgs of Austria. The major decline commenced in 1820 with the loss of Greece, followed in that decade by Russia acquiring regions in its southern parts and France occupying Algeria. Through the second half of the nineteenth century Turkey was weakened by the effects of the Crimean War against Russia (with Britain and France allied with Turkey) and later a separate war against Russia followed by war with Greece. These wars and the Balkans War of 1912 resulted in Turkey losing practically all her European territories.

After capturing Jerusalem, Allenby's forces continued on to defeat the Turks in towns in the north of Palestine and subsequently captured Damascus and Beirut. This brought to an end four hundred years of Turkish control of Palestine, Syria and Lebanon. At the same time, British troops were advancing through Mesopotamia (modern-day Iraq) up the valley of the Euphrates. That conquest was

7 T E Lawrence, *Seven Pillars of Wisdom*, page 455.

the final end of the Turkish Empire which had once extended into central Europe, southern Russia, the Middle East and North Africa.

Alternative opinions

The interpretation of the 'drying up' prophecy as expressed in this chapter has been in existence for at least three centuries, but longevity is not a guarantee of accuracy. It is important that opinions be tested against subsequent events in case they had been unduly coloured by contemporary events or attitudes. It is of interest that the interpretation explained in this chapter was in existence long before the Turkish Empire commenced its decline. However, it is still appropriate that it be re-evaluated.

One alternative opinion is that it applies literally and that a future cessation of water flow will cause massive economic hardship in Syria and Iraq which rely on the downstream flow of the Euphrates. This opinion is sometimes linked with the suggestion that "kings of the east" is a reference to Jewish captives returning to Israel from nations to which they had been taken after a successful Arab attack.[8] Another view is that, although the headwaters of the Euphrates are in Turkey, the river is sometimes used in scripture to represent Babylon (e.g., Jeremiah 13:4-7) and consequently the prophecy could apply to modern-day Iraq.

The authors consider that these are improbable intentions of the prophecy because:
- Revelation is a book of symbol; and
- its message applies primarily to believers under the new covenant and seldom applies to natural Israel. The traditional 'drying up' interpretation is one of the few occasions where there is a link to the land of Israel, but it occurs in the context

of preparing the way for events applicable to the household of Christ.

Other Bible students have applied the prophecy symbolically to the harlot Babylon, representative of the apostate church. This opinion links the sixth vial of Revelation 16 with the punishment of symbolic Babylon referred to a few verses later in Revelation 17, leading some to the opinion that the 'drying up' must be an event immediately preceding Armageddon and the destruction of the harlot Babylon.[9]

These events are close together in scripture but, as our review of other prophecies will show, fulfilment often does not occur within the time frame and order of events expected by men and women. The 'drying up' precedes, but does not necessarily have to precede immediately, the subsequent events. Applying the 'drying up' to the future means that those most significant political and military events that paved the way for the return of the Jews, and accepted by many as fulfilment of God's word, were merely incidental and not a specific prophecy. Moving much of Revelation into a future time frame runs perilously close to the Futurist interpretation under which the various visions are attributed to the last several years of Gentile times. Many who hold this view also consider that the events take place during a period in which the anti-Christ runs rampant upon the earth. This interpretation negates John's visions as a rolling-out of events affecting God's true household over many centuries.

On balance we consider that the 'drying up' events were a fulfilment of a key prophecy; one that opened the way for matters integral to God's plan with His called out people, both natural and spiritual.

---

8 www.christadelphianbooks.org/agora

9 See, for example, Brother A D Norris, *Apocalypse For Everyman*, pages 279,280.

6

PERSECUTION THEN THE HOLOCAUST

"Then Haman said to King Ahasuerus, 'There is a certain people scattered abroad and dispersed among the peoples in all the provinces of your kingdom. Their laws are different from those of every other people, and they do not keep the king's laws, so that it is not to the king's profit to tolerate them.'" (Esther 3:8)

PERSECUTION was a feature of life for the Jews of Europe and Russia. It was not necessarily constant or widespread, but at any given time a Jewish community somewhere was likely to be experiencing persecution in one form or another.

The persecution could comprise:
- small unrecorded acts of aggression;
- banishment from towns or whole countries;
- restriction to specified parts of a town or areas within a country;
- widespread organised attacks causing many injuries and fatalities;
- exclusion from education and certain forms of employment;
- cancellation of debts owed by Christians to Jews;
- compulsory military conscription of young men.

The difficulties faced by the dispersed Jews should not have come as a surprise as they were foretold by God through Moses during their time in the wilderness. Blessings were specified for obedience and curses for disobedience. The Jews may not have expected a continuing application through many centuries but God had not placed a time limit on the response to their behaviour. In regard to their scattering among the nations God said:

"And among these nations you shall find no respite, and there shall be no resting-place for the sole of your foot, but the LORD will give you there a trembling heart and failing eyes and a languishing soul. Your life shall hang in doubt before you. Night and day you shall be in dread and have no assurance of your life. In the morning you shall say, 'If only it were evening!' and at evening you shall say, 'If only it were morning!' because of the dread that your heart shall feel, and the sights that your eyes shall see." (Deuteronomy 28:65-67)

Daily life was often difficult and challenging with Jewish communities at times fearing for their survival. Some of the particularly significant events that affected them are set out below:

The First Crusade

In November 1095 Pope Urban II called for a crusade to defend the Christian Byzantine Empire from invading Muslim Turks and then to continue on to rescue Jerusalem from the Egyptian Muslims. After a recruiting programme, five armies headed by noblemen departed from France in 1096 for Constantinople. They were joined by large numbers of untrained townspeople and peasants inspired by the concept of protecting Christianity and the Holy Land from Muslim control. As the armies entered

Germany the idea took hold of attacking Jewish communities in retribution for their role as so-called 'Christ killers'. The enthusiasm of the crusaders for this was enhanced by ideas of spiritual benefits that would accrue to them. "It was spread abroad that killing a Jew would secure atonement for one's sins. Certain of the leaders took an oath not to leave the country before they killed a Jew with their own hands."[1] The outcome was that many Jews in Germany were murdered and their houses and synagogues burnt. In a number of locations the Jewish communities took their own lives to avoid falling into the hands of the mobs.

Final outcome of the Crusades

Many in the Crusade died on the way or returned home but the remaining members of the armies reached Constantinople by May 1097 where they assisted the Byzantines (Eastern Roman Empire) in defeating the Turkish Muslims. A much reduced number of Crusaders proceeded to Jerusalem and in July 1099 defeated the Egyptian Muslims in a great slaughter. A Crusader kingdom was established in Jerusalem but it ceased in 1144 when the Muslims regained control.

A further two Crusades took place over the next century and, although various cities were conquered and occupied until the fifteenth century, no lasting Crusader kingdom could be established. In 1187 the Muslims under Saladin regained control of Jerusalem and most of the surrounding region. The Fourth Crusade (1202-04) included a reversal of form by the Europeans who, on that occasion, attacked Constantinople and looted much of its treasure. The Byzantines regained control in 1261 and a much weakened Eastern Empire continued until conquered by the Ottoman Turks in 1453.

1 Max Margolis and Alexander Marx, *History of the Jewish People*, page 360.

The blame game

A recurring problem for the Jews was that of being blamed for engaging in anti-Christian activities or for being the instigators of plagues and other calamities. In superstitious times it was not difficult to whip up hysteria about the alleged devious activities of a people generally viewed with suspicion by others.

Blood libels

The first recorded accusation of ritual murder took place in 1144 in Norwich, England, where it was alleged that the Jews had killed a local boy to use his blood in a Passover meal. This resulted in an uprising against the Jews but with no reported deaths. However, in 1190 in the same city the accusation was repeated, leading to the murder of many Jews. Similar accusations were levelled against Jews in Europe, an early recorded occasion being in 1171 in Blois, France, resulting in thirty-three Jews being burnt at the stake.[2]

Blood libel accusations against the Jewish community in Sandomierz, Poland, were made in 1698 and 1710 and on the second occasion seven Jews were executed and the remainder expelled. A painting by Charles de Prevot depicting the supposed murders can still be seen in the Sandomierz Cathedral. Frequent viewing of the painting by regular participants in the Mass would have reinforced a belief in the validity of such accusations against the Jews.

Interestingly, in 2005 a research team from the University of Warsaw interviewed many inhabitants of the district to ascertain their impressions of the painting. Some were not aware of its existence, but others knew of it and the message it portrayed and

2 Chaim Potok, *Wanderings*, page 309.

responded with comments to the effect that "as it hangs in a church the event must be true".[3]

Surprisingly, for a concept steeped in superstition, blood libel accusations occurred at times in the nineteenth century and even the early twentieth century. Charges were laid against Jews in 1840 in Syria, 1853 in Russia, 1882 in Hungary, 1891 in Germany and again in Russia in 1913. These events did not produce the hysterical reactions of the Middle Ages, but in each case Jews were imprisoned with some dying under torture and others, although ultimately acquitted, enduring criminal trials and public humiliation. The publicity from the trials markedly contributed to anti-Jewish sentiment in those countries.[4]

Desecration of the host

Similar in concept to blood libel accusations were the host desecration charges that commenced in the twelfth century following the declaration of the Doctrine of Transubstantiation. This doctrine contends that the bread (the wafer) and the wine used in the Mass become the literal body and blood of Jesus Christ. Rumours began circulating throughout Europe that Jews were stealing the wafer and piercing it to re-enact the Crucifixion. Common reactions were for crowds to burn synagogues or for city authorities to declare that debts owed to Jews did not have to be repaid. The latter was an extremely popular move which raises the question of whether many of the accusations were contrived with economic gain in mind.

Host desecration charges reached a peak in Germany in the fourteenth century. One instigator of trouble, named Rindfleisch, led mobs on a murder spree through the Jewish quarters of several towns. Jews began leaving Germany and the authorities, fearful of the economic consequences of their departure, had Rindfleisch hanged, thus bringing host stealing accusations to an end.[5]

The Black Plague

Bubonic plague carried by fleas from infected rats entered Europe in 1348, possibly carried by traders from China and India. As the plague spread the populace was in terror and many fanciful ideas developed about its cause. A common opinion in these superstitious times was that it originated from bad air generated by astrological forces.

The plague continued on and off throughout Europe for approximately fifty years with catastrophic outcomes. Some sources estimate that it reduced the world population by 100 million to near 350 million.[6]

In some cities Jewish death rates were lower, possibly because of their greater cleanliness and separation from the general populace, and rumours soon began to circulate about them instigating the plague by poisoning wells and rivers. Under torture a number of Jews confessed that this was correct, resulting in the false accusations being deemed factual. The authorities in many cities in what are now the countries of Spain, France, Germany and Switzerland responded by arranging massacres or expulsions of their Jewish communities. Amongst the worst atrocities were the killing of six thousand Jews in Mainz and the burning alive of two thousand in Strasbourg.

---

3 Joanna Tokarska-Bakir, *Sandomierz Blood Libel Final Report 2006.*
4 *A Brief Chronology of anti-Semitism,* www.jewishagency.org
5 Max Margolis and Alexander Marx, *History of the Jewish People,* page 235.
6 United States Census Bureau, *Historical Estimates of World Population.*

The Inquisition

The Inquisition was a process established by the Roman Catholic Church for identifying and punishing Catholics who held 'heretical' opinions. Initially it focused on members of the Waldensians and Albigensians which were organisations that questioned certain doctrines and practices of the Catholic Church. The term 'Medieval Inquisition' is applied to various Inquisitions of the twelfth and thirteenth centuries.

Councils of bishops and archbishops conducted the early Inquisitions, the first of which took place in the south of France in 1184. Pope Gregory IX in 1231 transferred responsibility for conducting Inquisitions to the Dominican Order. Many thousands of so-called heretics were imprisoned or put to death as a consequence of conclusions reached sometimes on the basis of 'confessions' obtained under torture, the use of which was sanctioned by Pope Innocent IV in 1252.

Spanish and Portuguese Inquisitions

The Spanish Inquisition commenced in 1480 and differed from earlier Inquisitions in that it was under the authority of the Spanish monarchs, King Ferdinand and Queen Isabella, but thoroughly supported by the Pope. Jews who had converted to Catholicism were called 'conversos' and were the principal target of the inquisitors. Large numbers of Jews had converted over the preceding century, some to avoid anti-Jewish riots and others to obtain social acceptability. In 1492 a royal edict was issued expelling all Jews from Spain, resulting in more converting to Catholicism to remain in the country and consequently more appearances before the Inquisition. Many 'conversos' were imprisoned and sometimes tortured to obtain responses to accusations that they practised Judaism secretly and were not genuine converts. There is debate about the numbers but Jewish sources estimate that approximately 13,000 Jews were burned at the stake and 150,000 to 170,000 were forced to leave Spain.[7]

Many of the expelled Jews moved to Portugal and others to Turkey and parts of Africa. Portugal, however, was no place of respite and many of the new arrivals moved on quickly to other countries. Those who remained risked being sold into slavery or forcibly converted to Christianity which compounded their problems by making them targets for the Inquisition. The Portuguese Inquisition commenced in 1536 and, as with Spain, focused on identifying 'conversos' to determine if their conversion was genuine. Again there is debate about the number of deaths but it is estimated that 1,800 Jews were burned at the stake.[8]

In contrast to current Jewish/Islamic antagonism, Jews who fled to Turkey were warmly welcomed by the Muslims and Jewish communities were successfully established in Istanbul and other cities. Many individuals rose to prominence and appointments of Jews as physicians to the Sultans became common practice. This acceptance continued for centuries and, while there were some outrages against Jews in Palestine during World War One, in the Second World War the Jews of Turkey remained secure.

Massacres in Poland

The most brutal attacks against Jews after the Crusades occurred in 1648 at the hands of Cossack mercenaries and others who joined them. At that time the Ukraine was controlled by Poland and living within the region were Lithuanian refugees holding the Greek Orthodox faith and known as

7 Potok, page 317 and Margolis & Marx, page 472.
8 *The Inquisition*, Jewish Virtual Library, www.jewishvirtuallibrary.org

Cossacks. Oppression by the Catholic Polish rulers caused the Cossacks, led by Bogdan Chmielnicki, to rise against them and ultimately to defeat the Polish army.[9]

That defeat encouraged Ukrainian serfs to join with the Cossacks in attacking their Polish masters and the Jews who were often the administrators of the estates owned by the Polish gentry and the collectors of a repressive tax system.

A decade of unrestrained brutality followed during which up to 100,000 Jews and many more Poles were slaughtered. The methods of slaughter included sawing prisoners into pieces, flaying them alive, burning them over open fires and cutting them apart with swords. It is difficult in our age to perceive what drives people to such levels of cruelty and the terror it would bring upon those being persecuted.

Misery in Russia

Life for the Jews in Russia frequently measured up to the dire predictions of the prophets about sufferings during their period of dispersal:

"For thus says the LORD: Your hurt is incurable, and your wound is grievous. There is none to uphold your cause, no medicine for your wound, no healing for you. All your lovers have forgotten you; they care nothing for you; for I have dealt you the blow of an enemy, the punishment of a merciless foe, because your guilt is great, because your sin is flagrant."

(Jeremiah 30:12-14)

---

9 Cossacks are generally associated with Russia rather than Poland, the reason being that in 1654 Chmielnicki transferred his allegiance to the Czar of Russia. This resulted in the Cossack region of the Ukraine being incorporated into the Muscovite empire, which became part of Russia in 1700 under Peter the Great.

Intertwined with this message, however, is the promise that God would restore Israel to the land and bless them:

"Thus says the LORD: Behold, I will restore the fortunes of the tents of Jacob and have compassion on his dwellings; the city shall be rebuilt on its mound, and the palace shall stand where it used to be. Out of them shall come songs of thanksgiving, and the voices of those who celebrate. I will multiply them, and they shall not be few; I will make them honoured, and they shall not be small."   (verses 18,19)

This message of a restoration provided hope, but in the intervening centuries oppression had to be endured. In the seventeenth and eighteenth centuries Russia's practice of annexing surrounding lands resulted in the nation at times having the largest number of Jews in the world. Lithuania, Poland and former Swedish lands along the Baltic coast were included in the Russian census of 1897 counting 5,189,401 Jews, representing 4.13 per cent of the total population. Initially it was common practice to kill many of the Jews acquired by these expansionary activities or to expel them. Later they were permitted to move throughout the acquired regions, but in Great Russia they were restricted to a region on the western border known as the Pale of Settlement. Life for most Russians was very harsh but particularly so for the Jews who, in addition to the general privations, were restricted in regard to locality, education and occupations and at times had to endure beatings and expulsion. We shall limit our review to the nineteenth and twentieth centuries, the period in which some of the harshest measures were applied.

Czar Alexander I (1801-1825) initially relaxed some restrictions by allowing Jews to move to the cities, to have access to education and to pursue any occupation. However, in 1821 the government reverted to banning Jews from schooling and professional positions and forced them to leave Great Russia and return to the Pale. His successor, Czar Nicholas I, continued the policy of oppression and, in 1827, introduced the particularly cruel practice of requiring each community to provide a certain quota of boys aged between twelve and eighteen to serve a twenty-five year period of conscription in the Russian army. Conditions were very harsh with many conscripts not surviving the twenty-five years and those who did often lost all contact with their families and Judaism.

In 1881 Czar Alexander II was killed in St. Petersburg by a home-made bomb thrown under his carriage. This event was a key factor in the commencement of a period of unprecedented upheaval in Russia culminating in the Boleshevik Revolution in 1917. Among the group held responsible for the assassination was Gesia Gelfman, a woman of Jewish origin. This provided the spark for widespread anti-Jewish riots, known as pogroms. There is debate about whether they were instigated by the authorities, but it is indisputable that the police were unwilling to interfere and that troops were often called out late and responded passively. Pogroms took place in many towns with the rioters usually comprising local labourers supported by peasants from outlying areas. Although numerous attacks took place over a period of approximately three years relatively few Jews were killed. However, many were beaten, communities were terrorised and thousands of homes were burned or looted causing severe hardship for many families.

A second and more brutal wave of pogroms took place between 1903 and 1906 in many Russian cities, with one of the worst at Odessa in 1905 in which four hundred Jews were killed and much property destroyed.[10] At Easter 1903 a pogrom in Kishinev, Moldova, resulted in fifty deaths and is significant in that the mob was incited by Russian Orthodox priests. A third wave of pogroms accompanied the civil war that raged across Russia for five years after the 1917 Revolution. The death toll during this period was severe as Jews were deliberately targeted by armed forces from each of the opposing armies. The Jewish author and sociologist, Nahum Gergel (1887-1931), in a detailed analysis calculated that up to 250,000 Jewish civilians were killed in that five-year period.[11] The frequency of violence convinced many Jews that they had no future in Russia and between 1880 and 1920 two million emigrated, the majority to the United States. In the same period a further one million Jews from other European nations migrated to the United States. Only about 50,000 European Jews moved to Palestine during this time.

An open door but few enter

Despite the defeat of the occupying Turks in 1917 and Britain's declaration of Palestine as a homeland for the Jews, relatively few migrated to the land. For some, especially those in Russia, travel costs and emigration restrictions were a factor, but for most Jews in Europe assimilation was a preferred option. For those who did decide to emigrate, as before the war, the destination of choice was the United States, the perceived modern 'Promised Land'.

Most Bible students assumed that the opening up of opportunities would cause many Jews to migrate to the land. Few, if any, perceived that unprecedented events would be needed to convince

10 John Klier and Sholome Lambrozo, *Pogroms: Anti-Jewish Violence in Modern Russian History*, pages 248-289.
11 Nahum Gergel, *Article on pogroms in the Ukraine 1918-1921*, Yiddish 1928, English 1951.

the Jews that there was no future for them in the countries in which they had lived for centuries. Likewise, there was no expectation that Britain and most other nations would refuse to accept significant numbers of Jewish immigrants when they did commence fleeing from Europe. However, in retrospect it is evident that this lack of support forced the Jews to recognise Palestine as their only option.

Germany the ultimate aggressor

Germany was to be the instrument to fulfil one of Jeremiah's prophecies about the return to the land:

> "Behold, I am sending for many fishers, declares the LORD, and they shall catch them. And afterwards I will send for many hunters, and they shall hunt them from every mountain and every hill, and out of the clefts of the rocks."
>
> (Jeremiah 16:16)

Born in 1889, Adolf Hitler served in the German army during the First World War. Bitterly upset about Germany's defeat, and the economic decline of the nation caused by reparation payments to the victorious nations, Hitler set out to elevate Germany to his perception of the nation's role in the world. He became leader of the National Socialist (Nazi) Party in 1921 and in many party meetings and at large rallies spoke with extreme vitriol about Jews and the need to rid Germany of them.

In 1925 he published *Mein Kampf (My Struggle)* in which he expressed his political and military aims for Germany, together with his distaste for the Jews. He had fertile ground on which to work for many Germans had been influenced by Lutheran anti-Semitism, based on Martin Luther's disdain for Jews and by Catholic opinion of Jews as 'Christ killers'. Hatred of the Jews was also fuelled by the economic depression of the late 1920s which Hitler and others attributed to Jewish financial manipulation.

Oppression of the Jews commenced in the early 1920s with attacks on Jewish cemeteries and synagogues and escalated throughout that decade into destruction of Jewish properties and attacks on individuals. In 1933, after much political manoeuvring, Hitler became Chancellor of Germany (see also Chapter 7) and anti-Jewish activity became more severe, including the removal of Jews from public sector positions and from many professions such as Law and Medicine. The infamous racial legislation, known as the Nuremberg Laws, passed in 1935, stated that citizenship only applied to "a national of German or kindred blood" with Jews defined as not being of German blood. Exploitation of Jews, including confiscation of properties and the transfer of their businesses to Germans, increased with the legal support provided by these laws.

Under Nazi rule prior to the Second World War, concentration camps were built in Germany for imprisoning citizens who opposed the regime along with selected Jews, usually those in positions of prominence. Those sent to camps such as Dachau and Buchenwald endured hard work with beatings and sometimes torture. Many died in these camps, but much worse was to come after 1939 with the mass extermination camps built in Poland.

Additional to these acts of brutality and exploitation the Jews of Germany and Austria, which was annexed in 1938, ran the daily risk of being rounded up for menial and humiliating tasks. These activities were arranged by Nazi storm troopers but, disconcertingly, many German and Austrian citizens, who had previously lived harmoniously with the Jews, enjoyed watching and participating in their humiliation.

An eye-witness in Vienna described the scene:

> "Nazi storm troopers, surrounded by jostling, jeering and laughing mobs of 'golden Viennese hearts', dragged Jews from shops, offices and

Yellow star that Jews were ordered to wear from September 1, 1941.

Buchenwald Concentration Camp

Photo: Sid Levett

homes, men and women, put scrubbing-brushes in their hands, splashed them well with acid, and made them go down on their knees and scrub away for hours at the hopeless task of removing anti-Nazi propaganda ... Every morning in the Habsburger gasse the SS squads were told how many Jews to round up that day for menial tasks."[12]

Many Jews realised that there was no future for them under these conditions, and

12 Richard J Evans, *The Third Reich In Power*, page 658.

by the time the borders were closed at the outbreak of war in 1939 approximately half of the 500,000 Jews in Germany and the 200,000 in Austria had fled.

The Holocaust commences

Germany invaded Poland in 1939 and as the army advanced eastwards it was followed by specialist death squads manned by volunteers under instruction to locate and kill the Polish intelligentsia, Jews and gypsies. The Jewish communities of each town and village were rounded up then marched to a site where they dug their own graves and were shot. Volunteers were sought for these callous activities and many Germans came forward,

supported by volunteers from Albania, Serbo-Croatia and Bosnia, many at the bidding of Mohammad Amin al-Husayni, the Grand Mufti of Jerusalem. A similar practice was adopted after the invasion of Russia in 1941 with killings of Soviet political officials and entire Jewish communities.

The official records of the death squads identify that they killed one million people as they moved across Poland and Russia behind the German army. However, it became apparent to the German leaders that a more efficient method would be needed to dispose of Polish and Soviet officials and the millions of Jews in Europe and Russia.

Hans Schweitzer ("Mjölnir"). Poster in the German Federal Archives, Koblenz.
Photo courtesy of Dr. Robert D. Brooks.

Nazi propaganda poster:
"The Jew – War inciter – War prolonger"

parts of the Occupied Countries to be killed on a mass scale by gassing and their bodies burned in large crematoria. A department headed by Adolf Eichmann set about the huge task of building the camps, obtaining rolling stock, arranging timetables and deportation schedules from numerous locations. From this process came camps such as Auschwitz, Birkenau and Treblinka, names which are synonymous with mass killings and acts of appalling brutality. Much has been written about this period in history and it is not our intention to write in detail here about these events.

The chilling feature of this planned annihilation of a race of people is that it was directed by the German Government and required meticulous planning and the input of thousands of participants. Most Germans, if unaware of the methods used, were well aware that Jews were disappearing and most treated the matter with indifference. Germans, as well as many Ukrainians, Latvians and Lithuanians, were guards at the camps and apparently had no qualms about participating in mass murder and acts of senseless brutality to people who were of no threat to them at all.

The end result of the Holocaust was that six million Jews and approximately one million other civilians were killed by the death squads or at the concentration camps. The Nazis also took particularly harsh measures against Russian prisoners of war; three million were deliberately killed or died from cold or hunger during captivity.

The prophets could not perceive the methods that would be used but the outcome was foretold:

"I will scatter them among the nations whom neither they nor their fathers have known, and I will send the sword after them, until I have consumed them." (Jeremiah 9:16)

'The Final Solution'

Senior Nazi officials met in January 1942 and devised a scheme known as 'The Final Solution'. Under a well documented plan, camps would be constructed near rail networks in Poland and Jews transported to the camps by trains from all

Where was God during the Holocaust?

After events in which there has been much loss of life, either by natural causes or from the actions of men, the question of why God allows such events to occur is often asked. This entirely understandable query has been raised about the Holocaust both by Jews who suffered through it and by others stunned at its enormity.

Even with a knowledge that Jews would have to endure persecution, we can struggle to understand why the Holocaust had to be so severe. We cannot fully perceive the way in which God works in the nations and why each prophesied event is necessary, but we can gain a level of understanding. A key fact to remember is that through lengthy periods of history oppression by authorities and attack by invading nations was a feature of life for many people. The Jews faced those standard challenges as well as specific punishments brought upon them by God for disobeying His instructions.

From their early days in Canaan the Israelites suffered punishment from surrounding nations for their disobedience, with much misery and deportation occurring at the hands of the Assyrians in 721 BC and the Babylonians in 587 BC. Much later in AD 70 the siege and subsequent conquest of Jerusalem by the Romans caused unimaginable horrors. The European and Russian persecutions described in this chapter brought great misery upon the Jews over an extensive period of time.

More Jews died in the Holocaust than in any previous period of persecution, but the number of deaths in no way worsens the suffering of each individual affected by a particular event. The terror and anguish of those caught up in the Holocaust would have been intense, but the effect of being attacked by marauding Crusaders or cut to pieces by Cossacks would have been no less appalling. The inescapable conclusion, perhaps difficult to perceive in our time, is that over the centuries men have regularly committed terrible atrocities upon their fellows.

A common explanation by the churches is that the Holocaust was the work of Satan entering into the minds of men causing them to do such terrible things. Given their culpability in creating a culture in which anti-Semitism could thrive it is perhaps understandable that the churches would look for someone to blame. As we do not believe there is a literal Satan, we do not have the luxury of allocating the cause to an external agent of evil. The human race is perfectly capable of committing great acts of evil without supernatural influence. Apart from that there is an absurdity in the logic, for it would mean that Satan brought about the fulfilment of God's prophecies of punishment and the subsequent restoration of Israel.

The answer is that God 'allowed' evil men free rein for a period of time to convince His people that there was no future for them in Europe and that they should return to their own land. The event to bring this about had to be terrible; it had to be widespread and it had to exceed previous persecutions which they had endured and then shrugged off as the price to pay for maintaining a separate identity in a foreign land. It had to be sufficiently intense to make the Jews realise that they would never be assimilated into the nations in which they lived.

The principle of evil existing only because it is 'allowed' by God is expressed as:

"I form light and create darkness, I make well-being and create calamity ('evil', KJV), I am the LORD, who does all these things." (Isaiah 45:7)

God did not have to 'program' a group of exceptionally evil men to bring this about. All that was needed was for God to 'allow' those with evil intent against His people to have their way for a period of time. Although exceptionally chilling in its widespread activity and meticulous planning, the evil nature of the perpetrators of the Holocaust is similar to that displayed by others around that time. For example:

- In the Spanish Civil War of the 1930s approximately 500,000 Spaniards were killed by their own countrymen in military action and by execution.
- Civilian and prisoner of war deaths from the Japanese invasion of Manchuria and occupation of countries in the Pacific region during the 1940s are counted in the many millions.
- Stalin's aim to eliminate every trace of political dissent and punish peasants opposed to collectivisation of their farms is estimated to have cost the lives of between ten and twenty million Russians and Ukrainians by execution, forced labour in Siberian camps and by re-settlement of entire communities to areas in which they starved to death.

People do not have to be raised up to commit exceptionally evil acts; for many all that is needed is opportunity. Since the beginning of time God has 'allowed' opportunity to occur generally and specifically when necessary, to bring about required outcomes, including against His own people. An example of this was God's use of the barbaric Assyrians to punish the "godless" people in Judah (Isaiah 10:5-12), after which God punished Assyria also for its "arrogant heart" in acting so callously.

We have the privilege of knowing that the concept of the inherent goodness of man is incorrect. We also know that when major evil occurs it is not at the direction of a fallen angel battling for supremacy over God. This understanding places a responsibility on those in the household of God to serve Him by battling against the sin that dwells within.

The Holocaust in prophecy

Reference was made earlier to Jeremiah 16 where God is seen as taking steps to encourage his people to return to their ancient homeland:

"'As the LORD lives who brought up the people of Israel out of the north country and out of all the countries where he had driven them. *For I will bring them back to their own land that I gave to their fathers*. Behold, I am sending for many *fishers*, declares the LORD, and they shall catch them. And afterwards I will send for many *hunters*, and they shall hunt them from every mountain and every hill, and out of the clefts of the rocks. For my eyes are on all their ways. They are not hidden from me, nor is their iniquity concealed from my eyes. But first I will doubly repay their iniquity and their sin, because they have polluted my land with the carcasses of their detestable idols, and have filled my inheritance with their abominations.' O LORD, my strength and my stronghold, my refuge in the day of trouble, to you shall the nations come from the ends of the earth and say: 'Our fathers have inherited nothing but lies, worthless things in which there is no profit. Can man make for himself gods? Such are not gods!' Therefore, behold, I will make them know, this once I will make them know my power and my might, and they shall know that my name is the LORD."

(Jeremiah 16:15-21)

Verse 15 promises that God will bring His people back to their homeland from "the north country" (Russia and Europe), and from other lands. Verse 16 refers to two agents sent by God for this purpose – fishers and hunters. A fisher seeks to lure his prey, whereas a hunter actively stalks or entraps his prey.

Perhaps we can see in the fishers a reference to the Zionist movement which arose at about the turn of the twentieth century and which sought to encourage Jewish migration, in particular from Europe to Israel. This would lead us to see the hunters as those more aggressive and hostile forces in Europe which culminated in the full brutality of the Nazi regime in Germany and occupied Europe which hunted down the Jews and ultimately forced reluctant Jewry to view migration to Israel more favourably.[13] Appalling as it was, the Holocaust was an instrument by which God brought His people back to the land because He could see their iniquity (their assimilation in Western culture?) (verse 17), with the eventual objective of turning them back to Him (verse 21), an aspect of the prophecy that will be fulfilled only when the chastened Jews accept the rule of their Messiah. Might we have the wisdom to heed the lesson for ourselves and our own walk towards Zion.

---

13 Writing of this passage in 1930 (prior to the rise of Hitler and the Holocaust), Brother C C Walker could see its relevance to events then unfolding in Europe: "The true nature of this latter-day crisis is very little understood in 'Christendom', which is faithless concerning 'the purpose of God according to election' (Romans 9). Nevertheless there is some suspicion that a Jewish crisis is at hand, in which the fate of the nations of Christendom will be very deeply involved. And the inevitable tendency of the nations to burden themselves with Jerusalem and the Holy Land for the sake of conquering world-dominion is a most cheering sign of the times to those who, like Jeremiah, have the hope of Israel in the knowledge of the purpose of God, and the endeavour to conform to His will" (*The Christadelphian*, 1930, page 434). An appreciation of prophecy in accordance with the promises to the patriarchs can help us to appreciate events as they unfold under the direction of the angels.

7

CATHOLIC COMPLICITY WITH HITLER

THE narrow streets of Vienna's Jewish Quarter and its central square, the Judenplatz, lie in the shadows of St. Stephen's, the city's major cathedral built between the thirteenth and fifteenth centuries. Mosaic tiles on its roof depict the double-headed eagle, symbol of the Holy Roman Empire ruled from Vienna by the Habsburg dynasty. How incongruous that for centuries the Catholic Mass was conducted in the vicinity of the Jewish Quarter. How particularly incongruous that part of the large Catholic community of this city met in a location where they could not miss the destruction of Jewish property on *Crystal Night* in 1938 and the rounding up of Jewish inhabitants for deportation in the 1940s.

Thus it was across Germany and the occupied countries of Europe. In the shadows of great cathedrals, in the vicinity of village churches, Jewish property was destroyed or confiscated; Jews were beaten and later rounded up for the death camps. In large cities and towns and in small villages of Catholic dominated Europe oppression of the Jews was apparent, yet little objection came from an organisation whose adherents were numbered in the many millions. Events in Vienna, Rome, Avignon and Croatia, mentioned in this chapter, are but a few examples of occurrences common throughout Europe.

Jewish communities in Catholic cities

The process behind the collection and deportation of Jewish communities was ruthlessly efficient, spreading from large cities to provincial towns and villages. In some cities and towns the gathering points for deportation are marked by signs which, to Bible students, stand as sober reminders that prophecies of Jeremiah, given twenty-six centuries ago, were fulfilled in recent history

In Rome, the centre of the Catholic world, a sign in what has been the Jewish Quarter since the 1500s marks the assembly point for deportation to the death camps on October 16, 1943. Jews are first recorded in Rome in the second century BC, establishing it as the oldest Jewish community in the world outside the Holy Land. The size of the community increased when slaves were taken there after the Roman conquests in Judea in the first and second centuries AD. The longevity of that community provided no immunity.

The city of Avignon in Southern France, gateway to the region of Provence, has had Jewish inhabitants since the second century, arriving with or shortly after the Roman invasion, making it one of the oldest Jewish communities in Europe. In the thirteenth century the Jewish community moved to the section of the city in which a synagogue is still located and where streets have names such as Place Jerusalem, Rue Abraham and Rue Jacob. In the elevated part of Avignon is the Palace of the Popes. This palace/fortress was constructed in stages throughout the fourteenth century after Clement V was elected Pope in 1305 and moved the papal court to Avignon. It remained the centre of the Catholic world for seventy years during which there were seven Popes, all French. After much political pressure and threats of violence an Italian was elected as Pope in 1378 and, taking the title of Urban VI, he returned the papal court to Rome. The French cardinals were less than happy with this outcome and elected their own rival Pope, Clement VII. He and several successors continued to function as 'Popes' for a forty-year period known as the Western Schism or the period of the antipopes.

In this most Catholic of Catholic cities the Jewish community, after a presence spanning nearly twenty centuries, was rounded up in 1944 and transported to death camps in Poland. A sign at the gathering point near the synagogue is particularly poignant, especially in French: *Mort En Deportation, 1944*.

Rounding up and deportation of Jewish communities, which had been in southern Europe for up to twenty centuries and in the North for around ten centuries, took place in countries where Catholicism was dominant or, as in Germany where, though smaller than Lutheranism, it was still a major force. The question we must ask is, Why was the Catholic Church so silent about the oppression of the Jews? We answer this question not just for historical interest but to see the hand of God in many events, additional to the Holocaust itself, to bring about the return of the Jews to the Promised Land. We also need to consider how we would have reacted in such terrible times when a totalitarian force was ready to crush any opposition ruthlessly, including the expression of alternative opinions.

In forming an opinion on this apparent failure to act, we must remember that the reaction involved many people in a number of countries over several years and there is no one simple answer. There are, however, several key factors, many of which have only become apparent in recent years. A change in thinking about the supposed valuable assistance of the Vatican during the Second World War commenced in 1963 with Rolf Hochhuth's play *The*

Deputy. Although containing a number of factual errors, it opened discussion on the topic and led to a review of relevant archives of the period.

Catholics and emerging political trends

In the 1920s and 1930s the Vatican focused on dealing politically with Fascism in Italy, National Socialism (Nazism) in Germany and Bolshevism in Russia. As well as providing instructions to local bishops and priests, extensive meetings took place at diplomatic levels as the Vatican attempted to maintain its influence in Italy and Germany and to constrain the spread of revolutionary thought from Russia. This is a subject far too broad to consider in detail in this book. Suffice it to say that it considered Bolshevism (or Communism) to be the greatest political threat because of its blatantly anti-religious concepts. That point is particularly relevant to the Vatican's subsequent responses to Nazi aggression and anti-Semitism.

Some individual Catholic bishops and priests were significantly concerned about the rise of Nazism and expressed opposition to it. In 1931 a Catholic journal *Die Arbeit* stated that the theology of the National Socialists "stood in blatant, explicit contrast to the Catholic Church". A parish priest in a small town advised his parishioners that members of the National Socialist Party could not attend funerals or other parish activities or participate in the sacraments. The Party raised complaints with the Bishop of Mainz who supported the priest and added that he was acting in accordance with diocesan thinking. In a letter the bishop stated that Nazi cultural policy could not be reconciled with Catholic Christianity.

His response was discussed by the bishops of Germany at their annual conference, with the conclusion being reached that his approach "lacked tactical prudence". No definitive statement was issued on the topic. A minority group of the bishops did, however, subsequently express, in clear terms, that National Socialism and Catholicism were incompatible.

Others, especially at a local level, expressed similar opinions. Several Catholic publications voiced strong opposition to the developments of the early 1930s but, as Nazi influence increased, most of these publications were shut down. What clearly stands out though is the lack of support from the collective Bishops of Germany or the Vatican for locally voiced opposition. This lack of high level input continued through the worsening situation of the late 1930s and beyond. There were occasional exceptions, one being Bishop Galen of Munster who, in a series of sermons in July 1941, put himself at serious personal risk by attacking the Nazi practice of euthanasia and 'mercy killings' of the disabled and intellectually impaired (there was, however, no criticism of oppression of the Jewish community). The Nazis were infuriated and wanted to imprison him but decided not to do so for fear of a Catholic backlash. This suggests that opposition from high levels could possibly have had some ameliorating effects. The issue of significance is, What was the reason for the low-key reaction from the hierarchy of the Catholic Church? That brings us to Eugenio Pacelli.

Eugenio Pacelli

In 1930 Eugenio Pacelli was promoted from his role as Papal representative in Berlin to Cardinal Secretary of State, the second most senior post in the Vatican. This was just one year after the revival of Papal temporal power when the Vatican City was established as an internationally recognised sovereign state under the Lateran Treaty of 1929. Pacelli had responsibility for foreign policy and state relations during a period in which the then

Eugenio Pacelli in Bavaria, 1924

Photo: Unknown – Wikimedia Commons

Pope, Pius XI, was seriously ill and unable to direct his full attention to major issues. In 1939 Pius XI died. With World War Two looming, Pacelli was elected Pope, being crowned on March 12, 1939 and taking the title of Pius XII. Thus, during the years of the growth of National Socialism, followed by the War years, through to his death in 1958, Pacelli was the dominant influence on Vatican diplomacy in Europe. The hand of God is evident in this. Additional to the Holocaust itself, numerous events came into play to bring about the return of God's people. One of these events was the election at the outbreak of war of a Pope who was more anti-Semitic than his predecessor, thus creating a situation in which the head of the religion that dominated much of Europe would be less inclined than others might have been to express an opinion on Hitler's so-called 'Final Solution'.

Pacelli had been influential in preventing the hierarchy of the Catholic Church from supporting the initial local Catholic opposition to the rise of National Socialism in Germany. Born in 1876 to a staunch Catholic family with long term service to the Vatican in the role of lawyers, from an early age he was fascinated with the ceremonies of the Church and maintained that interest after being ordained a priest at age twenty-three in 1899. His scholastic strengths were noticed; two years after his ordination he was invited to work in the Secretariat of State at the Vatican, a department that specialised in canon law and concordat law.[1]

In 1904, in strictest secrecy, the Vatican commenced compiling the Code of Canon Law. This was a process to codify the countless decrees, rules and regulations the Catholic Church had issued over many centuries. Pacelli was one of the principal architects of the process which took thirteen years. Issued globally in 1917, the Code was to be applied without local discretion or favour. Coupled with the 1870 declaration of papal infallibility it added to the Vatican's authoritarian, centralist control, an attitude endorsed by Pacelli and reflected in his later dealings in establishing concordats with other nations.

On May 13, 1917 Pacelli was consecrated as a bishop. Coincidentally that same day three children in Fatima, Portugal, announced that they had seen a vision of and received messages from Mary. This had a profound effect on Pacelli and influenced his later emphasis on Mary worship and his Papal declaration in 1950 about the Bodily Assumption of Mary.

Catholic influence on World War One
Although not directly linked to the response to Hitler, the political manoeuvring of the Catholic Church prior to the First World War and the unintended consequences are fascinating.

Pacelli, despite his young age, was involved in two key decisions. In 1904 the Vatican removed the long-held right of Austria-Hungary, France and Spain to apply a veto in papal elections. In 1914 a concordat was established between the Vatican and Serbia, a country which previously took direction from Austria on matters relating to Catholicism. Among other things it provided for bishops to be nominated by the Vatican rather than by Austria and removed the necessity to offer a prayer for the Austrian Emperor during the Mass.

Four days after the signing of the concordat Franz Ferdinand, the Habsburg heir to the Austrian throne, was murdered in Sarajevo by a Serbian. This was the final straw for Austria, already annoyed by the weakening of its political and religious influence. Austria declared war on Serbia and shortly thereafter Germany declared war on Russia and then France.

It is reported that the then Pope, Pius X, was profoundly depressed by the declaration of war that followed the signing. There is no report of Pacelli being similarly affected. Catholic politics significantly contributed to the commencement of war, but prevailing circumstances in Europe would have caused a war at some stage:

> "The fundamental causes of this development were the unbridled sovereignty of national states, now rendered more dangerous by popular nationalism; the profound maladjustment of European economic life, and the ambition of united Germany."[2]

This description of the situation in 1914 is particularly interesting given the similarities with the recent European debt crisis.

---

1 Concordats are agreements between the Vatican and sovereign states on matters relating to relationships with Catholics, including such things as funding of schools and electing bishops.

2 John Bowle, *The Unity of European History*, 1970 edition, page 305.

Catholic diplomacy with Germany

In 1917 Pacelli took up residence in Munich upon being appointed Apostolic Nuncio (papal ambassador) to Bavaria. It was a role with full diplomatic accreditation and Pacelli met with heads of state and senior government officials. Pacelli's initial role was to establish a concordat with Bavaria which at that time, along with Prussia, retained separate diplomatic and governmental structures, but under the Third Reich became part of a united Germany. Despite Bavaria being the predominantly Catholic region of Germany, negotiations were complicated and agreement was not reached until 1924. Opportunity soon arose for Pacelli to focus on his major purpose in Germany, that being the establishment of a concordat with the German Government. Promoted to Nuncio for the German State, on June 30, 1920, he was the first diplomat to present his credentials to the newly established Weimar Government. As Apostolic Nuncio he was the senior diplomat in Berlin, an honour he enjoyed with all the formality of European diplomatic life of the 1920s.

Negotiations for a national concordat were tortuous, commencing in 1920 and not concluding until 1933. They were complicated by the parlous economic circumstances in Germany and the complex and brutal political situation caused by the rise of National Socialism. Attitudes outside Bavaria were not so conducive to negotiation with the Catholic Church. In 1872 Chancellor Bismarck, in response to the dogma of papal infallibility, had stated that Germany would never enter into a concordat with the Vatican.

After years of negotiations between Pacelli and senior government officials with no conclusion, Hitler personally intervened sensing that he could use the situation to his advantage by negotiating the withdrawal of Catholic political opposition.

Negotiations from this point were to see two authoritarians aiming to achieve totalitarian, centralist control for their respective persuasions. Pacelli achieved his desire for greater Vatican control over Catholics in Germany and Hitler achieved his aim of removing the Catholic Church from political influence. In this, Hitler achieved the more significant outcome when the concordat was finally signed in July 1933.

In 1930 Pacelli was appointed Cardinal Secretary of State, the most powerful post in the Catholic Church next to the Pope. He returned to Rome to take up this position and from that time the concordat negotiations were conducted by emissaries with documents despatched back and forth between Berlin and Rome.

Effect of the Concordat

In essence the result of the concordat was that the Vatican rather than the German bishops would henceforth handle key negotiations with the Reich and be responsible for pronouncements. Hitler could proceed to marginalise Catholic input to the political scene. The results of this in major events leading up to the signing of the concordat and in the years following are very telling.

As previously mentioned, there was initial local Catholic opposition to the Nazi Party but after the signing of the concordat this all but disappeared. In 1933, in the wake of the growing boycott of Jewish businesses and escalating violence, the German bishops were requested to intervene. They declined to do so on the grounds it was "an economic struggle in a circle of interests not near to us ecclesiastically".

1933 also saw the significant event of the Reichstag passing the Enabling Act that granted Hitler powers of dictatorship. Bitterly opposed by some, the legislation only received the necessary two-thirds majority by the support of the Catholic controlled Centre Party, a decision endorsed by Pacelli. Thus, through the support of the Catholics, Hitler gained approval to pass laws without the consent of the Reichstag and to make treaties with foreign governments. Nazi leader Goebbels later stated that the Catholic support was in exchange for the government's agreement to negotiate a concordat with the Holy See.

The infamous 'Night of the Long Knives', in which an estimated eighty-five Germans opposed to Hitler were murdered, took place on June 30, 1934. The toll included a number of Catholics but, constrained by Pacelli, the German bishops uttered no word of protest. In September 1935 Hitler issued the Nuremberg Laws which defined German citizenship and prepared the way for isolating those of Jewish origin, including Jews who had converted to

Warsaw Ghetto captives, April-May 1943

Catholicism. Again, there was not a word of protest from the Catholic hierarchy. The Second World War began on September 1, 1939 with the German invasion of Poland, a country of thirty-five million mainly Catholic people. To the amazement of the British, French and Polish governments, not a word of protest came forth from the Vatican. By this time Pacelli had occupied the Papal office for six months.

Atrocities in Europe

There is reliable evidence that throughout 1942 the Vatican was receiving intelligence that the deportation of Jews to camps was for the purpose of exterminating them. Despatches came into the Vatican from sources in Europe describing the fate of Jewish communities. By June 1942 the Allies also were becoming aware of the purpose of the camps and the London *Daily Telegraph* ran a series of articles contending that more than 700,000 Polish Jews had been killed. The Vatican continued with its policy of silence, much to the frustration of the Allies. Diplomats from Britain, France, Poland, Brazil and the United States requested the Pope to denounce German atrocities specifically mentioning the killing of Jews.

The United States decided to exert further pressure. In 1942 President Roosevelt sent Myron Taylor to convince the Pope that a statement was desperately needed. Taylor, controversially appointed by Roosevelt as his personal representative to the Vatican in 1939, remained in the role until 1950. This first time appointment of a US representative to the Vatican was bitterly opposed by Protestant churches who considered that no recognition should be provided. Taylor temporarily left Rome in September 1941 and returned to the US. Negotiations with Mussolini allowed him to be slipped back into Rome a year later, much to the displeasure of the Germans. During

Taylor's meetings with the Pope in September 1942 news came through of the destruction of the Warsaw Ghetto and the extermination of its inmates. Pacelli maintained his silence.

The Allies wanted a message from the Pope to make it clear to Germany that they were aware of what was occurring and because his unique position could potentially influence the large Catholic populations of the Occupied Countries. A statement from the Pope would have been believed whereas statements from the Allies could be dismissed as propaganda.

Incidentally, after the conclusion of Taylor's appointment in 1950, no official US representative to the Vatican was accredited until 1969 when President Nixon appointed a personal representative. Formal diplomatic relations did not begin until President Reagan's appointment of a US Ambassador to the Vatican in 1984. Subsequent presidents have maintained ambassadorial appointments.

Outside Germany, one of the most brutally anti-Semitic regimes during World War Two was the puppet government in Croatia. A Fascist and Catholic terrorist group known as the Ustase, led by Ante Pavelic with clear support from Rome and Berlin, proclaimed Croatia's independence in 1941. Between then and the end of the war this regime was notorious for the atrocities it perpetrated against Serbs, Jews, Muslims and Communists. For the Ustase, relations with the Vatican were as important as relations with Germany. Croat dictator Pavelic was granted a private audience with the Pope in May 1941. In spite of the Pope having received direct intelligence of the atrocities Pavelic's regime was inflicting he was granted another private audience in 1943. A British Foreign Office memo on this meeting described Pacelli as "the greatest moral coward of our age".

The Catholic Church did not just turn a blind eye to the appalling violence of the Pavelic regime; many Catholic clergy actively supported and participated in forced conversions and slaughter of Jews and adherents of the Serbian Orthodox Church. One Croatian bishop, Ivan Saric wrote in his diocesan newspaper: "The movement of liberation of the world from the Jews is a movement for the renewal of human dignity. Omniscient and omnipotent God stands behind this movement." Another Catholic priest, Mate Mugos, wrote that clergy should put down the prayer book and take up the revolver, while another clergyman, Dyonisy Juricev, said that to kill seven-year-olds was not a sin!

At the end of the war the Ustase puppet government in Croatia was overthrown. Many of its leaders and its clerical supporters such as Bishop Saric, fled to Rome, carrying gold looted from Jews and others who had been murdered. The gold was deposited in financial institutions controlled by the Vatican. Pavelic arrived in Rome in 1946 and was granted sanctuary by the Vatican. The Church subsequently facilitated his relocation to Argentina in 1948 via the so-called "ratline" the Vatican used to help many fascist sympathisers flee to South America to escape trial for war crimes.

Catholic defence of Pacelli

In the face of mounting evidence of Pacelli's intransigence the Catholic Church has had to defend his actions, especially as he is under consideration for sainthood. The argument in his defence is essentially that criticism of the Nazis would have worsened the situation for Catholics and Jews and that statements had been made calling for both sides to exercise restraint. The Papal statements that were issued were so vague that no specific conclusion could be drawn from them. It is probable that Pacelli wanted to maintain neutrality in case

the Axis powers won the war. Whatever his expectations, the inescapable conclusion is that he viewed the fate of the Jews with indifference.

The Lutheran Church also voiced only marginal objection to Nazi policies and, as with the Catholics, millions of its members voted for the National Socialists in the 1933 elections. Having in mind the extreme anti-Semitic views of its founder, and its German nationalism, the Lutheran Church was unlikely to be supportive of the Jewish community. Although they could not influence political outcomes, the small Christadelphian and Jehovah's Witness communities were amongst the very few in Germany to refuse military service and paid dearly, in this life, for their stand.

The lesser of two evils

By any objective measure it seems reasonable to conclude that the Catholic Church was prepared to cease objecting to Nazi policy once it became clear that a concordat to their satisfaction could be negotiated. Later they realised that their expectations would not be fully met but still they did not protest. Apparently they considered it better to support the perceived lesser evil of National Socialism rather than Communism.

In an era in which 'unity', irrespective of doctrine, is endorsed by the major religions it is important that we continue to see the Catholic Church for what it is: an authoritarian, centralist organisation that seeks growth in membership rather than true converts to Christ and will support totalitarian regimes in pursuit of its goal. That is not a characteristic which passed with the conclusion of the Second World War. In more recent times it has been prepared to support, particularly in South America, despotic regimes that oppose dissent, provided the regime is prepared to offer political support to the Catholic Church.

"For all nations have drunk the wine of her impure passion, and the kings of the earth have committed fornication with her, and the merchants of the earth have grown rich with the wealth of her wantonness."

(Revelation 18:3, RSV)

Followers of Christ must oppose all evil rather than choose 'the lesser of two evils'. Like our brethren in Germany during this period we hopefully would have the faith and courage to make the ultimate stand against governments or regimes that refuse to allow conscientious objection to unholy ways.

Further Reading

John Cornwell, *Hitler's Pope*.
Gerhard Besier, *The Holy See and Hitler's Germany*.

8

THE PALESTINIANS: MYTHICAL YET REAL

FEAR has become a constant in the modern world. The Olivet Prophecy warned that at the time of the end men's hearts would fail them for fear (Luke 21:26). While the fear in that context is linked to the myriad insurmountable problems facing the world (verse 25), in recent years that sense of foreboding has been accentuated by the fear of terrorism.

Terrorism is not new. Fenian terrorists committed numerous atrocities in the United Kingdom and as far afield as Australia in the nineteenth century. There were many outbreaks of terrorism throughout the twentieth century and Israelis have lived with this problem since before the establishment of the Jewish state. But since September 11, 2001 and the launch of the war against terrorism the world has focused on it as never before. Wanton destruction of life in New York, Baghdad, Bali, Mombasa and so many other places has shaken the confidence of people across the globe. Fear is an entirely rational response to the events unfolding in the world. It is only the insight we gain from the prophets that allows us to overcome these fears and face the future with hope.

Reasons for the rise in terrorism in recent years are many and complex. It is evident, however, that much of the tension in the world today is firmly rooted in the soil of the Holy Land, in the tensions between Arabs and Jews over the right to all or part of Palestine. Opening the conference of the Non-Aligned Movement in Kuala Lumpur in February 2003, Malaysia's Prime Minister Dr.

Mahathir described the victims of the October 2002 Bali bombing as "collateral casualties in the war over Palestine." Osama bin Laden stated repeatedly that a key driver for his organisation's activities was the continued presence of a Jewish state in Palestine and the support of the West for Israel. Along with Hamas, Hezbollah and other extremist organisations, he refused to concede that Jews have a right to a homeland in Israel. Some moderate forces on the Arab side might be willing to negotiate a compromise with Israel, but the more extreme elements will settle for nothing less than Israel's annihilation.

The intractable nature of the tension in this region does not surprise students of prophecy. God determined that the Holy Land, and Jerusalem in particular, should be a centre of conflict at the time of the end. Zechariah 12:1-3 is clear – lasting and enduring peace and harmony in the land will be elusive until after the Messiah returns to establish God's kingdom.

Verse 1 of Zechariah 12 is majestic. This message is about Israel, but the language used demonstrates that it is relevant to all men. This is not only a message from the *God of Israel*; it is a message from the *Creator of all mankind*. It is not surprising, therefore, that verses 2 and 3 confirm that all nations are going to find themselves enmeshed in the turmoil that surrounds Israel in the time of the end. And although verse 1 says that this is the burden for Israel, the focus in verses 2 and 3 is primarily the city of Jerusalem. Jerusalem is to be a burdensome stone and a cup of trembling for all nations. Verse 3 implies that, in spite of the intractable nature of the problem, all nations will be drawn into the vortex that is Jerusalem and Israel at the time of the end. Verse 7 confirms that this tension will only be resolved by divine intervention.

Israelis and Palestinians, with their competing claims over the Holy Land generally and Jerusalem in particular, are at the heart of the tension of which Zechariah 12 speaks. But who are the Palestinians? The answer to this question is fundamental to addressing the tensions that emanate from this region, yet this is a question that the world ignores.

The name Palestine

It is routinely accepted today that the Palestinians are a distinct people with a right to their own homeland. For the first time in its history a motion of the Security Council of the United Nations in March 2002 openly referred to a Palestinian state to be established in the Holy Land. Popular opinion accepts 'Palestine' and 'Palestinians' are real. Even Israel recognises the claims of the Palestinians to nationhood. History confirms, however, that 'Palestine' and 'Palestinians' in the sense of a distinct nation and nationality are myths.

The geographic title 'Palestine' was coined by Rome. Following the Jewish revolt led by Simon Bar-Kochba in AD 135 the Romans wanted a name dissociating the Jews from the Holy Land. They chose the name Palestina, linking the territory with the Philistines rather than the Jews. They based the name on a term coined by Herodotus about 600 years earlier to describe the area south of modern day Syria.

The name Palestine is found in the KJV in Joel 3:4: "Yea, and what have ye to do with me, O Tyre, and Zidon, and all the coasts of Palestine? (RV, NKJV, NIV and ESV, 'Philistia')". The Hebrew name used by Joel is *Pelesheth*, translated in the KJV three times as Palestina (Exodus 15:14; Isaiah 14:29 and 31), three times as Philistia (Psalms 60:8; 87:4 and 108:9) and once as Philistines (Psalm 83:7).

The Greek word for Palestine, although in existence since the sixth century BC, is not found in the Septuagint. The names Palestine, Palestina, Philistia or Philistines also do not appear in the New Testament, presumably because by that time the Philistines had ceased to exist as a separate people. When the New Testament refers to the Holy Land, the name Israel is used (eg., Matthew 2:20,21), even though Israel no longer existed as a political entity. Josephus used the name Palestine in the first century, but always in reference to the coastal plain which the Philistines had inhabited. Josephus carefully distinguished between Judea and the area of Palestine. Linguistic and historical evidence shows, therefore, that prior to the Roman adoption of the name in AD 135, Palestine was never understood as referring to the Holy Land.

The Roman name Palestine fell out of use and it was not until the nineteenth century that it re-emerged. In that century it was often used by English speaking scholars to refer to the Holy Land in general, and was commonly used in books of the time. Not all scholars followed this trend, however, with some such as George Adam Smith in his book *The Historical Geography of the Holy Land* using the name Syria to refer to the Holy Land. More importantly, Palestine was not adopted by Arabs living in the area at that time; they continued to refer to the land as southern Syria.

It is only since the early twentieth century that the name Palestine has been used to describe a distinct political entity. After World War One the name Palestine was assigned to a mandate territory administered by Britain that included the modern states of Israel, Jordan and what have been referred to since 1967 (when Israel wrested them from Jordan and Egypt) as the Occupied Territories. Jordan was separated from the mandate territory of Palestine in 1923.

Who are the Palestinians?

The term 'Palestinian' was first used to describe people in the early years of the twentieth century. At that time and throughout the period of the British mandate, 'Palestinian' was used to describe Jewish settlers and inhabitants of the land. Arab residents strongly objected to being called by this name. In 1937 an Arab leader, Auni Bey Abdul Hadi, told the British Peel Commission, "'Palestine' is a term the Zionists invented".

The name "Israel" was only selected for the new Jewish State immediately prior to the declaration of independence. It was in 1948, therefore, that Jews in the land ceased referring to themselves as Palestinians and started calling themselves Israelis. It has only been since Israel's independence, and in particular since the 1960s, that Arab residents and former residents of the Holy Land have begun referring to themselves as Palestinians. Prior to the middle of the twentieth century they referred to themselves as Arabs.

During the twentieth century it became widely accepted that all races had a right to national self-determination – a right to self-government and independence. After World War Two the United Nations placed special emphasis on the process of decolonisation, which involved the granting of independence to people who had formerly been subject to the control of an imperial power. This flourishing of new nations in particular since 1945, but really since the French Revolution, is referred to in a number of prophecies, including:

- Luke 21, where it speaks of "all the trees shooting forth";

- the sixth vial of Revelation 16, describing the work of the frog-like spirits which destabilise the world and in particular the Middle East; and
- Joel 3 where it refers to how "the weak say I am strong."

United Nations support for a Jewish homeland in 1947 reflected the widespread belief in the right of national self-determination, in that case for Jews. On this same basis many people argue that Palestinians are entitled to a homeland of their own. The Jews have their own homeland, so surely the Palestinians are also entitled to a homeland.

This sounds reasonable only if you ignore the fact that the Palestinians *are not* a distinct ethnic group. Arabs have lived in the Holy Land for centuries. They are, as Genesis shows, descendants of Abraham and his relatives. Some of those who now claim Palestine as their homeland can trace their roots in the Holy Land back to ancient times. Many others, however, cannot.

Rapid economic development of Palestine during the 1920s and 1930s as a result of both the British administration and of investment by Zionist settlers encouraged Jews to migrate to Palestine. It also encouraged significant numbers of Arabs from surrounding and more impoverished nations to move to Palestine in search of work and prosperity. There were job opportunities, educational facilities and a better standard of living in British administered Palestine. These were not available in Arab states nearby, especially in the years prior to World War Two when the oil reserves of the Arab nations had not been as widely exploited as they were later in the century. It is not surprising, therefore, that tens of thousands of Arabs moved to Palestine in the 1920s to 1940s in addition to the many Zionists who came to settle there.

When assessing Arab claims to Palestine it is also necessary to keep in mind the itinerant nature of many of the local people. For centuries it was the practice in this area to roam around; this is reflected in the lives of the Jewish patriarchs as described in Genesis. Loosely connected clans often were present in various places. When Zionists wanted to resettle their ancient homeland they had to buy real estate. Much of this was in the hands of absentee landlords, often based in Cairo or Beirut, who were only too pleased to offload barren and undeveloped tracts of land for ready cash. These people had a genuine connection with the land but did not live there.

The facts show that the Palestinian people are not a distinct race, nor do many of them have long-standing connections to the Holy Land. It is true that many Arab residents were displaced at the time of Israel's War of Independence (1948); many Jews also fled their homes in territory that ended up in Arab hands. It is also undeniable that many Palestinian refugees still endure appalling conditions in refugee camps, but this suffering does not alter the fact that the claims of their leaders about a Palestinian homeland are baseless.

Many of the leaders of the Palestinian movement were born outside the land. Yasser Arafat and Edward Said, a leading Palestinian academic, for instance, were born and educated in Cairo. Yet both of these men claimed that they were born in Jerusalem in a deliberate attempt falsely to bolster the Palestinian myth.

Palestinian autonomy

Regardless of the facts that the Palestinians are a mythical race and their claims to a homeland are baseless, in general the world accepts their right to national self-determination. Even the Israeli Government accepts that a Palestinian state of some

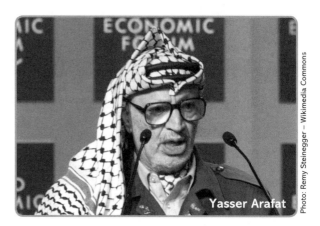

Yasser Arafat

Photo: Remy Steinegger – Wikimedia Commons

kind is inevitable. Had the Palestinians accepted what was offered at Camp David in July 2000 it is likely that an independent Palestinian state would have been established on much of the West Bank and the Gaza Strip within a few years.

Several places in the West Bank have strategic value for Israel, and negotiations for a Palestinian state have been hampered by Israeli attempts to retain control of certain key strategic sites. The Israeli Government has repeatedly stated, however, that it has no wish to annex all of the West Bank. Some extremist Jews vow that they will never give up the West Bank, but that is not the Israeli Government's position, and in October 2002 it began dismantling some of the Jewish settlements in the West Bank of which it does not approve.

The Gaza Strip is another story. Even at the height of Jewish settlement in the occupied territories it was home to over one million Arabs and only seven thousand Jews. It also has little strategic value. Whatever happens in relation to Palestinian independence, there is no incentive for Israel to re-conquer or annex the Gaza Strip, although it may be expected to intervene if extremist forces in Gaza threaten the security of Israelis living adjacent to the territory.

Peaceful co-existence?

Should we expect peace with the Palestinians? The answer appears to be no, at least in the long term. There seems to be diminishing goodwill on the part of Israel, and none on the part of the Arabs, on which to draw when negotiating peaceful co-existence. Palestinians remain openly hostile to Israel.

The PLO is the *Palestine* Liberation Organisation, not the West Bank and Gaza Strip liberation organisation. The true aspirations of the Palestinians are no secret. The PLO charter, which in spite of promises to the contrary has never been amended, calls for the "elimination of Zionism in Palestine" (article 15) and requires Palestine to have "the boundaries it had during the British mandate" (article 2). The al-Fatah faction of Mr Arafat and his successors is the dominant grouping in the PLO. Its constitution is also strongly anti-Israel, declaring that "this struggle will not cease unless the Zionist state is demolished and Palestine is completely liberated".

The Hamas charter is even blunter. It calls for the slaughter of the Jews (article 7) and declares: "There is no solution for the Palestinian question except through Jihad. Initiatives, proposals and international conferences are all a waste of time" (article 13).

These are not the sentiments of people with whom Israel could expect to negotiate a peaceful resolution to the current dispute. The PLO tells the West it is interested in peace, but simultaneously it indoctrinates its children with a gospel of hatred and violence towards Israel. Official video clips are produced encouraging children to become martyrs to the cause of destroying Israel. Textbooks used

Hamas leader, Khaled Mashal

Photo: Trango – Wikimedia Commons

in Palestine routinely omit any reference to Israel and are vehicles for anti-Semitic rhetoric. One book entitled "Our Country Palestine", prepared for sixth grade children in the 2000-1 school year openly proclaims on its title page, "There is no alternative to destroying Israel". The hostile images, words and policies of the Palestinian administration are not designed to engender peaceful co-existence.

Even when Palestinian leaders appear to support cooperation with Israel, the words they use often mislead the unwary. From time to time, for instance, there are reports of Palestinian leaders "condemning" suicide bombers who launch attacks in Israel. They will say something like, "We condemn attacks upon innocent civilians". To most people in the West that seems a straightforward statement, but the Palestinian public realise that their leaders do not regard Israelis as "innocent civilians." All Israelis are, in their eyes, active militant members of a hostile occupying force.

Palestinians in prophecy

Although the Palestinian people are an invention of the last forty years, the prophets anticipated

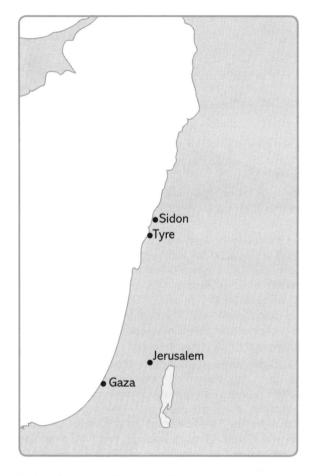

"Yea, and what have ye to do with me, O Tyre, and Zidon, and all the coasts of Palestine? (RV, NKJV, ESV and NIV, 'Philistia'). Will ye render me a recompence? And if ye recompence me, swiftly and speedily will I return your recompence upon your own head (KJV)."

Joel refers to "Tyre and Zidon, and all the coasts of Palestine", or Philistia. Tyre and Sidon, cities in southern Lebanon, are well-known strongholds of Palestinian extremists and their supporters such as the Hezbollah movement. The coasts of Philistia equate today to the Gaza Strip (Gaza was one of the five chief cities of the Philistines). Israel has been attacked repeatedly from these regions and it would be consistent with their recent behaviour for the Palestinians and their allies based in these areas to take advantage of the Gogian invasion to step up hostilities.

Many Palestinians celebrated when Iraqi missiles hit Israel during the 1991 Gulf War. There were also unedifying scenes of rejoicing in these same territories after the September 11 terrorist attacks in the United States in 2001. It is not hard to imagine these people taking advantage of Israel's distress when the northern invader sweeps down. The geography of verse 4 is explicit; it clearly identifies territory now under the control of the Palestinians or of forces sympathetic to the Palestinians.

Ezekiel 28:20-26: another key passage in relation to the Palestinians and their allies at the time of the end. Verse 21 draws attention specifically to Zidon. Verses 24-26 then speak of a period when Israel's immediate neighbours, those "round about them" (verses 24 and 26), are troubling Israel, and the harassment only comes to end when God intervenes to overturn Israel's enemies.

The phrase "round about them" is significant. In Deuteronomy 6:14 the same phrase is used to speak of the close neighbours of Israel, people

their influence at the time of the end in at least two passages:

Joel 3: a parallel passage to Ezekiel 38 or Zechariah 14, or both, depending on which interpretation is applied (for which see Chapter 14). Verse 4 suggests that at the time of the end invasion forces from current Palestinian strongholds will harass Israel:

with whom they might interact on a daily basis. In Ezekiel 28 these people around Israel harass her up until the time the Lord Jesus Christ manifests himself in the earth. These close neighbours are described as "pricking briers" and "thorns" in verse 24, language which also is reminiscent of words from Israel's past. In Numbers 33:55 God warned Israel that the gentile nations of the land would become "pricks" and "thorns" to them. In Joshua 23:13 similar language is used of the nations who occupied parts of the Holy Land when Israel was seeking to establish itself in the land. In the twentieth and twenty-first centuries we have seen that history repeat itself.

When Israel first attained independence all her neighbours could have been called "pricking briers" and "thorns." They certainly "despised" Israel, as Ezekiel 28:24 says, and all of them invaded Israel as soon as she declared independence. In 1979 Egypt signed a peace treaty and has been at peace (admittedly half-heartedly) with Israel ever since. With the removal in 2011 of Egypt's pro-Western leader, Mubarak, there is potential for that peace treaty to be cancelled or simply ignored. In 1994 peace was achieved with Jordan and with continuing unrest in the region the question of the treaty's continuance remains unanswered.

Even if peace with Egypt and Jordan is maintained, some of the "pricking briers" and "thorns" remain. From 2000 Israel became subjected to a spate of suicide bombers infiltrating from Palestinian controlled areas. Israel's construction of a security fence along the border with the West Bank led to a significant reduction in terrorist sorties from that region. It cannot, however, have any impact on rockets fired into Israel from the Gaza Strip and southern Lebanon. Palestinian sympathisers also have infiltrated Israel via Lebanon to fire on Israeli citizens near Israel's northern border. Southern Lebanon is a haven for the Hezbollah guerilla organisation and a base from which they launch attacks upon Israel.

In 1982 Israel invaded Lebanon and for some time occupied the southern portions of the country, in particular areas near Tyre and Sidon, in an effort to eliminate forces that were using southern Lebanon for attacks across her northern border. In 2006 Israel launched an offensive against Hezbollah in southern Lebanon (near Tyre and Sidon) in response to repeated attacks but with only limited success. In 2008 Israel launched a short-term invasion of Gaza in a bid to suppress repeated attacks on Israeli towns near the border, again with only limited success. Both of these incursions attracted considerable condemnation from the international community.

Ezekiel 28:26 says that these briers and thorns will only disappear completely and lastingly when Israel recognises and submits to God, or in other words when God delivers Israel through the intervention of Christ. The briers and thorns, however, seem likely to remain until that time, and this is consistent with the image in Joel 3 of harassment from Palestinian controlled areas. So the Palestinians have their place in prophecy around the time of the end – albeit a less than glorious one.

9

ISRAEL A NATION AGAIN

"Israel is a freak. It is a kind of Frankenstein creation, conceived on paper, blue-printed in the Mandate, hatched out in the diplomatic laboratory. But, in the last phase of its birth-process, violence was the decisive factor; and, as with other nations, its existence is ultimately based on an accomplished fact at the expense of the original native population."[1]

TWO millennia after expulsion from their land the Jews remained a distinct people. This proved to be at the same time beneficial and unfortunate – beneficial because it meant survival of their identity and their longing for the land of their fathers; unfortunate because it left them exposed to vicious anti-Semitic persecution, culminating in the horrors of the Holocaust. God had decreed that Israel was to be His witness (Isaiah 43:10,12). So it was that Israel survived two thousand years of exile, a feat not replicated by any other people expelled from their homeland. In the process Israel testified to the existence of God and to the veracity of the prophecy in Deuteronomy 28 about the consequences of disobedience and the rigours of life as a vagabond people cut off from home.

The Romans first referred to the Holy Land as Judea, thus recognising the Jews' connection to their land. But when they expelled Jewry from Judea they changed its name to Palestina, thus linking the territory with the Philistines and dissociating it from the descendents of Abraham. The Edict of Hadrian in 135 AD forbad Jews to live in or around Jerusalem. In a further effort to erase Jewish links to the land Hadrian renamed the city Aelia Capitolina.

A very small number of Jews remained in the Holy Land, especially in Galilee. Even today one Galilean village claims to have been inhabited continuously since ancient times by an extended family of Jews with the name Cohen. Over the centuries a trickle of Jews returned to their ancient homeland, but they were a pathetic remnant – for the most part poor and despised by their neighbours. In 1827 it is said that there were not more than five hundred Jews in all of Palestine.

As discussed in Chapter 3, in the nineteenth century a number of people started to speak and write about the return of the Jews to the Holy Land. Many, like Brother John Thomas, did so based on their reading of the Bible prophecies of the return of the Jews from exile. There were practical difficulties in giving effect to these ambitions. For instance, there were legal impediments; the Edict of Hadrian was not rescinded until 1856. The Sultan of Turkey was reluctant to permit Jews to migrate to the Holy Land and Jerusalem in particular. He only agreed under pressure from Western powers. His action was so unexpected that it shocked many observers. One British newspaper writer at the time pondered the significance for the Jews of the Sultan's act:

---

1 Arthur Koestler, *Promise and Fulfilment – Palestine 1917-1949*, page 21,22.

"Can this be the first decided movement towards the accomplishment of prophecy relative to the history of this wondrous people?"[2]

The story of Zionism and the return of the Jews in the nineteenth and early twentieth centuries is the subject of Chapter 3. In this chapter we shall consider the revival of an independent Jewish state.

The number of Jews returning to the land was modest at first, as the following table shows:

Table 1: Arrival of Jews in Palestine prior to World War Two

Waves	Years	Number of Jews arriving
First Aliyah Mostly from Russia and Romania	1882-1903	25,000
Second Aliyah Mostly from Eastern Europe	1904-1914	35,000
Third Aliyah Mostly from Eastern Europe	1919-1923	35,000
Fourth Aliyah Mostly from Eastern Europe, Yemen and Iraq	1924-1928	67,000
Fifth Aliyah Mostly from Europe (especially Germany)	1929-1939	>250,000

It was not until after Israel became a nation in 1948 that Jews began returning in really large numbers. Many of the earliest immigrants, especially those who arrived in advance of the formal establishment of the Zionist Organisation in 1897, were drawn to Palestine by both religious motives and a desire to flee persecution. Those merely fleeing persecution and who lacked a religious motive usually chose the United States or Britain over Palestine. In fact, these early Jewish

---

2 Quoted by Brother F G Jannaway, *Palestine and the Jews*, page 11.

settlers often expressed hostility to the objectives of Zionism. In 1903 the British Government offered Uganda as a homeland for Jews. This proposal was not well received by most Zionists. It did have some supporters, however, and some of the most enthusiastic were Jews in Palestine who did not want their fairly tenuous situation disturbed by an influx of nationalistic Zionists!

British Mandate

As described in more detail in Chapter 5, British Empire troops were successful in pushing the Turks out of Palestine during the First World War. After the war the British administered Palestine as occupied enemy territory, applying Ottoman Law. The Paris Peace Conference in 1919 and the San Remo Conference in 1920 confirmed that Palestine should become a Mandate territory administered by Britain.

The League of Nations ratified the British Mandate over Palestine and a civilian administration took over. In part, the terms of the Mandate reflected the terms of the Balfour Declaration issued by Britain in 1917, that Britain should promote Palestine as a homeland for the Jews, while at the same time guaranteeing the rights of existing non-Jewish residents. Even at the time, these two ambitious objectives were recognised by many as mutually incompatible: history proved this to be the case.

Britain's decision in July 1920 to appoint Sir Herbert Samuel as the first High Commissioner in Palestine was a curious one. A leading politician prior to and during World War One and again in the 1930s, Sir Herbert was born a Jew but renounced his religion while at university. He remained a Jew culturally, however, keeping the Sabbath and eating only kosher foods for what he called "hygienic reasons". Thus he typified many of the Jews who would relocate to the Holy Land during the twentieth century, men and women with a Jewish heritage but who for the most part did not practise their religion and were largely secular.

In spite of Sir Herbert's renunciation of the religious aspects of Judaism, many Arabs in Palestine reacted with suspicion to his appointment for obvious reasons, especially as his predecessor as representative of the British Government, Sir Ronald Storrs, had been an opponent of Zionism. Many criticised the inclusion in the terms of the Mandate of any reference to a "national home" for the Jews. In an attempt to mollify these concerns, the British Government published in June 1922 a White Paper, known as the "Churchill White Paper" after Winston Churchill, Colonial Secretary at the time.[3] The White Paper sought to explain the broader objectives of the Mandate. One of the steps outlined to address the reservations of those opposed to a "national home" for the Jews was the separation of those parts of Palestine east of the River Jordan and the establishment on that land of the (nominally independent) Hashemite Kingdom

of (Trans-)Jordan.[4] This was the first of several proposals in modern times to partition the land promised to Abraham. Joel 3:2 draws attention to this intention to divide the territory as a trigger for events leading to Armageddon:

"I will gather all the nations and bring them down to the Valley of Jehoshaphat. And I will enter into judgment with them there, on behalf of my people and my heritage Israel, because they have scattered them among the nations and have *divided up my land* ..."

Just as many non-Jews were concerned about pro-Jewish aspects of the Mandate, many Jews had reservations about its inclusive nature and about the separation of the territory west of the Jordan. It was with a degree of apprehension, therefore, that the Zionist Executive accepted the final terms of the Mandate, which was ratified by the League of Nations on July 24,1924.

Subsequent British High Commissioners in Palestine were not always as sympathetic to the Jews as Sir Herbert Samuel. Most were at best ambivalent towards them and some were quite hostile. Official British policy towards Palestine was inconsistent throughout the course of the Mandate. The Arabs discovered quite early that the British would make concessions in response to unrest. As Jewish immigrants continued to arrive in Palestine the Arab population became increasingly restive, with violent riots erupting periodically.

Article 4 of the Mandate provided for an official Jewish agency to advise and co-operate with the government "in such matters as may affect the administration of the Jewish national home and the

---

3 In spite of its name it is accepted that Sir Herbert Samuel had a decisive influence on the Churchill White Paper.

4 Full details are mapped by Sir Martin Gilbert, *The Routledge Atlas of Jewish History*, Eighth Edition, Map 88, "Britain and the Jewish National Home: Pledges and Border Changes, 1917-1923".

interests of the Jewish population in Palestine, and subject always to the control of the Administration, to assist and take part in the development of the country". Initially this agency was the Zionist Organisation but in August 1929 an official Jewish Agency was established to pursue the work. The provisions of Article 4 created an almost insuperable difficulty for the government. Providing one part of the community special privileges in relation to public administration inevitably created tension. As tension grew, so the willingness of both parties to co-operate declined. Arthur Koestler observes:

> "For within a few years the Jewish Agency, by force of circumstances, had developed into a shadow Government, a state within a State. It controlled the Jewish economic sector of the country, it had its own hospitals and social services, it ran its own schools, its own intelligence service with virtually all Jewish Government officials as voluntary informers, and controlled its own paramilitary organization, the famous Haganah, nucleus of the future Army of Israel."[5]

The Jewish Agency, in effect, was the embryo of the Jewish state that would arise with the Declaration of Independence of Israel in May 1948. The ethos of the League of Nations, and later of the United Nations meant that the Mandate administration was never intended to be open-ended. It was always expected that the mandatory power should work towards independence for the territory administered. It is likely that the officials who devised the Mandate of Palestine envisioned a single, independent state of Palestine in which both Jews and Arab would live in peaceful co-existence. By the end of the 1920s it was becoming evident that such a unified, peaceful state was unlikely to eventuate.

Major riots in 1929, in particular in Hebron and Safed, resulted in the slaughter of many Jews. In response the British Government considered options for reducing inter-communal conflict in Palestine. This led to publication in 1930 of the Passfield White Paper which expressed concern about the impact on Arabs of Jewish land purchases in Palestine and reservations about Jewish immigration. Zionist reaction to this White Paper was so strong that in early 1931 the government of Ramsay MacDonald largely ignored its terms.

Building a viable community

A true national home is more than just a political entity. Economic, cultural and social foundations put flesh on the bones of any political skeleton. The Jews were conscious of this, and the early Zionists strove to develop agricultural, industrial, commercial, educational and artistic skills that would underpin a viable, vibrant Jewish community in the Holy Land.

In the late nineteenth century Eliezer Ben Yehuda[6] (1858-1922), against considerable opposition, revived the Hebrew language as a language for day-to-day use. For centuries Hebrew had been confined to religious purposes, with Jews using Yiddish or other languages or dialects for daily business. Ben Yehuda's efforts saw Hebrew become a language suitable for daily use in commerce and social life. So successful was he that Hebrew was recognised, along with Arabic and English, as one of the official languages of Palestine under the British Mandate. This arrangement would

5 Arthur Koestler, *Promise and Fulfilment – Palestine 1917-1949*, page 12.

6 The fascinating and inspiring story of Eliezer Ben Yehuda is told in Robert St. John's book, *Tongue of the Prophets*.

Hebrew language and prophecy

SOME students have seen in the revival of the Hebrew language a possible fulfilment of Zephaniah 3:9: "For at that time I will change the speech of the peoples to a pure speech, that all of them may call upon the name of the LORD and serve him with one accord." The context of this prophecy, however, suggests that it has more to do with acceptable worship than with the language used to express that worship. The statement would appear to be the reversal of the circumstances mentioned in Zephaniah 1:5 where men in Judah and Jerusalem were swearing by Malcham, while in the broader Biblical context it represents the reversal of the curse of Babel. Brother John Thomas probably captures the significance of the passage when he suggests that the pure language describes the "one religious language"[1] which will be employed in the kingdom age. That language may well be Hebrew, but that is not the point being made by Zephaniah.

There is, however, another prophecy which suggests that revival of Hebrew as the day-to-day language of Israel may be significant. Revelation 16:14-16 says that the place where the "battle of that great day of God Almighty" takes place is "called *in the Hebrew tongue* Armageddon". This helps locate Armageddon in Israel but also may indicate that this is the language in use in that area at the time when the prophecy is fulfilled.

1 Brother John Thomas, *Elpis Israel*, page 454 (14th edition).

continue after Israel was established, with all three languages being recognised for official purposes.

Jews in many parts of Europe were legally barred from many of the professions, from owning rural land and from certain trades. In the ghettos of Eastern Europe these Jews had few alternative avenues of employment beyond commerce, trade and money-lending. This meant that many of the Jews who sought refuge in Palestine in the early waves of immigration had few skills to equip them as pioneers in a harsh and unfamiliar land. As early as 1870 an agricultural experimental station and farm school was established at Mikveh Israel ('Hope of Israel'), near Jaffa. This was followed by the Jewish Agricultural Experiment Station at Haifa, founded in 1910. Farm skills are not the only

requirements for a modern economy, and work on a Jewish Technical College in Haifa, intended to train Jewish immigrants in mechanical skills, commenced in 1912 but the war intervened and it was not until 1921 that it became operational. These efforts to impart practical, nation-building skills were effective. By 1943, in a reversal of the situation in the ghettos of Europe, fifty-five per cent of the Jewish working population in Palestine were engaged in manual labour, while only eleven per cent were engaged in commerce.

Higher education was not overlooked. In a great act of faith, the foundation stone for the Hebrew University had been laid in July 1918, before the war had even concluded (guns were firing a mere ten miles away at the time). The University opened on April 1, 1925 on Mount Scopus, north-east of Jerusalem. The opening ceremony was attended by Arthur Balfour, Lord Allenby and Dr Chaim Weizmann, all closely associated with Britain's interest in Palestine in the First World War. Development of the primary campus on Mount Scopus ensured that the university would be at the heart of the struggle to establish Israel during the War of Independence in 1948-49, when Mount Scopus was behind the Jordanian lines.

Improved medical services were also a feature of Jewish settlement in Palestine. For example, in 1934-35 expenditure on health by the Mandate government in Palestine amounted to £166,000, while expenditure by the Jewish Agency (the "shadow government") amounted to £350,000. Although not the objective of the Jewish Agency, it is the fact that vital health statistics for the Muslim population in various regions of Palestine were strongly linked to the proportion of Jews in that region, as infant mortality rates illustrate.[7]

The Jews made a conscious effort to settle the land, buying land from its Arab owners, many of them absentee landlords who lived in cities such as Beirut and Cairo. Much of the land they purchased had been uncultivated up to that point. Great swathes of the coastal plain and in the Valley of Jezreel, which were to be key parts of the independent state of Israel, had been, until the arrival of the Jewish settlers, sand dunes, marshes

Opening of the Hebrew University

Photo: Unknown – Wikimedia Commons

or stony desert and very sparsely populated. There was a remarkable transformation of the landscape. The hill country of Palestine, once regarded as uncultivable, became very productive during the

7 **Table 2: Arab infant mortality rates 1937-39**

	Jaffa	Haifa	Ramleh	Safed	Ramallah	Bethlehem
Percentage of Jews in total population	71.9	52.3	22.0	9.9	0.0	0.0
Arab infant mortality per thousand live births	81.4	118.7	114.8	177.0	171.5	176.4
N.B. The town names stand for capitals of rural sub-districts						

Mandate years. Between 1931-41 the area planted to fruit trees in the hill districts grew from 33,200 hectares to 83,200 hectares. Malarial swamps in the valleys were drained by extensive manual labour and converted into productive land for crops.[8]

This pattern of settlement was a key to the eventual viability of the Israeli state when it was proclaimed in 1948. Arthur Koestler commented:

"Had Jewish immigration been confined to the towns and to industrial occupations, the Jewish State would never have come into existence. The decisive factor was the conquest of the land, both in a metaphoric and literal sense. Without possession of the strategic key positions along the coastal belt and in the valley of Jezreel, and of the frontier outposts scattered over Galilee, Judea and the Negeb, the Jews would have been unable to defend themselves. Without their achievement of transforming desert, swamp and dune unto the material basis of the National Home, they would have had no moral claim to its possession. They had started building their country from scratch, in the wilderness, which had been unexploited by its native owners and had been willingly yielded by them against material benefits, despite every warning and legal and administrative hindrance."[9]

Of course the Bible had foreshadowed this process of nation-building. The words of Jeremiah are apt and while it is true they apply in their fullest sense to the time when Christ is reigning in Jerusalem, we may see in the events leading up to 1948 at least a preliminary fulfilment:

"Behold, the days are coming, declares the LORD, when I will sow the house of Israel and the house of Judah with the seed of man and the seed of beast. And it shall come to pass that as I have watched over them to pluck up and break down, to overthrow, destroy, and bring harm, so I will watch over them to build and to plant, declares the LORD."   (Jeremiah 31:27,28)

Yet another partition proposal

In 1934 40,000 Jews migrated to Palestine, and a further 62,000 arrived the following year. As tensions intensified between the Arab and Jewish communities in Palestine the British Government struggled to find the circuit-breaker needed to restore harmony. In 1936, by which time there were 400,000 Jews in Palestine, it appointed the Peel Royal Commission to investigate the causes of the tensions and suggest solutions. Having heard extensive evidence from all sides, the Commission concluded that the conflicting expectations of the Arabs and the Jews meant the Mandate was unworkable. Building on the approach taken in the Churchill White Paper, it proposed partitioning what was left after the separation of Trans-Jordan of the Palestinian Mandate territory to establish separate Jewish and Arab states, with Jerusalem, Bethlehem and Nazareth to be controlled by the League of Nations.

The Commission acknowledged that its partition plan was inadequate but argued that it was the only possible solution. The report said this of the plan: "If it offers neither party all it wants, offers each what it wants most, namely freedom and security … and the inestimable boon of peace."[10] This same naive hope has been a hallmark of all proposals for partitioning the land, including modern demands

8 Full details are mapped by Sir Martin Gilbert, *The Routledge Atlas of Jewish History*, Eighth Edition, Map106, "Jewish owned land in Palestine by 1942".

9 Arthur Koestler, *Promise and Fulfilment – Palestine 1917-1949*

10 *Palestine (Peel) Royal Commission Report*, 1937, page 296.

for a "two state solution". History reinforces the message of Joel 3 that partitioning the land will never bring peace but only create a climate where war is inevitable.

The proposed partition plan was formally rejected by the Zionist Congress in 1937 and was abandoned by the government in November 1938. A conference of Jews and Arabs to discuss a way forward was convened at St James's Palace, London, in February 1939. In a bad sign for any hopes of peaceful co-existence, the Arabs refused to sit with the Jews. As a consequence of this refusal, Prime Minister Neville Chamberlain was obliged to give his address of welcome twice! Following that conference a further White Paper was prepared which:

- foreshadowed an independent state of Palestine jointly governed by Arabs and Jews but expressly declared that it is not the government's "policy that Palestine should become a Jewish State";
- limited Jewish immigration to Palestine to 75,000 over the next five years and aimed to ensure that Jews would always remain a minority in Palestine. On July 13, 1939 the British Government actually suspended all Jewish immigration into Palestine until March 1940, at a time when tens of thousands were seeking to flee Europe ahead of impending war with Germany; and
- provided for restrictions on the right of Jews to purchase land in Palestine from Arabs.

In the debate on the White Paper in the House of Commons in April 1939 Winston Churchill, Conservative Party, called it a "base betrayal, a petition in moral bankruptcy", while Herbert Morrison, Labour Party, described it as "a cynical breach of faith, a breach of British honour".

Drawing on the Chamberlain Government's betrayal of Czechoslovakia in the 1938 Munich Agreement, the Opposition Labour Party derided it as the "Palestine Munich". This colourful phrase was not entirely unfair. The same ethos of appeasement which prompted the British Government at Munich in 1938 to agree to Germany's demands in relation to Czechoslovakia was influencing its approach to the hostile demands of the Arab population in Palestine. It is worth recognising, however, that the folly of a policy of appeasement is much more obvious in retrospect than it was in the late 1930s, when the leaders of the United Kingdom were men who had been severely scarred by the appalling savagery of the Great War.

The provisions of the 1939 White Paper were clearly inconsistent with the terms of the Mandate about a national home for the Jews, but in March 1940 the High Commissioner in Jerusalem issued an edict to give effect to its terms with respect to effectively forbidding land transfers to Jews in most parts of Palestine. This edict led to the remarkable situation in which the only two countries in the world in which Jews were effectively denied the right to acquire real estate were Palestine and Nazi Germany!

The war changes everything

Debate about the future of Palestine was overshadowed by the outbreak of the Second World War. With the possible exception of the Russian peasantry, Jews subject to Nazi control suffered more unspeakable atrocities during the war than any other group. Although Winston Churchill succeeded Neville Chamberlain as British Prime Minister in 1940, there was little change in the policies of the British Administration in Palestine.

Immediately after the outbreak of war in 1939, some 130,000 Palestinian Jews of military age voluntarily registered for military service, albeit through the Jewish Agency rather than directly with the Army. A Jewish Regiment had fought with the British in the Great War and it was hoped that this might be repeated. British authorities actively discouraged Jewish enlistment in the armed forces, not because they did not need the support but because they could see that this would enhance Jewish claims to the land. In the end they did allow 30,000 Palestinian Jews to enlist, but did everything to suppress their connection with Palestine. The Arab community, on the other hand, had little enthusiasm for the Allied cause and many were quite sympathetic to the Axis powers. The Grand Mufti of Jerusalem had been openly courted by Hitler and ended up travelling to Berlin during the war from where he broadcast anti-British and anti-Jewish propaganda. Even this was not enough to discourage the British from their pro-Arab and anti-Jewish policies in Palestine.

By 1942 there were about 500,000 Jews in Palestine, a large proportion of them immigrants. The Arab population also grew during the Mandate, roughly doubling between 1922 and 1942 from about 600,000 to 1,200,000. Much of this growth was due to improved health conditions under the British administration, but much also was due to immigration of Arabs from other parts of the Middle East attracted by the booming economy in Palestine, fuelled to a large extent by the influx of Jewish migrants. By way of contrast, the population of Egypt, another Arab state where Britain exercised considerable influence, grew by just twenty-five per cent during the same period.

Jewish migration to Palestine slowed to a trickle during the war, under the explicitly declared policy that "nothing whatever will be done to facilitate the arrival of Jewish refugees". The statistics tell a sorry tale; the numbers of Jews arriving while Hitler was at the height of his power were:

1939	27,500
1940	8,000
1941	6,000
1942	3,700
1943	8,500
1944	14,500

The name of the official militia of the Jewish Agency, the Haganah, means 'defence'. In its early years it almost exclusively confined itself to acts of self-defence, protecting Jewish settlements from hostile raids by their Arab neighbours. The Jewish Agency adopted a stance of Havlagah, meaning 'self-restraint', in the face of provocation, but this policy became unacceptable to an increasing number of Palestinian Jews.

From the late 1930s growing frustration in the Jewish community fuelled extremism in some elements which was manifested in acts of terrorism. In 1938 one such group, Irgun Z'vai Leumi (National Military Organisation) split from the Haganah to pursue a more militant policy. An ideological struggle ensued between the two groups. The Haganah issued a leaflet attacking the policy of the Irgun headed by the Sixth Commandment: "Thou shalt not kill" (Exodus 20:13). In a reply transmitted by radio the Irgun quoted: "life for life, eye for eye, tooth for tooth, hand for hand, foot for foot, burning for burning, wound for wound, stripe for stripe" (Exodus 21:23-25).

As conditions deteriorated, the policy of self-restraint became less sustainable. Dissatisfaction with the implementation of the 1939 White Paper and anguish over the fate of Jews condemned to death in Europe because they were denied entry into Palestine led to an escalation of Jewish terrorism in the 1940s.[11] This was exacerbated by the increasing number of desperate Jewish refugees perishing while attempting to reach Palestine in unseaworthy vessels.

In spite of the war and the 1939 White Paper, and perhaps because of the growing awareness of the excesses of the Holocaust, at least some political leaders in Britain remained interested in the concept of a Jewish home in Palestine. At the Labour Party's annual conference in 1944 the issue of Palestine was debated. In a conference resolution passed to rescind the 1939 White Paper and establish a Jewish state in Palestine the following was stated:

> "There is surely neither hope nor meaning in a 'Jewish national home' unless we are prepared to let the Jews, if they wish, enter this tiny land in such numbers as to become a majority. There was a case for this before the war. There is an irresistible case now, after the unspeakable atrocities of the cold and calculated German Nazi plan to kill all Jews in Europe."

Birth pangs

Germany surrendered to the allies in May 1945. Her defeat can be seen as consistent with the terms of the promise to Abraham in Genesis 12 which said that those who cursed Abraham would themselves be cursed. If that was true of Nazi Germany it must be asked whether it also came to be true of Britain in the light of its administration of Palestine, particularly in the dying days of the Mandate.

Britain went to the polls in July 1945. In the lead-up to the election Dr Hugh Dalton, who would

Bombing of the King David Hotel

Photo: Unknown – Wikimedia Commons

become Chancellor of the Exchequer in the Labour Government of Clement Atlee, stated:

> "It is morally wrong and politically indefensible to impose obstacles to the entry into Palestine now of any Jews who desire to go there. We consider Jewish immigration into Palestine should be permitted without the present limitations which obstruct it."

One can imagine Zionists taking heart from these words, and when the Labour Party won the election they could have been forgiven for expecting a change of policy in relation to Jewish migration to Palestine, especially in view of the vast numbers of displaced Jewish survivors of the Nazi concentration camps looking for refuge. Alas, their expectations were dashed. Labour Foreign Secretary, Ernest Bevin, known for his antipathy towards the Jews, persisted with the policies embodied in the White

---

11 The King David Hotel in Jerusalem, site of the British Mandatory Authority Headquarters, was bombed on July 22,1946 by the right-wing Zionist underground movement, Irgun, with the loss of ninety-one lives.

Paper right up until the end of the Mandate and the declaration of Israel's independence.

Of Europe's estimated seven million Jews (excluding Jews in the Soviet Union), only about one million survived the war. About 100,000 of these, mostly survivors of the Nazi death camps, were housed in official Displaced Persons Camps. Few countries were willing to take these people and for many the obvious answer was relocation to Palestine.

In September 1945 President Truman wrote to Prime Minister Attlee urging him to allow the 100,000 displaced persons to settle immediately in Palestine. No reply to that letter was ever sent. The same month, however, the Colonial Office told Dr. Weizmann that rather than allowing 100,000 into Palestine it was prepared to issue 1,500 immigration certificates, "the last available under the White Paper". This was later extended to 1,500 per month.

It was clear that the British were unwilling to compromise. Signalling a more aggressive stance, the Jewish Agency began referring to the Haganah as the "Jewish Resistance Movement". In October it undertook its first officially sanctioned act of armed revolt against the Palestine administration.

The uncompromising British attitude to the plight of the Jewish refugees began to threaten bilateral relations with the United States. In a bid to counter this, Ernest Bevin announced on November 14, 1945 the establishment of "The Anglo-American Committee of Enquiry regarding the Problems of European Jewry and Palestine". This was the eighteenth committee appointed by His Majesty's Government to provide advice on Palestine! Mr Bevin committed himself to implementing the Committee's recommendations if they were unanimous.

The Committee's unanimous recommendations in April 1946 called for:

- 100,000 displaced persons to be allowed to enter Palestine;
- abolition of the 1940 land transfer regulations; and
- adoption of a United Nations trusteeship for Palestine. That is, the Committee did not recommend either an independent Palestine state or separate Jewish and Arab states.

Notwithstanding Mr Bevin's commitment, the British Government rejected these recommendations. In August 1946 the British Government floated the Morrison Grady Plan,[12] its own proposal for resolving problems in Palestine. The plan was to establish a federal model with discrete cantons for Arabs and Jews, yet another proposed partition proposal. The Jewish Agency had always been willing to compromise about partition plans, but this was a bridge too far even for the moderate wing. It was abhorrent to the growing number now committed to a militant solution.

In January 1947 the British Government convened a conference in London to discuss options for Palestine. The Jewish delegation, evidently untroubled by their own prophet Joel, was prepared to accept partition of the land. The Arab delegates, however, would only sign up to a unitary state which, of course, would have an Arab majority. Neither side was willing to accept ongoing continuation of British rule. Ernest Bevin, in an effort to break the deadlock, threatened to refer the matter to the United Nations. It is said that

---

12 This scheme was developed by Herbert Morrison (who had been so passionate in the debate about the 1939 White Paper) and who was now the Deputy Prime Minister, and Henry Grady, United States Ambassador to the United Kingdom.

the Jews thought Bevin was bluffing and that the Arabs thought that the United Nations would side with them. Both sides were wrong. Britain did refer the question of Palestine to the newly established United Nations which established the United Nations Special Committee on Palestine (UNSCOP). The Committee could not reach agreement on a solution and majority and minority reports were issued. The majority report proposed yet another scheme for partitioning the land, calling for independent Arab and Jewish States with Jerusalem to be an "international city" (i.e., not controlled by either Arabs or Jews).

From the perspective of prophecy, this proposal also flew in the face of the terms of Joel 3 with respect to partition. Its proposal regarding Jerusalem also stood condemned by a prophecy in Zechariah, while at the same time highlighting the relevance of it for the days in which we live:

> "The burden of the word of the LORD concerning Israel: Thus declares the LORD, who stretched out the heavens and founded the earth and formed the spirit of man within him: 'Behold, I am about to make Jerusalem a cup of staggering to all the surrounding peoples. The siege of Jerusalem will also be against Judah. On that day I will make Jerusalem a heavy stone for all the peoples. All who lift it will surely hurt themselves. And all the nations of the earth will gather against it.'" (Zechariah 12:1-3)

Zechariah says that his "burden" (utterance) in chapter 12 relates to Israel, yet the chapter goes on to speak overwhelmingly about Jerusalem. In fact, the city is mentioned eleven times in the chapter. The message is unmistakeable: there is no Israel without Jerusalem. Verse 2 says as much: "The siege of Jerusalem will also be against Judah." From the divine perspective it is this fact as much as any other that explains why a lasting and peaceful solution to the Palestine question was elusive in the days of the Mandate, remains so today and will continue to be problematic until Christ returns.

On November 29, 1947 the United Nations General Assembly met to vote on the partitioning of Palestine as recommended in the UNSCOP majority report.[13] Jews in Palestine and Bible students throughout the world held their breath in anticipation as they listened to the live radio broadcast. It did not commence positively for the Jews: Afghanistan voted no, Argentina abstained; then came Australia with the first 'yes' followed by several more, including Canada. Voting continued alphabetically with most European countries supporting partition and all Arab and other Muslim nations voting against. Of the major powers, the United States and the Soviet Union voted in favour whilst the United Kingdom abstained. The final tally was thirty in favour, thirteen against and ten abstentions. The result was greeted with joy by Jews and anger by Arabs with gangs immediately attacking Jews in Palestine. Bible students observed another step towards the prophesied restoration of God's people.

The vote to support the majority report called for its provisions to be implemented by August 1948. The British Government, exasperated by the challenges of Palestine, pulled out well ahead of this deadline. The last High Commissioner departed Haifa on May 14, 1948 and the same day in Tel Aviv David Ben-Gurion proclaimed the establishment of the State of Israel. On the following day the massed armies of the Arab nations crossed the borders of the new state.

---

13 Full details are mapped by Sir Martin Gilbert, *The Routledge Atlas of Jewish History*, Eighth Edition, Map 108, "The United Nations Partition Plan, November 29, 1947".

Up until the proclamation it was not known what the state would be called: postage stamps prepared in advance for the new state used the words Hebrew Post. Jews in the land referred to themselves as Palestinians, a term the Arab residents refused to adopt for themselves, so many had assumed it would continue to be known as Palestine. Many of the Zionist leaders were secular Jews. It may have been unintentional, but invoking the ancient name of their patriarch and the united kingdom of David underlined the Biblical basis for what was transpiring before the nations – the budding of the Israelite fig tree, the great sign that the return of Christ was drawing near.

Retrospective

The years of the Mandate had been challenging for all concerned – Jews, Arabs and British. This fact, however, should not be allowed to obscure the reality that the Mandate years had also been a period of great prosperity and growth in the Holy Land. During the period the population trebled to 1,800,000, two-thirds of them Arabs. In addition to agriculturalists, among the Jewish immigrants were eminent scientists and industrialists, many fleeing persecution in Europe. The vicissitudes experienced by Jews both within and outside Palestine during these years were being overseen by Almighty God. Angels were at work to ensure that the gestation of the embryonic Jewish state could be brought to a successful birth.

Brother Cyril Cooper quotes remarkable words by Norman Bentwich[14] which are perhaps truer than their author realised: "the combination of head and heart, faith and science, worked miracles". Bro Cooper further quotes Mr Bentwich:

"The story of the thirty years of the Mandate is, then, marked on the one hand by signal achievement: the development of Palestine by agriculture and industry, and by social, artistic and cultural efforts, to a prosperity it had not known for nearly two thousand years, and on the other hand, by political frustration and despair, by turmoil and strife, such as it had known in many periods of the past. Looking in retrospect at the history of the thirty years we see that, under the aegis of the British Mandate, the foundation of the National Home had been well laid, and that the last period of the conflict was the travail of the birth of the State. Palestine of the Mandate was the womb of the Jewish creation. There was a fruitful marriage of Jewish enthusiasm and British caution. Happily both the British and Israel governments and the two peoples cultivated the art of forgetting the troubles of the last decade of the Mandate. Jewish leaders recognise the immense debt Israel owes to the Administration which gave the Jews the opportunity of self-government and preparing for the State."[15]

A successful birth is the first step in life, but there are many other challenges to be met during infancy. These are the subject of the next chapter.

14 Norman Bentwich, a barrister and moderate Zionist, had been employed in the British Administration in Palestine, initially as Senior Judicial Officer during the military occupation and then as Attorney-General in the civilian government until 1931. From 1932 to 1951 he occupied the Chair of International Relations at the Hebrew University.

15 Norman Bentwich, *Israel Resurgent*, quoted by Cyril Cooper, *Modern Israel*, page 26.

Further Reading

Brother Cyril Cooper, *Modern Israel*, The Christadelphian, 1973. Now out-of-print and dated, it is still useful for its overview, from a Biblical perspective, of the events leading up to the establishment of Israel and those which followed in the state's first twenty-five years.

Brother John V Collyer, *Israel: Land and People of Destiny*, The Christadelphian, 1988.

Arthur Koestler, *Promise and Fulfilment – Palestine 1917-1949*, MacMillan, London, 1949.

Sir Martin Gilbert, *Israel*, Doubleday, London 1998.

Sir Martin Gilbert, *Jerusalem Illustrated History Atlas,* MacMillan, New York, 1977.

Sir Martin Gilbert, *Jewish History Atlas*, Weidenfeld and Nicolson, London 1985.

10

CHALLENGES TO EXISTENCE: 1948 TO 1973

THE day Israel was proclaimed a nation its Arab neighbours attacked, intent on driving the fledgling Jewish state into the Mediterranean and out of existence. As noted in the previous chapter, both the United States and the Soviet Union were quick to recognise the legitimacy of Israel as an independent nation, but in those early days the Jews in the land were left largely to fend for themselves against hostile neighbours.

By dawn on the day after the proclamation of independence Egyptian bombers were over Tel Aviv and a desperate battle for survival was under way on land and in the sky. Although (from a human perspective hopelessly) outnumbered and outgunned, the Israeli forces gradually prevailed against their enemies. Male and female, young and old were pressed into military service to secure Israel's future.

In June the United Nations appointed mediator Count Bernadotte negotiated a one month ceasefire. This may have provided the breathing space for Israel to regroup without which the nation may not have survived. Why did the Arabs agree? Perhaps the angels were at work influencing their strategy as they had been in the days of Daniel (Daniel 10:13). Although Israel expressed willingness to extend the ceasefire the Arab side refused and fighting resumed on July 9, 1948.

Count Bernadotte renewed his efforts to secure a further ceasefire and this was accepted by both sides. While still formulating a scheme for a more lasting agreement Count Bernadotte was assassinated by Jewish terrorists and was succeeded by his deputy, Dr Bunche. An armistice was finally agreed in July 1949, by which time Israel had conquered Galilee and driven the Egyptians from the Negev, although Egypt was able to retain the sliver of territory known as the Gaza Strip.

The borders established by the armistice were in many respects more favourable to Israel than the borders that had been proposed under the Mandate, which would have created a fragmented Jewish state. They were, however, inherently vulnerable and difficult to defend. In the narrowest parts of the land it was a mere eleven miles from Jordanian-seized territory in the hill country of the West Bank to Tel Aviv, Israel's largest city, and a mere nine miles to Netanya. In the north the hostile Syrians occupying the heights above the Sea of Galilee could easily fire on Jewish settlements below.

While Israel's successes in 1948 were impressive they were somewhat overshadowed by its failure to secure control of much of Jerusalem, in particular the Old City and the Temple Mount, which was seized by Jordan. The Jordanians expelled Jews from the Jewish quarter of the Old City and denied them access to the Western Wall. For two thousand years Jews at Passover had yearned, "Next year in Jerusalem": with the signing of the armistice in 1949 they would have to wait almost two more decades until that plea could again be met without impediment. The 1947 partition plan had called for Jerusalem to be an international city, but by the time of the armistice it was split between Jordanian and Israeli controlled sectors.[1] Thus the scene was set for Jerusalem to be the "burdensome stone" to which Zechariah 12 refers.

Even as the fight for survival went on, Israel made progress in the development of the secular state. At the time of independence a Provisional Council was established to run the government. David Ben-Gurion was Prime Minister and Dr. Chaim Weizmann, who had played a role in the development of the Balfour Declaration in 1917, was President of the Council. Elections for the first Knesset (Parliament) and for the Presidency were held in January 1949 and Dr Weizmann became the first elected President of Israel. The Knesset's first meeting was held on March 10, 1949.

Realising the importance of staking its claim to the Holy City, Israel quickly relocated the Knesset and as many government offices as possible to Jerusalem. This policy helped to ensure that Jerusalem would remain at the heart of tension in the Middle East as the prophets had predicted.

1 Full details are mapped by Sir Martin Gilbert, *The Routledge Atlas of Jewish History*, Eighth Edition, Map 111, "Jerusalem: Divided City 1948-1967".

Declaration of the State of Israel by Ben-Gurion

Photo: Zoltan Kluger – Israeli Government Press Office

Despite this early establishment of government facilities, debate over the legal status of Jerusalem continues to this day.

UN Resolution 181 issued in 1947 which provided for the partitioning of Palestine established Jerusalem as a *corpus separatum* (separated body) administered by the UN. Israel contends that it is of non-effect because partitioning was rejected by the Arabs and borders were established by the outcome of the 1948 war. Resolution 242 issued after the 1967 war called for the withdrawal of Israeli forces from all territories occupied in the conflict. Technically that would

include East Jerusalem, but there has been much debate about the intent and Israel considers that retention is legitimate. In 1980 the Knesset passed a law declaring Jerusalem to be the "eternal and indivisible" capital of Israel. The UN passed further resolutions stating that this was a violation of international law and that member states should not recognise Jerusalem as the capital. For these reasons, nations with embassies in Israel have located them in Tel Aviv.

Arab hostility a constant threat

Even before Israel's Declaration of Independence in May 1948,

87

convoys moving between the Jewish sectors of Jerusalem and the Mount Scopus campus of the Hebrew University were harassed by hostile Arabs. On April 13, 1948 a convoy bringing supplies and personnel to the Hadassah Hospital in the university grounds was attacked by Arabs. Seventy-nine doctors and nurses and one British soldier were massacred. The location of the hospital and adjacent university behind enemy lines was untenable. Even though the 1949 armistice agreement which ended the War of Independence established Mount Scopus as a demilitarised Israeli enclave within the Jordanian controlled West Bank, it was not possible to operate facilities on the site until the Israelis captured East Jerusalem in the Six-Day War in 1967.

Of all her Arab enemies, Lebanon alone honoured its commitments under the armistice agreement. Egypt in particular remained especially hostile, refusing Israeli ships access to the Suez Canal and impeding access to the Israeli port of Eilat on the Red Sea. Egypt also sought to interfere with ships from other nations attempting to bring goods to Israel.

As discussed in Chapter 8, prophets had warned that Israel would suffer harassment from aggressive neighbours until the Lord Jesus Christ returns and re-establishes the throne of David in Jerusalem. Ironically, incessant threats and harassment of the young Jewish state were key factors which facilitated its early progress. Constant border raids and infiltration by marauders provided necessary practice and training for a new army, cobbled together from a motley array of partisan forces, as it honed its skills as a united fighting force. They also made the new state conscious of the need to develop the more remote parts of the country as a means of reinforcing its claim to disputed territory. Industrial facilities were built at centres such as Arad, Lakish, Beersheba and Eilat as much for military as for commercial reasons. In 1954 David Ben-Gurion resigned as Prime Minister and moved to a kibbutz in the Negev which occupied a strategic position overlooking the highway to Eilat as an example to his fellow Israelis to occupy territory the state had claimed, although he was later to return to high office.

While the United States, Britain and the Soviet Union all recognised the Jewish state, they hampered its access to arms while simultaneously continuing to provide its enemies with weapons. In 1951 Britain, France and the United States signed a tripartite pact under which they agreed not to supply arms to Israel for "aggressive purposes" while continuing the supply of arms to the Arabs, although it is known that the French secretly provided more arms to Israel than was contemplated under the agreement.

Covert French support for Israel became open and official following the election of Guy Mollet as Prime Minister of France in 1956, with warm relations between the two nations to last for twelve years until 1968 during a crucial period in Israel's history. Some students of prophecy will see in French involvement in Israel's struggle to survive evidence of the outworking of the sixth vial (Revelation 16:12-16 – see chapter 5). Regardless of the extent to which this action reflected the terms of the sixth vial we may be confident that this was another example of the angels manipulating events in accordance with the divine will.

The Suez Crisis

While Israel was troubled by cross-border raids ever since the 1949 armistice, it was not until 1956 that it launched a full military strike against its neighbours. In July 1956 Egypt's President Nasser nationalised the Suez Canal and denied access for ships travelling to or from Israel. Not surprisingly this takeover angered Britain and France, the Canal's owners, and gave them an incentive to co-operate with Israel to wrest back control of the waterway.

At a meeting in London on August 1, 1956, John Foster Dulles, the American Secretary of State, agreed that Egypt must reverse its actions even if it required force to bring this about. Emboldened by such sentiments an international conference was convened in London later that month at which eighteen nations with a vital interest in the Canal considered options for responding to the Egyptian aggression. The broad range of nations represented at this conference reflected the fact that God is ensuring that at the time of the end all nations will be inextricably enmeshed in the affairs of the Middle East.

Australian Prime Minister Robert Menzies, the appointed representative of the conference, conveyed its views to President Nasser, but the Egyptian leader was unmoved. While Mr Menzies was in Cairo the French were discussing with Israeli military leaders means by which the Canal could be seized.

As tension increased in the Middle East Israel launched a pre-emptive strike against Jordan, a friend of Egypt, on October 10. Jordan asked Egypt for help and at about that time French Prime Minister Mollet announced plans for a joint Anglo-French-Israeli attack on Egypt to wrest back control of the Canal Zone. France also delivered to Israel a substantial number of fighter aircraft.

Late in October, Israel invaded Egypt and advanced rapidly towards the Canal. In just five days the Israelis seized the Gaza Strip and almost the entire Sinai Peninsula. Britain and France attacked and destroyed much of the Egyptian air force and then issued a pre-arranged ultimatum to both Egypt and Israel calling for the Canal Zone to be cleared to allow British and French troops to occupy the area.

Supporters of Egypt and the Arabs such as the Soviet Union were enraged by the Anglo-French-Israeli action. This had been expected. What was not quite so expected was the strong opposition expressed by the United States, notwithstanding the views expressed by Secretary of State Dulles on August 1. Under pressure from the United Nations, and in particular from the United States, Israel withdrew from all the territory it had occupied and, later, France and Britain halted their campaign in the Canal Zone.

The Suez Crisis often is regarded, with good reason, as a debacle. It certainly was a major factor in the later fall from office of British Prime Minister Anthony Eden. It did, however, lead to United Nations control of the strategically important Tiran Straits, thus ensuring for Israel unrestricted access to the Red Sea which the Egyptians had previously frustrated. Destruction of much of the Egyptian military, until that time the greatest threat to the Jewish state, also delivered a period of relative peace for Israel. Professor Dan Vittorio Segre made this observation about the value to Israel of the Suez campaign:

"They had achieved almost complete peace around the frontiers for the first time since the establishment of the State ... They had also won time. How much nobody could say, but enough, it was hoped, to integrate the thousands of newcomers still living in temporary accommodation; time to reap the fruits of economic investments; time for a new generation of indigenous Israelis to grow up; time, above all, to think and plan the future of a State whose real nature and vocation nobody could as yet tell."[2]

Not all commentators were so sanguine about the legacy of the Crisis for Israel. Writing just one year afterwards two British analysts made this observation about Israel and the Arabs:

"Israel, by the success of its army in the November fighting, has renewed Arab fears that it may enormously enlarge its borders, and has confirmed the Arabs in their intention to make the extermination of Israel the first claim upon national policy. The Israelis have beaten all the Arabs once and the Egyptians twice. Perhaps they could do so again, but no state can survive if it has to fight against superior numbers every five or six years. In the end the 40 million Arabs must prevail over the 1½ million Israelis if the Arabs are determined and united and become just a little less inefficient."[3]

On the surface this observation about the relative size of the protagonists in the Arab-Israeli dispute seems quite reasonable. But it was based on human logic and made no allowance for divine oversight. Israel is God's witness, and earlier in the chapter where that declaration is made the prophet records this promise to Israel:

"When you pass through the waters, I will be with you; and through the rivers, they shall not overwhelm you; when you walk through fire you shall not be burned, and the flame shall not consume you."   (Isaiah 43:2)

Obviously this promised protection is not absolute as there are prophecies which speak of God bringing enemies against His people to punish them for their disobedience in both ancient times (e.g., Isaiah 10:5,6) and modern times (e.g., Ezekiel 39:23,24). It does suggest, however, that the fact that Israel is God's witness helps to explain why modern Israel has survived and even thrived in spite of many challenges to its existence.

Consolidation

As Professor Segre pointed out, the years following the Suez Crisis relieved the pressure under which Israel had struggled in its early years. The warm relationship with France provided Israel with access to military hardware which had not been so readily available previously. Israel was also able during this period to build close ties with West Germany, a nation whose sense of guilt about the Holocaust made it eager to assist the Jewish state. In addition to the sizable reparation payments West Germany was making to Israel as compensation for the sufferings under the Holocaust, it became a supplier of arms.

Supplies of arms from Europe were complemented by local efforts to develop an armaments industry. This led to the launch on July 7, 1960 of the Fouga, the first Israeli designed and built fighter plane. Since then Israel has become one the world's leading arms exporters. Interestingly this trade underpins the commercial ties between Israel and India which have flourished since diplomatic relations between the two nations were established in 1992: this may be significant in the light of the reference to Tarshish in Ezekiel 38.[4]

The Arab economic boycott of Israel, designed to frustrate the commercial success of the Jewish state, had some benefits because it forced Israel to develop its own international shipping line and

2 V D Segre, *Israel: A Society in Transition*, quoted in Brother Cyril Cooper, *Modern Israel*, pages 48,49.
3 Peter Calvocoressi and Guy Wint, *Middle East Crisis*, Penguin, 1957, page 121.

4 For further information on the possible prophetic significance of relations between Israel and India, see the article "India and Israel" in *The Testimony*, August 1997.

airline to negate as far as possible the impact of the boycott. Israel also made a point of cultivating relationships with emerging Third World countries where it found a ready market for its technical expertise in agriculture (especially dry land and irrigated agriculture) and, over time, in a range of industries such as armaments, pharmaceuticals, optics, electronics and even diamonds.

Why have Israelis been so successful in developing a diverse range of goods and services in high demand around the world? We must not rule out divine oversight. Even though for the most part the Jews have returned to the land in disbelief, with little regard for God and with a focus on commercial success (as Brother John Thomas had anticipated in *Elpis Israel*), they are God's witnesses and He watches over both the people and the land of Israel (Deuteronomy 11:12).

Adversity can be a powerful impetus to innovation and would appear to have been a key factor in the technological and commercial success of Israel. In 2009 Dan Senor, a former US foreign policy official and venture capital expert, and Saul Singer, an Israeli journalist, published a book entitled *Start-Up Nation*. They sought to explain how a sixty-year-old country of less than eight million, with (up to that time) extremely limited natural resources and surrounded by hostile enemies, could have achieved the distinction by early 2009 of having sixty-three companies listed on the NASDAQ exchange in New York. Also, it could produce more successful start-up companies than much larger and wealthy nations such as Japan, Canada and the United Kingdom.

The authors reject the suggestion that "ethnic or religious exceptionalism" on the part of Jews is a reason for the remarkable commercial success of so many Israeli businesses. They argue that the main factors responsible for this success are:

- **Immigration**: Ninety per cent of Israelis in 2013 are immigrants or first or second generation descendents of immigrants. Immigrants are by nature risk takers, especially those who have had to battle intransigent bureaucrats to be allowed to leave their homeland as did so many who came from Russia. It has been said that a nation of immigrants is a nation of entrepreneurs. Israel in this regard provides an extreme example of a phenomenon which can also be seen in Australia, Canada, the United States and other nations which have welcomed large numbers of immigrants.

- **Mandatory military service**: seen as playing a part in the entrepreneurial nature of Israeli society because it encourages individual initiative and risk-taking. The Israeli military is also renowned for its relatively unhierarchical environment which fosters creativity and improvisation. In the Israeli army it is common for junior officers to address their superiors by their first name and soldiers may vote to oust their unit leaders. This rather unorthodox military culture reflects the fact that almost all adults – male and female – are expected to serve in the armed forces, which means that the army inevitably mirrors the robustly egalitarian nature of Israeli society. Israeli soldiers are used to taking the initiative and, given the fact that active combatant service is the reality for many of them, doing so when the stakes are high. This creates a competitive desire to win at all costs and a culture which is seldom daunted by the challenges ahead. There is perhaps a delicious irony in the fact that the intransigent opposition of its enemies has contributed to Israel's resilience and success.

The cross-fertilisation between Israel's military and its technology sector is exemplified by the

"To seize spoil and carry off plunder ..."

"Thus says the Lord GOD: On that day, thoughts will come into your mind, and you will devise an evil scheme and say, 'I will go up against the land of unwalled villages. I will fall upon the quiet people who dwell securely, all of them dwelling without walls, and having no bars or gates, *to seize spoil and carry off plunder,* to turn your hand against the waste places that are now inhabited, and the people who were gathered from the nations, who have acquired livestock and goods, who dwell at the centre of the earth.'" (Ezekiel 38:10-12)

EZEKIEL 38 describes an invasion of Israel by the Gogian host. It is clear that Gog is motivated by the prospects of spoil and plunder, which implies that Israel at the time of the end must be a prosperous nation. This is in stark contrast to its condition during the two thousand years the Jews were exiled from the land. Since 1948, in spite of many impediments, Israel has developed a strong economy and a high standard of living, underpinned by the export of quality goods and services.

In addition to traditional fields of expertise such as agriculture, by the early twenty-first century Israeli businesses were world leaders in a diverse range of fields. For example, in 2013 Teva Pharmaceuticals was the largest generic drug company in the world. It is the company that developed Copaxone, one of the most efficient medicines used in the treatment of multiple sclerosis. AZT and other leading drugs used in the treatment of HIV and AIDS were developed or enhanced by researchers at the Weizmann Institute of Science or the Hebrew University. Israeli scientists have developed advanced devices for measuring and injecting insulin and Israeli researchers are at the forefront of developing medications for Parkinson's Disease, strokes, Alzheimer's Disease, epilepsy, glaucoma and brain tumours. They are also responsible for the highly regarded capsule endoscopy technology which has revolutionised the treatment of gastrointestinal conditions.

At one time Israelis would joke that Moses led the Israelites to the only land in the Middle East that had no oil reserves. That is no longer the case. In 2009 the Tamar and Leviathan Gas Fields were discovered 80 and 130 km respectively offshore from Haifa. The Tamar field came into production in March 2013. Also in 2009 geologists confirmed the existence of large oil shale deposits in Israel which are described as being of very high quality. It has been suggested that they contain oil reserves similar in size to those in Saudi Arabia. The oil shale reserves extend beyond Israel's borders into Jordan and Egypt and the economic benefits arising from joint development might in the future foster more constructive relationships between Israel and Jordan and Egypt, the only two countries with which the Jewish state has been able to establish formal peace treaties up to 2013.

Will resources and skills such as these make Israel an attractive target for Gog when he launches the invasion described in Ezekiel 38 and 39? It is a tantalising thought!

fact that, in 2013, the largest single unit in the Israeli Defence Forces, is focused on cyber-warfare. The potential for commercial application of such expertise in the modern world is significant.[5]

Six days in June 1967

After Suez, Israel did its best to meet the competing challenges imposed by rapid population growth due to immigration and the need to assimilate so many migrants in a short space of time, while also funding the crippling cost of defence in the face of hostile neighbours. Inevitably, however, the stress became too severe for the young nation and by the mid-1960s the economy was in serious trouble. While immigrants continued to arrive, a growing number of Israelis became despondent about the state's future and emigration began to increase.

It was at about this time that the Palestine Liberation Organisation was established to become a focus for Arab resistance to Israel, and belligerent Arab states such as Syria and Egypt stepped up their anti-Israel rhetoric. Israel's enemies had never accepted her right to exist and it was only fear of a further defeat that kept them from attacking. In such an environment peace was never going to last long.

On May 17, 1967 Egypt demanded that the UN withdraw its peacekeeping forces from the Sinai Peninsula. The UN complied promptly and on May 22, Egypt closed the Straits of Tiran, denying Israel access to the Red Sea from its port of Eilat. Quickly after this Jordan, Saudi Arabia, Syria, Iraq and the PLO aligned themselves with Egypt. It was noted at the time that this alliance reflected the catalogue of nations listed in Psalm 83 as threatening Israel. Whatever historical application may apply to that Psalm it became evident that a latter-day application might also be possible.

5 *The Economist*, August 10, 2013, page 38.

As the threat to the Jewish state continued to grow its leaders recognised that the best form of defence is offence. Thus on June 5, Israel launched a blitzkrieg against its enemies. Within sixty hours Israel seized the Sinai desert and reopened the Straits of Tiran, conquered most territory held by Jordan on the West Bank of the river Jordan and, most significantly, wrested control of Jerusalem from Jordan.

Within days of the capture of the Old City the municipal authorities in the Israeli section of Jerusalem were making arrangements for the provision of sanitation and other services necessary for civilian life. One of their first acts was to reinstate the public bus route to Mount Scopus which had been suspended when that enclave became isolated behind enemy lines following the War of Independence.

Although Israel from June 7, indicated its willingness to accept a ceasefire, it was determined to continue fighting until it had secured its objectives in the Sinai, the West Bank and the Golan Heights. As will be seen in chapter 11, US President Johnson, a man strongly influenced by Bible teaching on Israel's place in God's purpose, helped to delay the enforcement of a ceasefire until Israel gained the upper hand. This was despite Israel attacking in error the U.S. Navy's USS Liberty, off the Sinai coast.

Fighting came to a halt on June 10, appropriately a Sabbath day. The war left Israel more secure than the nation had ever been. It had to be a quick war because every available man and woman was called up for service. The economy could not have continued operating had the fighting extended even for a few weeks. Israel's success was remarkable and it was recognised as such by journalists. As the *Jewish Observer* commented:

Paratroopers at the Western Wall

Photo: David Rubinger – Israeli Government Press Office

"Seven days ago we wrote that the Jewish people cannot rely on miracles. But what has happened since then cannot be comprehended in any other terms."[6]

The journalist was perhaps more correct than he realised. This was not, however, a view shared by many in Israel at the time. *The Christadelphian* in July 1967 summed up the situation:

"The present victory is so dramatic as to have the look of a divine deliverance, but will it be seen that way in Israel? From their point of view,

6 *Jewish Observer*, June 9, 1967.

their own hand has done it. In an Israel self-assured and largely secular, pride in their own powers and their great traditions – now enlarged by one more tale of valour – are likely to mean more than fear of the Lord."[7]

Israel is to be humbled, but 1967 was not the time appointed by God. Jews in the Diaspora celebrated Israel's success by increasing their support for the nation both morally and financially. Winning the Six-Day War emboldened the state and the war's effect on Israel was profound and long-lasting:

"Moribund before the war, Israel's economy suddenly flourished as tourists and donations flooded the country, and oil was extracted from Sinai wells. Emigration all but ceased, and thousands of new immigrants hastened to partake of the glory."[8]

June 1967 without question was a time of miracle, and students of prophecy recognised that fact. It is instructive, however, to browse the pages of *The Christadelphian* magazine of 1967. There is commentary about the significance of the developments in the Middle East but the tone is somewhat subdued. The editor, Brother L G Sargent, observed that:

"In general one saw less intensity in the reaction to critical happenings than would have been shown in years gone by ... Perhaps a greater sense of detachment is in part the effect of over-confident predictions which have been discredited, but that alone would not account for the change between the profound emotion with which the Brotherhood in 1917 greeted the Balfour Declaration and the capture of Jerusalem,

7 *The Christadelphian*, July 1967, page 324.
8 Michael B Oren, *Six Days of War: June 1967 and the Making of the Modern Middle East*, page 309.

and the comparative placidity of many in the present day."[9]

Those eagerly watching the signs of the times today – and that should be all of us – need to take care that they maintain a sober perspective. The signs are given to remind us to be always watchful. That is how our Lord sums up the significance of the Olivet Prophecy:

> "But watch yourselves lest your hearts be weighed down with dissipation and drunkenness and cares of this life, and that day come upon you suddenly like a trap. For it will come upon all who dwell on the face of the whole earth. But stay awake at all times, praying that you may have strength to escape all these things that are going to take place, and to stand before the Son of Man."   (Luke 21:34-36)

We need to watch the signs and watch our own lifestyle to ensure that we are ready for our Master. It may be a mistake to be overly confident in relation to the signs of the times, but it is an even bigger and more serious mistake to be too placid and relaxed about these things.

We shall consider further the prophetic significance of the Israeli capture of Jerusalem in Chapter 12.

Yom Kippur

In 1973 Israel's Arab enemies made another attempt to snuff out Israel in what was arguably the war which most threatened the Jewish state's existence. Early in October Syria and Egypt mobilised troops close to Israel's borders in what Jewish leaders assessed as military exercises. In retrospect it seems incredible that the defence officials should have been so relaxed. For instance, Syria was in the process of deploying 1,200 tanks

along its forty-mile front with Israel: by comparison, in 1941 the German army deployed 1,400 tanks along the thousand-mile front with Russia!

In a well-kept secret plan, Syria and Egypt agreed to launch simultaneous attacks on Israel at 2.00 pm on Saturday, October 6. Not only was this a Sabbath, but it was Yom Kippur (Day of Atonement), the holiest day in the Jewish calendar. The intention, of course, was to catch the Israelis unprepared and in this regard the enemies enjoyed some success.

Israel became aware that invasion was imminent only at 4.00 am that morning. At that time Yom Kippur was very solemnly observed in Israel. There was no broadcasting, no commercial activity and almost no travel other than pedestrian traffic between homes and synagogues. Ironically, although the enemies had chosen Yom Kippur to maximise the element of surprise, that day meant the Israeli response was easier than it would have been on any other day of the year. That Israeli soldiers and reservists could only be at one of two places on Yom Kippur – at home or at a synagogue – greatly assisted the task of mobilisation in the very short time available. There was still the challenge of moving troops to the front line, which in the case of the Egyptian attack was the Suez Canal, but at least the men and women could be located easily. It has been suggested that it was this fact which saved the nation.[10]

Having started on the back foot, Israel lost ground in the first week of the war. By the second week the tide was turning in Israel's favour. By the third week of the conflict Israeli forces had not only repulsed Egyptian attacks in the Sinai but had crossed the Canal and were moving towards Cairo. In the north they advanced from the Golan Heights

---

9 *The Christadelphian*, July 1967, page 319.

10 Sir Martin Gilbert, *Israel A History*, page 432.

into Syria towards Damascus. Notwithstanding support provided to Syria and Egypt in particular by the Soviet Union, Iraq and Jordan, Israel continued to hold its ground and advance on several fronts. It soon became obvious that the Arab cause was hopeless and a ceasefire was implemented on both fronts on October 24.

The Yom Kippur War had several profound consequences for Israel and others, including:

- It underlined the crucial importance for Israel of the support of the United States. The huge cost of the war forced Israel to depend even more on American economic aid, becoming by far the largest recipient of US foreign aid.
- Many Third World countries, whose friendship had been assiduously courted over the past decade, broke off diplomatic relations with Israel, thus isolating the state even further and hampering its access to export markets.
- Egypt's initial success in the war helped that country to recover a sense of honour and created an environment which allowed President Sadat to pursue a political rather than a military settlement to the conflict with Israel.
- Oil-producing states in the Middle East discovered they could use oil as a tool to influence nations in their relationships with Israel.
- The harrowing close call shook Israeli confidence and influenced Israeli politics for several decades. It did not, however, cause the people to reconsider their relationship with God and the state remained as secular as ever.

After 1973 Israel was able to secure peace treaties with Egypt (in 1979) and with Jordan (in 1994). It was also able to secure the first of several (so far ineffectual) agreements with the PLO in the Oslo Accords of 1994. These agreements have delivered varying degrees of harmony. In the case of the Palestinians in particular tension and conflict remain features of the relationship (this is discussed in more detail in other chapters).

Negotiations between Israel and the Palestinians since the 1990s have been viewed sceptically by hard-liners on both sides. In Israel this is reflected in tension about the future of Israeli settlements in the occupied territories. On the Palestinian side this has resulted in the rise of the more radical Hamas movement. Neither of these developments augurs well for peace in the future.

In 1982 Israel launched an inconclusive and unpopular invasion of Lebanon in an effort to neutralize PLO forces ensconced in southern Lebanon. Although the PLO was removed from the area it was far from defeated and since then the area has become a stronghold of Hezbollah, which arguably poses an even greater threat to Israel. This has led to a number of border skirmishes in recent decades which have not been successful in relieving the threat. Perhaps we may see in the 1982 Lebanon campaign another example of how God manipulates events to produce outcomes that none of the human agents involved intend or could foresee.

The exiles return

In spite of ongoing tension on her borders and threats posed by hostile neighbours, including militant Palestinian forces, Israel has continued to flourish as a modern and highly advanced economy. Even today Jews are returning to Israel from all parts of the globe.

Many prophecies speak of the return of the Jews to their ancient homeland. For example:

"I will restore the fortunes of my people Israel, and they shall rebuild the ruined cities and inhabit them; they shall plant vineyards and drink their wine, and they shall make gardens and eat their fruit. I will plant them on their land, and they shall never again be uprooted out of the land that I have given them," says the LORD your God. (Amos 9:14,15)

The ultimate fulfilment of these stirring words and similar prophecies will be seen in the kingdom age, but the return of Jews to Israel since the late nineteenth century is at least an initial fulfilment.

Passing in July 1950 of the Law of Return provided all Jews a right of admission to Israel and automatic citizenship for those who came. A vast number took advantage of this privilege. By the end of Israel's first decade the Jewish population had increased from 650,000 to about 1,810,000 (out of a total population of 2,032,000).

Ill-prepared for such a rapid increase in population the government needed to find creative solutions, especially as so much government expenditure had to be diverted to defence needs. There was a surge of immigrants in the first few years, many of them Jews who had survived the Holocaust and who had nowhere else to go. By 1951 it is claimed that a quarter of the Israeli population was living in properties that had been abandoned by Arabs who had fled their homes during the War of Independence. This would provide further fuel for ongoing tension between Arabs and Israelis that continues to modern times.

It was not just Arabs who were displaced by that war; many Jews also were obliged to flee their homes, in particular those whose settlements in what came to be called the West Bank were seized by Jordan. Further afield, the conflict in Israel led a number of Arab nations to expel many of their Jewish residents, or make it especially difficult for Jews to live in the nations where their families had

lived for so many generations. Yemen and Iraq were two nations that were especially hostile to Jews. In the first forty years of the state well over one million Jews from Arab countries found refuge in Israel, far exceeding the number of Arabs who fled the land during the War of Independence.

Jews in selected Arab nations

	1948	1988
Egypt	75,000	200
Iraq	140,000	300
Lebanon	2,000	200
Morocco	285,000	10-12,000
Syria	18,000	4,000
Yemen	55,000	1,200

Since 1988 the bulk of Jews making "aliyah" to Israel have come from the former Soviet Union and the former Warsaw Pact states in Eastern Europe. Many of the Jews that came from Russia and Europe were highly qualified and talented and their arrival had significant commercial and industrial benefits for Israel. The majority, however, were not exceptional in any particular way. And the Jews which preceded them from the Middle East were largely of peasant stock with limited financial resources and few qualifications. But wealthy or impoverished, skilled or unskilled, as Jews they all had a right to migrate to the land and to claim Israeli citizenship. It is not always easy or smooth going, but the Israeli Government and Jewish agencies labour tirelessly to integrate new settlers into Israeli society. As suggested earlier, the influx of vast numbers of Jews has been one of the key factors in Israel's ability to meet and overcome constant challenges to its existence.

The unseen hand of God

Shimon Peres, one of the greatest of Israel's leaders, has argued that the timing of Israel's rebirth as an independent nation was very significant and in fact crucial to the state's success. In *David's Sling*, published in 1970, he wrote:

> "It was Israel's fate that the period of her rebirth coincided with the period of tension in the Arab world. But it was her good fortune to be born in an age when quality can compensate somewhat for quantity. If Israel had been established a hundred or even fifty years ago, and Arab enmity were as intense then as it is now, pessimism rather than hope would have been the permanent Israeli mood."[11]

Israel's ability to harness technology has undoubtedly helped it to overcome the massive numerical imbalance between the Jewish state and its Arab enemies. But this has not been the only influence on the nation. One historian has commented on the impact of their Biblical heritage on Israel's leaders:

> "The part which archaeology, and the Bible, played in the minds and activities even of secular Israel was profound. Some of Israel's most respected secular leaders were the descendents – even the grandsons – of distinguished rabbis. The fascination of the Bible was enhanced by proximity to the towns and villages, valleys and battlefields, which are described in it."[12]

No nation has ever absorbed more immigrants as a proportion of its population in such a short time span than Israel has since 1948. The arrival of so many Jews over such a short period contributed enormously to the dynamism of the country and fuelled its economic development. It must be admitted that it has also fuelled a degree of arrogance among many Israelis. When the nation was poised on the banks of the Jordan and about to enter the Holy Land, Moses warned the people that they must not take for granted the blessings God would shower upon them:

> "And when the LORD your God brings you into the land that he swore to your fathers, to Abraham, to Isaac, and to Jacob, to give you – with great and good cities that you did not build, and houses full of all good things that you did not fill, and cisterns that you did not dig, and vineyards and olive trees that you did not plant – and when you eat and are full, then take care lest you forget the LORD, who brought you out of the land of Egypt, out of the house of slavery."
>
> (Deuteronomy 6:10-12)
>
> "Beware lest you say in your heart, 'My power and the might of my hand have gotten me this wealth.' You shall remember the LORD your God, for it is he who gives you power to get wealth, that he may confirm his covenant that he swore to your fathers, as it is this day."
>
> (8:17,18)

Alas, the majority of modern Israelis make the mistake to which Moses refers. They regard the success of the Jewish state as the product of their own ingenuity, industry, courage and commitment. Unquestionably Israel has enjoyed a healthy supply of all of these qualities, but the fact that it has not only survived but flourished in spite of the forces arrayed against it has been described by many commentators – not all of them religious – as a miracle, and so it is. The nation is God's witness (Isaiah 43) and the great sign that the return of Christ is imminent (Matthew 24:29-33; Luke 21:29-31). (Refer to Chapter 13 for further discussion on the nations of Psalm 83.)

---

11 Shimon Peres, *David's Sling*, quoted in Brother Cyril Cooper, *Modern Israel*, page 39.
12 Sir Martin Gilbert, *Israel A History*, page 341.

Further Reading

Sir Martin Gilbert, *Israel A History*.

Brother John V Collyer, *Israel – Land and People of Destiny*.

Brother Cyril Cooper, *Modern Israel*.

Michael B Oren, *Six Days of war: June 1967 and the Making of the Modern Middle East*.

Dan Senor and Saul Singer, *Start-Up Nation*.

11

U.S. PRESIDENTS AND ISRAEL

IN her book, *Bible and Sword*, American historian Barbara Tuchman outlines the remarkable cultural and religious forces which engendered in many leading British statesman a profound interest in the Jews, the Holy Land and the return of the Jews to their ancient homeland. These forces were a major influence on the development of the Balfour Declaration which played such a key role in the re-establishment of a Jewish state in the Middle East. Similar forces were also evident in the U.S.

Many American presidents contributed to the return of the Jews to the land and to the continuing existence of the nation. Some became involved because of religious belief and others through political necessity. Irrespective of what drove them, they were part of the myriad events manipulated by the angels over many years that brought about the fulfilment of prophecies contained in God's word.

The resolve of several presidents to achieve outcomes beneficial to Israel is all the more remarkable as, at times, the decisions taken were contrary to the U.S. State Department's official policy of providing minimal support to Israel, especially prior to 1967. It is reasonable to conclude that God ensured that men with a resolve to implement actions for the support of Israel were in office at appropriate times.

The Puritan doctrine of 'Restoration of the Jews' was taken by the Pilgrims to America in the seventeenth century. They believed that God would restore the Jews but also saw themselves as the New Israel delivered from slavery in the Old World to freedom in the New World to which God had brought them. Initially the 'Restoration' concept was a belief they held but not something in which they could actively be engaged. However, in the early 1800s the concept was enthusiastically accepted by many of the churches that had by then developed, leading to a great fervour for missionary work in Palestine. Their desire was to convert the small Jewish population there and to facilitate the return of the Jews, thus bringing about the return of Christ.

Practical difficulties substantially restricted the number who could engage in missionary work. Those who did travel to Palestine endured privations beyond anything they had imagined and far beyond conditions anyone would now contemplate enduring. Towards the end of the nineteenth century enthusiasm for the restorationist doctrine and missionary work among Jews began to wane, especially as the once separate Methodists and Presbyterians gravitated towards the mainstream churches. The belief, however, did not completely disappear and continued as an influencing factor in U.S. religious thought, particularly outside of the mainstream churches. It resurfaced around the 1970s as a key feature of the evangelical movement and was an influence on several presidents.

Towards the end of the nineteenth and in the early years of the twentieth century vast numbers of Jews migrated to the United States from Eastern Europe, many of them fleeing anti-Semitic persecution. These immigrants greatly increased the size of the Jewish community and thus ensured that Jews could wield a degree of political influence. The true power of the "Jewish lobby" in the United States is much debated but it clearly has some influence and this may be detected in the actions of the government at various times.

The following paragraphs provide an overview of the actions of several presidents in either supporting or disregarding the Jews or the nation of Israel at key points.

Woodrow Wilson (1913-1921)

During the presidential election campaign of 1912 Wilson stated:

> "If ever I have the occasion to help in the restoration of the Jewish People to Palestine I shall surely do so."[1]

Wilson made this statement with a view to obtaining support from the American Jewish community but it did reflect a genuinely held belief gained from his strict Presbyterian upbringing. Opportunity later arose for Wilson to play an active role in the restoration of God's people when in 1917 Britain sought his endorsement of the Balfour Declaration. The backing of the United States was seen as essential and, as explained in Chapter 4, the release of the Declaration was delayed until the wording was acceptable to Wilson. Of this event he said:

> "To think that I, the son of the manse, should be able to help restore the Holy Land to its people."[2]

Franklin D Roosevelt (1933-1945)

Roosevelt was a member of the Episcopalian Church (the U.S. Anglican Church) which had never embraced restorationism. His presidency included

1 Michael B Oren, *Power, Faith and Fantasy*, page 357.
2 *ibid*, page 361.

the period in which many Jews were attempting to flee Europe and migrate to other countries, most of which were reluctant to accept the numbers seeking entry. Influenced by State Department officials and oil company executives, Roosevelt saw no value in supporting Jews at the risk of alienating the Arabs and consequently did not endorse additional Jewish migration to the U.S. or oppose British restrictions on Jewish migration to Palestine. The lack of U.S. resolve on this issue is considered by some to have contributed to the British policy of further restrictions on Jews as outlined in the White Paper of 1939, details of which are contained in Chapter 9.

Popular with the people for a range of initiatives, including work programmes and relief during the Great Depression, Roosevelt became the longest serving president in U.S. history. He also had to deal with the overwhelming issues of America's entry into and the ongoing crises of World War Two. He died of a stroke in 1945, aged 63, raising the question of whether, despite his significant contributions in many matters, his falling short on support for the Jews meant he was not the right man to be in office for the pivotal event God's people were to face in 1948, which would have been the last year of Roosevelt's fourth term.

> "... the Most High rules the kingdom of men and gives it to whom he will."   (Daniel 4:25)

Harry S Truman (1945-1953)

Truman's opinion on Middle East affairs was influenced by his Baptist upbringing. Well versed in the Bible he accepted the concept of Jewish restoration and, in 1941, he joined the Zionist-minded American Christian Palestine Committee. He was, however, on occasions ambivalent towards the Jews – probably for domestic political reasons – and in 1944 when seventy-seven senators voted for a Jewish commonwealth he was not among them. He defended this decision by stating that his preference was "to make the whole world safe for Jews and not necessarily resettle them in Palestine."[3]

For a period of time Truman hardened his views against the Jews largely in response to relentless pressure from U.S. Zionists who he accused of acting as if Jews were the only people to have suffered during the Second World War and seeking advantage over other displaced persons. However, in a contrary reaction Truman disagreed with the British Prime Minister Clement Atlee, who was of the opinion that migration of Jews to Palestine would ignite a worldwide Muslim uprising and should therefore be prevented. Truman firmly opposed this opinion, especially after hearing of the state of Jews in displaced persons camps in Europe, and pressured Britain to admit 100,000 Jews – but to no avail. (Further information on Britain and the Mandate of Palestine is contained in Chapter 9.)

In 1947, at Truman's direction, the United States voted at the United Nations in favour of the partition of Palestine into Jewish and Arab regions, but a bigger decision on whether or not to recognise a national state would shortly have to be reached. By 1948, Truman had fortunately become fully committed to supporting the Jews in their quest for a homeland. The circumstances that led to this are remarkable. During military service in World War One, Truman met and formed a friendship with a Jew, Eddie Jacobson, and after the war they jointly ran a haberdashery business in Kansas City, Missouri. The business failed after some years and they went their separate ways but maintained contact even during Truman's years in the White House. Jewish leaders knew of the

3 *ibid*, page 484.

friendship and encouraged Jacobson to persuade Truman to provide full support to the Jewish cause.

In March 1948 Jacobson met with Truman and persuaded him to meet with Chaim Weizmann, a request previously rejected by the president who did not want to meet any more Zionists. Truman relented and after spending time with Weizmann became convinced of the need to provide his support to a Jewish homeland, a concept he believed in but needed persuasion to pursue in the face of opposition. He became another president to act against the advice of State Department officials who favoured providing support to the Arabs. With Truman's signature the U.S. was the first nation to grant diplomatic recognition to the new State of Israel when it was declared on May 14, 1948. It is highly improbable that the influence on Truman was by coincidence, for surely the hand of God was involved in the seemingly small matter of his friendship with Eddie Jacobson.

Dwight D Eisenhower (1953-1961)

With popularity gained from his wartime role as Supreme Commander of the Allied Forces in Europe, Eisenhower was elected in a landslide victory. With much of his time consumed with domestic policy initiatives and bringing the Korean War to a conclusion, foreign policy was largely directed by Secretary of State, John Foster Dulles. A pious Presbyterian he regarded the former Palestine as the Holy Land rather than the State of Israel, and supported State Department opinion that Israel should be pressured into ceding large portions of territory to the Arabs for the sake of peace in the region.

Like Britain beforehand, America at this time considered it quite appropriate to interfere in the internal affairs of Middle Eastern nations to suit its own purposes. With White House endorsement the

CIA engineered uprisings in Iran in 1953 to oust the elected prime minister, Mohammad Mossadegh, and reinstate the pro-Western shah he had replaced. In Egypt attempts were made to oust General Nasser who had replaced the corrupt monarchy in a coup. The end result was that both nations developed extreme anti-American attitudes contributing to the Iranian revolution of 1979 and more recent political upheavals in Egypt. The intention of the Americans was to curb communism and maintain oil supplies, but the lesson is that those who meddle in the Middle East, especially with proposals not helpful to Israel, often obtain unexpected outcomes.

John F Kennedy (1961-1963)

John Kennedy assumed the presidency in 1961 after narrowly defeating the Republican candidate, Richard Nixon. The wealth and influence of Kennedy's father, Joseph, played a major part in the campaign. Joseph Kennedy made his fortune from business ventures including motion pictures, shipbuilding, and real estate. After the conclusion of Prohibition in 1933 he consolidated his wealth by obtaining the sole U.S. distribution rights for a number of high profile brands of whisky and other spirits. He was appointed U.S. Ambassador to the United Kingdom in 1938 but was forced to resign in 1941 after making intemperate remarks about Britain and the Jews.

Brought up in a family that was immensely wealthy, but by many accounts morally and ethically bankrupt, John Kennedy at age 44 became the youngest ever president and the first Roman Catholic. In 1936, whilst a student at Harvard, he visited Palestine and endorsed the Peel Commission's proposal for partition of the land and restriction of Jewish immigration (see Chapter 9).

"After travelling through Palestine and witnessing the violence first-hand, Kennedy became convinced that partition was the only way to reconcile the 'arrogant attitude of the Jews' for 'complete domination' of the country with Arab fears of Jewish 'superiority' and conflicting British promises to both sides."[4]

His presidency, although short, was one of high profile because of his relative youth and the interest of his wife, Jacqueline, in fashion and the arts. Kennedy received global attention from his staring-down of the Soviet President, Nikita Khrushchev, causing the Russians to withdraw from their plan to install missiles in Cuba. On the domestic front he continued the desegregation of schools programme commenced by Eisenhower and was a leading proponent for civil rights legislation, a move that generated much dissent especially in the Southern States.

With a Catholic background and his views on the Jews and Palestine, he did not perceive Israel as part of God's plan, but could not avoid becoming involved in the politics of the region. A plan by Kennedy for water sharing in the Middle East was rejected by the Israeli leader, Ben-Gurion, and not even considered by the Arabs because it would require co-operation with Israel. He consequently reverted to the Middle East strategies of previous administrations to curb Russian influence and maintain the supply of oil to the U.S.

As a northerner and a Catholic, Kennedy chose as his vice-president Lyndon Johnson, a Protestant senator from Texas. He did not like Johnson but needed someone who could broaden the appeal of the Democrat ticket in the election and pragmatism won out over personal preferences. Kennedy was killed by an assassin's bullet whilst travelling in a motorcade through Dallas, Texas, on November 22, 1963.

4 *ibid*, page 427.

Lyndon Johnson (1963-1969)

Late in the day President Kennedy died Lyndon Johnson was sworn-in as president whilst returning to Washington from Dallas on Air Force One.

His elevation to a presidential role caused much interest in Christadelphian circles because of his close association with family members who were Christadelphians. *The Testimony* magazine allocated several pages to his appointment and questioned if he was to be a latter-day Cyrus to assist Israel, a most insightful observation to make prior to the Six-Day War of 1967.

> "His scriptural knowledge and recognition of his dependence upon the providence of God stems undoubtedly upon his early boyhood training in Houston, Texas, when he was practically 'brought up' by his aunt Sister Jessie Hatcher, a life-long Christadelphian."[5]

Brother George Booker from Texas has links to the Johnson family and has written several very interesting articles about the Christadelphian influence upon Lyndon Johnson. Influence at an early age came from his grandfather, Brother Sam Ealy Johnson Snr., but the person with the greatest influence upon him was his previously mentioned aunt, Sister Jessie Johnson Hatcher, the grandmother of Brother Booker who wrote:

> "… he (Johnson) was just a little barefoot boy from the hill country, attending Sunday School and hearing Bible stories from his grandfather and aunts; and a tall, gangling young college graduate teaching school in Houston and living with my grandmother and my mother (just a teenager then). How often I remember my grandmother saying, 'I always told Lyndon,

Lyndon Johnson

Photo: Unknown – Executive Office of the President of the United States

Watch the Jews. Take care of them anyway you can. They're God's chosen people'."[6]

During his teenage years Johnson was a member of the Disciples of Christ (which had its origins in the Campbellites with which Brother Thomas was associated early in his life), apparently being baptized by them at age 14. His parents were not Christadelphians although it has been said his father "recognized and acknowledged the Truth he never embraced".[7] Johnson did not continue as a participating member of the Disciples of Christ throughout his life but Christadelphian influence, especially about the Jews being God's people, remained with him. An article in *Time* magazine about Johnson's faith early in his presidency drew attention to the influence on his thinking of what

5 *The Testimony*, March 1964, Vol. 34, page 92.

6 *The Testimony*, January 1992 , Vol. 62, page 30.
7 *The Christadelphian*, January 1964, page 26. See also page 36.

it called the "hyperfundamentalist" Christadelphian sect.[8]

Kept secret for years were Johnson's actions, whilst a senator, in using his influence and connections in assisting Jews to flee from Europe. In 1938 he provided forty pre-approved visas to a Jewish friend who was travelling to Poland to use in enabling Jews to migrate to the U.S. In 1940 he used rather dubious legal means to enable approximately four hundred Jewish refugees to enter the Texas port of Galveston via Cuba, Mexico and other Latin American Countries.

Alan Steinberg, a U.S. political commentator with a Jewish background, published an article on Johnson's assistance to the Jews in which he contends that he deserves to be included in Israel's catalogue of Righteous Gentiles for the contribution he made at great risk to his political career:

"Johnson's actions are even more remarkable when viewed in the context of America at that time. During the late 1930s and early 1940s, anti-Semitism was still a highly significant force in American life. Indeed, the prevalence of American anti-Semitism intimidated many leading Jewish figures from raising their voices on behalf of their European brethren. It was fear of anti-Semitic political retribution that caused President Franklin D Roosevelt and his State Department to refrain from any actions to either rescue European Jews or provide a safe haven for those Jews who overcame overwhelming odds to actually elude their Nazi persecutors."[9]

Before he became vice-president, Senator Johnson was known for his strong support for Israel, even though this was unpopular in Texas.

He supported Jewish aspirations for nationhood in the 1940s and when the state was established he fought for increased financial assistance for Israel under the Foreign Aid Program. During the Suez Crisis in 1956 Johnson was a key figure in preventing the imposition of economic sanctions against Israel and later he worked to thwart as far as possible the effect of the Arab economic boycott of the Jewish state.

However, it was the Six-Day War in 1967 that was to bring Johnson's support for Israel to the fore. It was Israel's most critical hour since the Arab opposition to the formation of the State in 1948 and U.S. support was going to be crucial. The effect of religion on Johnson's pro-Israel stance is not just a Christadelphian opinion and has been acknowledged by political observers including Michael Oren, an Israeli Ambassador to the United States, who has written of the influence of Johnson's grandfather and aunt. Oren contends that it was Johnson's religious outlook that emboldened him to disregard State Department advice that providing support for Israel would alienate the Arabs and jeopardize oil supplies.[10] On several occasions prior to 1967 Johnson ignored objections from the State Department and the Pentagon and personally approved aid packages for Israel, declaring that he "was a friend of Israel in the true sense of the word".[11] When war appeared imminent in 1967 Johnson warned Israel that the U.S. could not provide support if it attacked first but he subsequently disregarded that statement, which had probably been made for the sake of diplomacy, and made certain that military equipment was delivered to Israel to ensure its survival. Later, when Israel was gaining territory held by Arab nations, he

---

8 *Time*, Friday, April 3, 1964.

9 Alan J Steinberg, www.newjerseynewsroom.com, May 2, 2011.

10 Oren, page 523.

11 Michael B Oren, *Six Days Of War*, page 112.

delayed approving a UN ceasefire until Arab defeat was evident.

As in the case of Cyrus in ancient times, Johnson's elevation to the presidency ensured that a man with the necessary resolve was in office at the appropriate time.

Jimmy Carter (1977-1981)

A Baptist from the Southern States, Jimmy Carter read the Bible daily and had a passion for the State of Israel and with this outlook he initially received much support from evangelical Christians. However, he also believed in providing support for the other occupants in the region and applied pressure on Israel to withdraw from sections of the Occupied Territories. This put him at odds with Israel and many evangelicals who believed that there should be no negotiation with the Palestinians.

Carter was desperately keen to negotiate a Middle East peace treaty and sought an international conference to structure, improbably, a broad-based agreement. The Egyptian President, Anwar El Sadat, and Israeli Prime Minister, Menachem Begin, were unconvinced about the value of an international conference and commenced negotiations in secret in 1977. When their talks became deadlocked they sought Carter's mediation, resulting in their being invited to the U.S. for discussions. Carter was soon to learn, as would subsequent presidents, that achieving agreement between Israelis and Arabs was an almost insuperable problem. Nevertheless, Carter persevered and after thirteen days of intense negotiations achieved the signing of an agreement known as the Camp David Accords, on September 17, 1978.

Some parts of the agreement, such as those to recognize the "legitimate rights of the Palestinian people", were interpreted differently by Egypt, Israel and the U.S. and are still debated. There

Sadat, Begin & Carter

Photo: Moshe Milner –
Israeli Government Press Office

were, however, specifics including Israel agreeing to withdraw from the Sinai in return for Egypt establishing diplomatic relations and guaranteeing freedom of passage through the Suez Canal. This led to the signing of the Israel-Egypt Peace Treaty in March 1979, an agreement that continues to the present day. Most of the Arab world denounced the treaty and Egypt was suspended from the Arab League until 1989. Sadat and Begin received the 1978 Nobel Peace Prize but in 1981 Sadat was gunned down in Cairo by Egyptian members of an Islamic Jihad organisation. He was succeeded by Hosni Mubarak.

Despite the civil unrest in Egypt that led to the ousting of the pro-Western President Mubarak in February 2011 and the election of Mohamed Morsi of the Muslim Brotherhood Party in June 2012, the peace treaty with Israel was not revoked. Surprisingly, what appeared to be a national move towards a fundamentalist Islamic state, was brought to a halt by the Egyptian military removing Morsi from office in July 2013 and imprisoning leaders of the Muslim Brotherhood. The final outcome of this political upheaval is yet to be seen. We can conclude from scripture that punishment is to come upon Egypt in the latter days, but that there is also to be a restoration. There are a number of prophecies about punishment, one example being in Joel's dramatic "day of the LORD" message:

"Egypt shall become a desolation and Edom a desolate wilderness, for the violence done to the people of Judah, because they have shed innocent blood in their land." (Joel 3:19)

In contrast there is Isaiah's description of restoration apparently following acceptance of the Lord Jesus Christ after his return:

"And the LORD will strike Egypt, striking and healing, and they will return to the LORD, and he will listen to their pleas for mercy and heal them. In that day there will be a highway from Egypt to Assyria, and Assyria will come into Egypt, and Egypt into Assyria, and the Egyptians will worship with the Assyrians. In that day Israel will be the third with Egypt and Assyria, a blessing in the midst of the earth, whom the LORD of hosts has blessed, saying, 'Blessed be Egypt my people, and Assyria the work of my hands, and Israel my inheritance'." (Isaiah 19:22-25)

Carter's presidency was marred by the Iranian revolution of 1979, a legacy of interference in Iranian affairs during the Eisenhower era. His inability to obtain, either by diplomatic or military means, release of U.S. embassy staff taken hostage during the revolution contributed to his being one of the few one-term presidents. Iran's extreme anti-American and anti-Israeli attitudes continue to the present and it is no surprise that this nation, previously known as Persia, is listed in Ezekiel 38 amongst those that come against Israel in the latter days.

After he left the White House Jimmy Carter wrote a book entitled, *The Blood of Abraham*, with a subtitle, *Insights into the Middle East*, in which he sought to explain the tensions in the Middle East in the context of history and God's promises to the Patriarchs as they are interpreted by the protagonists in the region.

George H Bush (1989-1993)

In 1844 a professor of Hebrew at New York University published a paper, *The Dry Bones of Israel Revived* in which he called for the re-creation of a Jewish state in Palestine for the benefit not only of Jews but all mankind. The professor was George Bush, a predecessor of the two presidents of the same name. His views were criticised by the *Princetown Review* which reflected mainstream church views and denounced the "belief in the literal Restoration of the Jews."[12]

George H Bush, an Episcopalian (Anglican), followed mainstream views and did not perceive Israel from a religious perspective. In fact his involvement in certain Middle East affairs produced unintended consequences for the U.S. As vice-president to Ronald Reagan he assisted in the supply of arms to Iraq which benefited armament manufacturers in the U.S. and helped maintain the Iran-Iraq war. As president he continued to provide aid to Saddam Hussein, but subsequently entered into a war to free Kuwait from an invasion by the Iraqi military machine he had helped to create.

George Bush Senior's son, George W Bush, held religious views similar to his nineteenth century forebear and he also declared war on Iraq in response to terrorist attacks by militant Islamists whose anti-Western views had been fuelled by the presence of U.S. troops in Kuwait. Manipulated no doubt by the angels, both Presidents Bush took steps that ensured the U.S. remained enmeshed in Middle East affairs, often contrary to the nation's interest.

12 Michael B Oren, *Power, Faith and Fantasy*, page 141.

Bill Clinton (1993-2001)

Although influenced by the pro-Israel views of southern states evangelicals, Clinton did not see Middle East affairs as a key plank of his presidency. He was, however, to find that as U.S. President it was difficult to remain detached from the region's issues and, as with Carter, he became involved in peace negotiations commenced by others.

Israeli Prime Minister Yitzhak Rabin informed Clinton on September 9, 1993 that his government had been in secret negotiations with the Palestinian Liberation Organisation (PLO) and it was now appropriate for Clinton to assist in finalising the details and arranging a signing by Rabin and Yasser Arafat.

Rabin and Arafat received the Nobel Peace Prize for their efforts but the document they initialled at the White House was far from explicit. Known as the Oslo Process from the location of the initial talks, it provided for mutual recognition between Israel and the PLO and the renouncement of terror and incitement. However, it did not specify when Israel would vacate the West Bank and Gaza or how those areas would revert to Arab rule. Crucially, it explicitly delayed any negotiations about sovereignty of Jerusalem until the very end of the negotiation process. Israel utilised this ambiguity to expand settlements in the territories and development in Jerusalem, while the PLO made only token gestures towards ceasing terrorist activities or in recognising

Rabin, Clinton & Arafat

Photo: Vince Musi –
Executive Office of the President of the United States

Israel's right to exist. Decades later the arguments continued.

Disappointed with the outcome Clinton worked on negotiating a meaningful peace treaty, but not with the PLO. In October 1994, in front of the world press in the Judean desert, he presided over the signing of the Israel-Jordan peace treaty, an agreement that has been maintained to the present time. Encouraged by this outcome, Clinton rather ambitiously sought to establish a Syrian-Israeli peace treaty with the return of the Golan Heights to Syria as its basis for their reconciliation with Israel.

The return of the Golan Heights to the Syrians was unacceptable to secular Jews who saw the region as essential for defence and to religious Jews who regarded it as land granted to them by God. On November 4, 1995, at a peace rally in Tel Aviv, Rabin was shot and killed by a Jewish gunman opposed to his peace proposals. Clinton, who thought very highly of Rabin, was very upset at his death and the failure of the peace initiatives. Rabin was succeeded by Shimon Peres who tried to restore the peace process but was thwarted by Yasser Arafat who failed to constrain the increasing violence of radical Palestinians. This was a key factor in Peres losing

the 1996 election to the right-wing Benjamin Netanyahu who, with prompting from Clinton, entered into an interim peace accord in which Israel agreed to cede certain territory in return for Palestinian pledges of peace. These pledges were not extensively implemented and negotiations collapsed.

The revolving door of Israeli prime ministers continued and Ehud Barak was elected in 1999, comprehensively defeating Netanyahu. In July 2000 Clinton mediated meetings between Barak and Arafat at Camp David. After much debate Arafat was presented with the best offer ever tabled at Arab-Israeli peace negotiations. Israel agreed to concede ninety per cent of the West Bank and all of Gaza to the Palestinians and to restrict settlements to areas adjacent to the 1967 border. To the amazement of all involved, particularly Clinton, Arafat rejected the deal and departed Camp David. As is to be expected, there are conflicting explanations for the collapse of the talks. The Arabs contend that Arafat justifiably rejected the deal because it did not guarantee a 'right of return' for all Palestinians into Israel proper or grant them sovereignty over the Temple Mount. The alternative view is

that he walked away because signing a peace treaty with Israel would acknowledge its existence, whereas his only real intention was always a single Arab state encompassing all of 'Historic Palestine'.

U.S. presidents may seek the acclamation of concluding a Middle East peace treaty, and Israeli prime ministers may aim to achieve peace without conceding more territory than is politically acceptable within the nation, but Bible students know that there will be no lasting peace "until he come whose right it is" (Ezekiel 21:27, KJV).

George W Bush (2001-2009)

The presidency of George W Bush is defined by the terrorist attacks of September 11, 2001

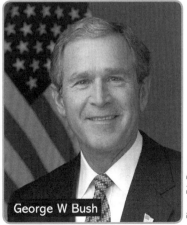

George W Bush

on the World Trade Centre, the Pentagon and an airliner in Pennsylvania, and by the nation's response in sending troops to Afghanistan and Iraq. Controversy continues over whether or not the military responses were warranted and whether the enormous cost and the deaths of many American and allied troops achieved a meaningful outcome.

Bush's response to the attacks was influenced by his religious attitude to the Middle East and his perception of 'good' and 'evil'. His views reflect those of the Religious Right,[13] a large and influential group consisting mainly of evangelicals, whose support was integral to Bush's election as president. The influence of evangelicals in presidential elections began in the 1970s with the election of Jimmy Carter and in the following decades the movement grew into a major political force reaching a peak in the election of George W Bush, the effect being:

"The secularism of Bill Clinton and Al Gore had given way to the Bible-based presidency of George W Bush. The new president of the United States saw himself as an instrument of God, his path as divinely ordained. The absolute nature of his faith meant that the values of secular democracy would take a back-seat to his Christian beliefs."[14]

Similar to the political leaders who brought about the Balfour Declaration, Bush believes that God has a purpose with Israel but also that it is the duty of those in power to engage in warfare against those deemed to be 'evil'. Christadelphians will see the shortfall in that reasoning and some secular writers have also queried the logic of conducting a war against 'evil' knowing that innocent civilians will also be killed. Among those is the Australian ethicist, Peter Singer, a Professor of Bioethics at Princeton University, who questioned:

"Is it consistent for someone who holds Bush's views about the sanctity of human life to be the supreme commander of armed forces that use bombs and missiles in areas where civilians are sure to be killed?"[15]

The rationale for wars against oppressive regimes is based, in part, on a belief that democracy is an integral part of Christianity and therefore a war to 'liberate' the population is justified and the death of some civilians is simply 'collateral damage'. George W Bush and many of the Religious Right hold this opinion, as Peter Singer has observed:

"When, in discussing the looming war with Iraq with the Australian Prime Minister John Howard in February 2003, he (Bush) said that liberty for the people of Iraq would not be a gift that the United States could provide, but 'God's gift to every human being in the world', he seemed to be suggesting that there was divine endorsement for a war to overthrow Saddam Hussein."[16]

A true believer understands that we are not to participate in the world's conflicts or politics and instead are to follow the words of Jesus:

"My kingdom is not of this world. If my kingdom were of this world, my servants would have been fighting, that I might not be delivered over to the Jews. But my kingdom is not from the world." (John 18:36)

---

13 See Appendix, page 162.
14 Craig Unger, *The Fall Of The House Of Bush*, page 196.

15 Peter Singer, *The President of Good and Evil*, page 60.
16 *ibid*, page 246.

Further Reading

Michael B Oren, *Power, Faith and Fantasy* (this book by an Israeli Ambassador to the United States provides excellent commentary on America's involvement in the Middle East since 1776 and includes much information on the attitude of many presidents to Israeli affairs).

Numerous books are available on the lives of most presidents. For information on the recent influence of the Religious Right, *The Fall of the House of Bush*, by Craig Unger is recommended.

Jimmy Carter, *The Blood of Abraham*, Houghton Miffen Company, Boston, 1985.

12

PRAY FOR THE PEACE OF JERUSALEM

"Jerusalem was once regarded as the centre of the world and today that is more true than ever: the city is the focus of the struggle between the Abrahamic religions, the shrine for increasingly popular Christian, Jewish and Islamic fundamentalism, the strategic battlefield of clashing civilizations, the front line between atheism and faith, the cynosure of secular fascination, the object of giddy conspiracism and internet myth-making, and the illuminated stage for the cameras of the world in the age of twenty-four hour news. Religious, political and media interest feed on each other to make Jerusalem more intensely scrutinized today than ever before."[1]

JERUSALEM! For people all around the world the name evokes remarkable feelings. A psychiatric condition known as the Jerusalem Syndrome afflicts some visitors to the city. People who previously might have been relatively normal suddenly become overwhelmed by the emotion and atmosphere of the city. They might begin to imagine themselves as Messiah, David or some other key figure in the city's past and act irrationally and even, in extreme cases, dangerously. Even people who have never been there or ever seen the city feel drawn to Jerusalem. It is for many a metaphor for hope and glory.

1 *Jerusalem the Biography*, Simon Sebag Montefiore, page xxv.

In many respects it is a city of anomalies and contradictions:

"Jerusalem is the Holy City, yet it has always been a den of superstition, charlatanism and bigotry; the desire and prize of empires, yet of no strategic value; the cosmopolitan home of many sects, each of which believes the city belongs to them alone; a city of many names – yet each tradition is so sectarian it excludes any other."[2]

Even today Jerusalem is a relatively small city. fifteen miles (twenty-four kilometres) from the Jordan and thirty-one miles (fifty kilometres) from the Mediterranean, it has no harbour and is on no significant trade route. In mountainous terrain with very limited natural water supplies and few other resources nearby, it was only after the British conquest in 1917 that the city gained a reliable reticulated water supply. The Old City remained unsewered until after its capture by Israel in 1967.

For all natural purposes it should be an obscure backwater of little interest. Yet it captures the attention of people around the globe, and its name appears in the news almost daily.

Yearnings for Jerusalem

In the nineteenth century William Blake wrote a poem now known as "Jerusalem", which during the First World War was set to a stirring hymn tune by Hubert Parry. Blake was a mystic and the words of the poem are somewhat cryptic. Almost certainly

2 *ibid*, page xxv.

they are intended as commentary on failings in British society. In spite of this, in the emotional atmosphere of war, the poem with its new tune quickly became very popular; King George V is said to have preferred it to "God save the king" as an anthem![3]

Blake's poem speaks of building a Jerusalem in England's green and pleasant land. Why did a small, provincial city on the edge of a barren wilderness in a backwater of the Ottoman Empire evoke such strong feelings in Georgian and Edwardian England? Surely it is, at least in part, testimony to the influence of the Bible on English thought.[4]

What was true of the English at that time was true even more of the Jews. For 1,900 years in exile the plaintive plea each Passover was, "Next year in Jerusalem". They felt the irresistible spiritual pull of this small, distant city. In doing so, the Jews of the Diaspora gave voice to the spirit recorded in Psalm 137, although as noted in Chapter 6, after centuries of living in Europe most Jews showed little inclination towards actually moving to the land. When Psalm 137 was written they had not assimilated, and in Babylon were grieved at being cut off from their land. Their focus remained on Jerusalem:

"If I forget you, O Jerusalem, let my right hand forget its skill! Let my tongue stick to the roof of my mouth, if I do not remember you, if I do

3 The nationalistic sentiment associated with this hymn tune and the inclusion of words taken from legends rather than scripture are amongst the reasons why Christadelphians have preferred not to use the tune or the words in their worship.
4 The subject of the influence of the Bible and the Holy Land on British culture is developed by Barbara Tuchman in *Bible and Sword*, Papermac, London, 1982. See also comments in Chapter 4.

not set Jerusalem above my highest joy!"
(Psalm 137:5,6)

When they call on God to judge their enemies, it is for desecration of Jerusalem that the enemy is condemned:

"Remember, O LORD, against the Edomites the day of Jerusalem, how they said, 'Lay it bare, lay it bare, down to its foundations!'" (verse 7)

Jerusalem and the prophets

Daniel also was in exile in Babylon. In Daniel 6 the prophet was promoted to a position of great authority under Darius, just as he had been under Nebuchadnezzar. This honour did not diminish his focus on those things that are eternal. Daniel's rivals in the empire tricked Darius into making a law prohibiting the worship of any God other than the king. Daniel, of course, could not comply with such a decree. He continued to pray to God according to his conscience:

"When Daniel knew that the document had been signed, he went to his house where he had windows in his upper chamber open towards Jerusalem. He got down on his knees three times a day and prayed and gave thanks before his God, as he had done previously." (Daniel 6:10)

There is no need for an open window when praying; God would hear regardless. But Daniel was not prepared to conceal his devotion to his God. And his window was not merely open; it was open "towards Jerusalem". Why? It is impossible to see Jerusalem from Babylon – except with the mind's eye, except with the eye of faith. Daniel's hopes and expectations were centred on that same city that his comrades lamented in Psalm 137.

Although exiled in Babylon for decades Daniel remained focused on Jerusalem. The city is referred to by name ten times in the Book of Daniel. Several other places refer to the city without using its name. In Daniel 8 we have an example:

"Then I heard a holy one speaking, and another holy one said to the one who spoke, 'For how long is the vision concerning the regular burnt offering, the transgression that makes desolate, and the giving over of the sanctuary and host to be trampled underfoot?' And he said to me, 'For 2,300 evenings and mornings. Then the sanctuary shall be restored to its rightful state.'"

(Daniel 8:13,14)

The Aramaic word translated "sanctuary", *Kodesh*, can describe a person, a place or an object that is holy. In this context it refers to a place. Whenever Daniel uses this word *Kodesh* of a place he is referring to Jerusalem. To the Jews many places are holy: Hebron, Sinai, the entire "Holy Land" are all holy. But for Daniel one place is pre-eminently holy – Jerusalem.

In Daniel 9 *Kodesh* is used on five occasions in relation to a place (twice in verse 20 and once each in verses 16, 24 and 26). In the context these are references to Jerusalem, in particular to Jerusalem as a centre of worship at the temple. In Daniel 11 we have one final reference to a place described as "holy". In verse 45 the King of the North is said to establish himself near the glorious holy mountain, another obvious allusion to Jerusalem.

For Daniel, Jerusalem was at the centre of his thoughts. It was for Jonah, too, even though he was a prophet from the Northern Kingdom, not Judah. While in the "whale's belly" having sought to escape his duty to God, Jonah utters a prayer of repentance and rededication. In Jonah 2:4 the prophet expresses how, when he reached the depth of anguish and despair, he turned at last to God. Jonah expresses his determination to repent as turning towards God's temple. Even though he could have been no more removed from the temple

in Jerusalem than in the abdomen of a large sea-creature, his thoughts turn to that place where God met with men and where He placed His name. As the Psalmist said of the city:

"The LORD has chosen Zion; he has desired it for his dwelling place: this is my resting-place for ever; here I will dwell, for I have desired it."

(Psalm 132:13,14)

When Nebuchadnezzar finally captured Jerusalem, Jeremiah penned the haunting Book of Lamentations, a lament as much for Jerusalem as it is for Judah (see, for example, Lamentations 1:7,8,17).

For Jeremiah, Jonah, Daniel and so many prophets, Jerusalem was at the centre of their thoughts. This is not surprising because the city plays a central role in the prophetic word. Jeremiah encapsulates the centrality of Jerusalem to the Gospel of the kingdom of God in words which declare God's purpose for the city in the age to come:

"And when you have multiplied and increased in the land, in those days, declares the LORD, they shall no more say, 'The ark of the covenant of the LORD.' It shall not come to mind or be remembered or missed; it shall not be made again. At that time Jerusalem shall be called the throne of the LORD, and all nations shall gather to it, to the presence of the LORD in Jerusalem, and they shall no more stubbornly follow their own evil heart." (Jeremiah 3:16,17)

Jerusalem – city of peace?

Jerusalem means 'city or place of peace'. Paradoxically, it has been the centre of conflict throughout recorded history. For millennia competing forces have struggled for control of the city – and in the days when our Lord returns that struggle will reach its climax.

Tension and conflict appear as constants in the history of Jerusalem. The city is mentioned throughout the Bible, and from what almost certainly is the first reference to the Holy City (in Genesis 14) it is associated with war and conflict down to our own times:

BC

1004	David captures Jerusalem
701	Sennacherib besieges the city
586	Destroyed by Nebuchadnezzar
350	Captured by the Persians
332	Captured (peacefully) by Alexander the Great
313	Ptolemy I of Egypt assumes control of Jerusalem
170	Plundered by Antiochus Epiphanes
167	Maccabean revolts follow desecration of the temple by Antiochus
63	Roman invasion under Pompei
37	Herod appointed as king in Jerusalem

AD

70	First Jewish revolt – Romans sack Jerusalem
135	Second Jewish revolt – Jerusalem razed and Jews excluded
614	Jerusalem falls to the Persians
629	Jerusalem retaken by Byzantines (Eastern Roman Empire)
638	Caliph Omar Ben Hatav captures Jerusalem
1009	Caliph Hakim orders the destruction of churches and synagogues
1077	Turks capture Jerusalem
1096	First Crusade captures Jerusalem
1187	Saladin takes Jerusalem from the Crusaders
1192	Richard the Lionheart fails to conquer Jerusalem
1244	Jerusalem sacked by Tartars
1259	Jerusalem sacked by Mongols
1347	Jerusalem falls to the Mamelukes
1517	Sultan Selim conquers the city for the Ottoman Empire
1541	Muslims seal the Golden Gate to prevent Messiah's entrance!
1831	Mehmet Ali of Egypt conquers Jerusalem
1840	Jerusalem returns to Ottoman rule
1917	British under Allenby capture the city
1947	UN Partition Plan provides for the internationalisation of Jerusalem
1948	Israel War of Independence – Old City captured by Jordan
1949	Proclaimed capital of Israel
1951	Jordan's King Abdullah shot by Arab extremists on Temple Mount
1967	Israel wrests control of Old City from Jordan
1980	Jerusalem Law – Israel's indivisible and eternal capital

A battlefield in the war against the flesh

Genesis 14 records the invasion of the land by Chedorlaomer. This conflict appears to be a precursor or type of the great northern invasion at the time of the end. As a result of the war recorded in Genesis 14, Lot is taken prisoner; Abraham intervenes and rescues him. On their way home they meet and are blessed by Melchizedek (verses 16-20). Without introduction, and for no apparent reason Melchizedek, King of Salem, is introduced into the record. We encounter this remarkable personage again only in Psalm 110 and Hebrews 5-7. The comments in Hebrews prove that he is a man of sign.

Melchizedek, as we are told in Hebrews, is a title meaning "king of righteousness". He was also King of Salem, or "king of peace". He was a king-priest, as Genesis 14:18 makes plain. He blesses Abraham on his return from this war against the power of sin and involves him in a feast of "bread and wine". All of this imagery rings with allusions to the Lord Jesus Christ, who will establish God's kingdom from Jerusalem after the overthrow of the northern invading host (refer to Chapters 13 and 14 for further details). The application to Christ is confirmed for us when we are told in Hebrews that Jesus Christ is a "priest for ever, after the order of Melchizedek".

Melchizedek is described as King of Salem, not Jerusalem, but we can be fairly confident that the two places are identical. Genesis 14:17 provides an additional piece of information to identify the place where this encounter occurred: the Valley of Shaveh is described as being the same as the "King's Valley". The only other scriptural reference to this place is in 2 Samuel 18:18, where it is recorded that the King's Valley was where Absalom raised up a pillar; this appears to have been in the Hinnom Valley adjacent to Jerusalem.

Later in Abraham's life there is another remarkable incident in the vicinity of Jerusalem. In Genesis 22:2 Abraham is told to journey to the land of Moriah to offer his son in sacrifice to God. Where was the land of Moriah? To which mountain did God direct Abraham? There are no other references to a land of Moriah, but in 2 Chronicles 3:1 the Temple Mount is called Mount Moriah. Building the Temple on Mount Moriah would seem fitting in view of the words of Genesis 22:

> "Abraham called the name of that place, 'The LORD will provide'; as it is said to this day, 'On the mount of the LORD it shall be provided.'"
> (verse 14)

"The LORD will provide." On this occasion God provided a ram, obviating the need for Abraham to slay his only begotten son. Hebrews 11 describes Isaac as having been symbolically resurrected at this time. The incident is a figure of the sacrifice of our Lord Jesus Christ – the sacrifice provided by God that we might have redemption from death and the hope of life eternal.

In Genesis, the seedbed of the Bible, are these two early references to Jerusalem that speak of God's ability and determination to triumph over the flesh and bring deliverance to His servants.

In 1 Samuel 17 we have another interesting reference to Jerusalem that continues and builds on these themes from Genesis. The chapter records David's contest with Goliath. The arrogant Philistine challenges the Israelites, but no man of Israel feels equal to the task of engaging Goliath in battle.

David in righteous indignation takes up the challenge and defeats the giant Philistine. In verse 51, having felled Goliath with a stone from his sling, David decapitates the Philistine warrior, thus turning the tide of the battle – the Israelites take heart and the Philistines are routed. David did something curious with the grisly trophy of the head of Goliath:

> "David took the head of the Philistine and brought it to Jerusalem, but he put his armour in his tent." (verse 54)

Why should David want the head of Goliath at all? And why take it to Jerusalem? At this time Jerusalem is not even controlled by the Israelites, being still in the hands of the Jebusites. David would not capture the city for Israel until some years later.

David's action was a declaration that he understood something of God's purpose in relation to Jerusalem and the conquest of the flesh. This great triumph over the champion of Israel's enemy is symbolic of the triumph of the son of David over sin and death. In keeping with the promise to Eve (Genesis 3:15), David bruised the head of the seed of the serpent – even cutting it off and placarding his triumph over it.

Taking Goliath's head to Jerusalem appears to foreshadow that the final victory over sin and death would be in Jerusalem. And so it was that, a thousand years later, the son of David triumphed over the power of the flesh and brought to reality the hope of resurrection, as experienced in a figure by Isaac.

David's appreciation of Jerusalem's place in God's purpose was evident later in his life when he relocated his capital to the city following its capture from the Jebusites (2 Samuel 5). Towards the end of his reign, after he sinned by numbering the nation, David was directed by an angel to the threshing floor of Araunah the Jebusite as the place where he should raise an altar to the Lord (2 Samuel 24:18). Like Melchizedek before him, David acted as king and priest in offering a burnt offering and a peace offering (verse 25), but significantly no sin offering because, even though David was in need of it, this was an offering that only God could provide, as had been intimated to Abraham at this very spot in Genesis 22.

O Jerusalem, Jerusalem

Although the Jews came into possession of Jerusalem in the days of David, by the time of Jesus the city is well and truly back under the control of the flesh. The Jews controlling the city and the temple reject the Son of David, and as the hour of his sacrifice approaches the Lord utters a lament for the city:

"O Jerusalem, Jerusalem, the city that kills the prophets and stones those who are sent to it! How often would I have gathered your children together as a hen gathers her brood under her wings, and you would not! See, your house is left to you desolate." (Matthew 23:37,38)

These poignant words of despair and sadness speak of grief and anguish at the blindness of Israel. The people failed to hear the prophets and recognise the call of their Messiah. Indeed, as verse 38 says, their house would be left desolate. Forty years after they wickedly slew the greatest prophet ever sent, their Messiah, the nation was punished in AD 70 when God sent the Romans to raze the city, destroy the temple and send the Jews into exile.

The Olivet Prophecy incorporates a graphic description of the harrowing days of the Roman siege of Jerusalem (Luke 21:20-23). The desolation of the Holy City was to last for a prolonged time. Jerusalem was to be trodden down of the Gentiles until the time came near for the kingdom of God to be established, as the remainder of the prophecy declares (verses 24-32).

Having lost control of Jerusalem in AD 70, Jewish forces reclaimed the city during the Six-Day War in 1967. Many students of prophecy were thrilled to see Jews in control of the city of David once again. Israel had been required to give up the territory in the Sinai Peninsula it had captured in 1956, so there was good reason to think it unlikely the Jewish state would be allowed to retain control of Jerusalem after 1967. Brother L G Sargent reflected this in an editorial in *The Christadelphian* for July of that year:

"The capture of Jerusalem is an astonishing development which opens up all kinds of hopes, though in fact it is unlikely that the Powers will allow Israel to keep it, and there will be renewed demands for it to be made an international Holy City".[5]

Figures such as Pope Paul VI[6] called for Jerusalem to be taken from Israel and established as an international city. Israel, however, went on to annex Jerusalem, while it continued to administer the remainder of the West Bank it conquered from Jordan as occupied territory.

On the morning that Jewish forces seized control of the Old City of Jerusalem General Moshe Dayan, Israel's Defence Minister, announced:

"This morning Israeli defence forces liberated Jerusalem, and we have now united Jerusalem, the divided capital of Israel. We have returned to the holiest of our holy places, never to part from it again. To our Arab neighbours we extend, also at this hour – and with added emphasis on this hour – our hand in peace. And to our Christian and Muslim fellow citizens, we solemnly promise full religious freedom and rights."[7]

Dayan's statement is both assertive and conciliatory. He makes clear what subsequent history has confirmed, namely that Israel has no intention of ever willingly relinquishing control of

5 *The Christadelphian*, July 1967, page 318; see also page 323.
6 An editorial at the time in the Vatican weekly magazine *L'Osservatore Della Domenica*, stated: "The Church demands that an international authority, founded on the principles of the United Nations and the declaration of the rights of man, take over the city."
7 Statement of General Moshe Dayan, Israel's Defence Minister, on June 7, 1967, quoted by E Marcell, *Israel Thunders: Six Historical Days in June as it Occurred*, pages 58 and 59.

any part of Jerusalem. But he also makes clear that Israel has no intention of denying the rights of other religions in the Holy City. The then Israeli Prime Minister, Levi Eshkol, confirmed these sentiments in meetings with the religious leaders of Jerusalem in the weeks immediately after the war.

The time of the Gentiles fulfilled?

Our Lord stated in the Olivet Prophecy that "Jerusalem will be trampled underfoot by the Gentiles, until the times of the Gentiles are fulfilled" (Luke 21:24). Some have seen in Israel's wresting of control of Jerusalem in 1967 the fulfilment of the time of the Gentiles. But is this a reasonable interpretation?

While the Jewish state exercises authority over the city the Gentiles still control significant sites within its boundaries. Indeed, Muslim religious authorities retain control of arguably the most significant religious site in Jerusalem, the Temple Mount, which includes the site of Moriah where Abraham was to have offered up Isaac and the site of the threshing floor of Araunah the Jebusite which became the focal point of Solomon's Temple. Religious Jews are forbidden to set foot on this holy hill until their Messiah establishes himself in the city.

Like the restoration of Israel, which is the great sign of the Lord's coming, the Jewish capture of Jerusalem is undoubtedly a key milestone on the road towards the kingdom of God. But while buildings such as the Dome of the Rock and the Al Aksa mosque, not to mention Christian shrines like the Church of the Holy Sepulchre, remain in the control of non-Jewish authorities it cannot be said that the time of the Gentiles has been fulfilled.

Perhaps the challenge some Bible students face in relation to terms such as this is due to a desire for a level of precision that the prophecy was never

Modern-day Jerusalem

Photo: Judy Levett

meant to convey. The modern Western mindset is inclined to apply to words such as times, days and seasons a degree of exactitude with regard to commencement, duration and end date that the inspired writers of the Bible did not intend. While there is no doubt that there are cases where such terms do have very precise application, there are other times when we should view the prophecies as relating to an epoch or a process over time.

The word translated 'time' (KJV, "times") is the Greek *kairos*, which literally means 'season or opportunity' (compare its use in Galatians 6:10 and Hebrews 11:15). Thus we may be justified in seeing in the term "times of the Gentiles" a reference to the period during which Gentiles will be in the ascendency in so far as Jerusalem is concerned and during which they have the opportunity to respond to the Gospel message. This, of course, comes to a close (in so far as the current dispensation is concerned) when the Lord returns. Brother Thomas links the fulfilment of the "times of the Gentiles" with Israel's restoration under its Messiah.[8]

8 *Eureka*, Volume 1, page 35. Interestingly, Brother Thomas applies Luke 21:24 to both Jerusalem and the saints being trodden under foot.

The 1967 victory is a significant step in the process of bringing the "time of the Gentiles" to its fulfilment, but the prophecy will not be completely fulfilled until our Lord returns, after which he will re-establish David's throne in Jerusalem and put down all competing claims to the Holy City.

The set time to favour Zion

Jerusalem is mentioned twenty-two times by name in Zechariah chapters 12 to 14. Although Zechariah 12:1 says that the theme of this passage is the future of Israel, we find that the prophet refers most directly to Jerusalem:

> "The burden of the word of the LORD concerning Israel: Thus declares the LORD, who stretched out the heavens and founded the earth and formed the spirit of man within him: 'Behold, I am about to make Jerusalem a cup of staggering to all the surrounding peoples. The siege of Jerusalem will also be against Judah. On that day I will make Jerusalem a heavy stone for all the peoples. All who lift it will surely hurt themselves. And all the nations of the earth will gather against it.'"   (Zechariah 12:2,3)

Jerusalem is to be a heavy (KJV, "burdensome") stone and a cup of staggering (KJV, "trembling"). We know from verses 6 to 8 that this prophecy concerns the time of the end, when God intervenes to defeat Israel's enemies and re-establish the throne of David in Jerusalem. Immediately prior to that time of the peace of Jerusalem, then, we should expect the city to be a heavy or burdensome stone for all nations.

Ever since the Jews commenced returning to the land, and especially since Israel was re-established as an independent state, the presence of Jews in the Middle East has been a source of tension. Since Israel's capture of the old city of Jerusalem from Jordan in 1967 this tension has become more and more focused in particular on the city of Jerusalem itself.

The Oslo Pact

In 1994 the Israelis and Palestinians signed a remarkable pact negotiated at secret meetings in secluded venues throughout Norway and Sweden. This agreement, which became known as the Oslo Pact, provided for a series of negotiations on a range of contentious issues aimed at securing a level of autonomy for the Palestinians. The last issue scheduled to be resolved in these talks is the status of Jerusalem. (Refer also to the section on President Clinton in Chapter 11.)

This agreement is an example of a modern approach to resolving conflict known as Alternative Dispute Resolution. Unlike traditional adversarial systems of dispute resolution using force or legal coercion, this approach involves two seemingly irreconcilable parties identifying the few things on which they are agreed, and then using these to build a platform for wider agreement. The secret to

Photo: Judy Levett

The Western Wall

such negotiations is to defer for as long as possible discussion of those issues on which agreement is least likely in the hope that something will happen in the interim to remove any obstacles to agreement. That is why Jerusalem was scheduled as the last issue to be determined.

Most commentators recognised that the Israeli and Palestinian views on Jerusalem were apparently irreconcilable, and that if the Oslo Pact were to collapse it would do so over this issue. Even as the treaty was signed it was feared that it could lead to a war over the status of Jerusalem. Events since then have confirmed this view.

A burdensome stone

In July 1980 the Israeli Knesset passed the Jerusalem Law which amongst other things enunciated the following three principles:

1. Jerusalem, complete and united, is the capital of Israel.
2. Jerusalem is the seat of the President of the State, the Knesset, the government, and the Supreme Court.
3. The holy places will be protected against desecration and any other offence, and against anything liable to infringe on the free access of adherents of religions to their holy places or on their sentiments towards those places.

In essence this merely codified what had been expressed by General Dayan and Prime Minister Eshkol in 1967. In 1998 the Israeli Government took steps further to strengthen its control over Jerusalem and surrounding areas by extending the boundaries of the city. This provoked a rebuke from the United Nations, which has never recognised Israel's control of the city.

In early 1999, during an Israeli election campaign, the government of Benjamin Netanyahu vowed to retain full control of Jerusalem. This was in response to a statement issued by the European Union questioning Israel's right to sovereignty over that city which is at the heart of the Holy Land. It is significant that, although Mr Netanyahu and his Likud Party lost the May 1999 election in Israel, the victor in that election, Ehud Barak, immediately confirmed his commitment to retaining full Israeli control over all of Jerusalem.

Continuing challenges

In addition to criticism from the international community, other pressures add to the headaches for Israel in relation to Jerusalem. One of these is demography – the make-up of the population of Jerusalem. Two adjacent articles in *The Jerusalem Post* (International edition) on June 7, 1997 reported that the city's Jewish growth rate was dropping, while at the same time Jerusalem's Arab population was growing four times faster than the Jewish population. A demographic time bomb does have a longer fuse than a terrorist bomb, but might in the end be much more devastating. And if you add to this the influence of extremists on both the Arab and Jewish side you have a very volatile mix indeed. Israeli police have foiled many plans by Jewish extremists to attack the Temple Mount, now occupied by Moslem mosques.[9]

Given the tensions that exist in this region and that are focused on Jerusalem, it would not take much to ignite a major conflict. Such a conflict is envisioned and predicted in the prophets, and the burdensome or heavy stone that is Jerusalem may well be the trigger.

---

9 For example, *The Jerusalem Post* (International edition), February 27, 1999 reported that "Jerusalem police foil five attacks on Temple Mount".

And it need not be a deliberate act that lights the fuse. It was reported in 1998 that the Mosque compound on the Temple Mount might be in danger of collapse due to the extensive excavations under much of the city and the seismic instability of the area.[10] Since then Muslim authorities have commissioned additional excavation work under the Temple Mount. While the Bible does refer to a massive earthquake affecting the area of Jerusalem after the return of Christ (Zechariah 14:4,5), there might also be an earthquake prior to that time. Many seismologists believe that a significant earthquake is likely in the region soon.

Jerusalem is now a burdensome stone and a cup of trembling. It is at the centre of world tension. A secular essay on the city made this remarkable statement about Jerusalem:

> "It is extraordinary how much human error attends virtually all major developments with regard to Jerusalem, as though ordinary men are not in control of events governing the destiny of the city holy to three faiths."[11]

The author, Daniel Mandel, is absolutely correct. Man is not in control of the future of that city, or indeed any other part of the globe. God has a purpose with this earth and at the centre of that purpose is Israel and Jerusalem.

---

10 Reported in the *Sydney Morning Herald*, March 7, 1998 under the headline, "Experts warn of mosque compound collapse".
11 *The Review* (known previously as the *Australia Israel Review*), May 1999.

13

WARFARE IN THE LAST DAYS

EVENTS that fulfil prophecy are important as they enable us to see the hand of God in action. We can also perceive in them the often extensive number of steps taken to reach the conclusion. Events that are yet to take place have an added level of intrigue as we ponder just how the conclusion will be reached and whether it will occur in our lifetime.

In moving on to consider future events we do so keeping in mind two lessons from fulfilled prophecy:

- the confidence we can have that future events will indeed occur; and
- that prophesied events do not necessarily occur in the precise format or time frame that we may expect. For example, who would have anticipated the broad range of events that brought about the restoration of the state of Israel?

The great event on the horizon is the return of the Lord Jesus Christ which will be accompanied by dramatic and, in many respects, disconcerting events even for believers as they may not necessarily be spared the effect of them all. Having witnessed the restoration of Israel, a key theme of the Olivet Prophecy, it is reasonable to contend that we also are seeing the beginnings of the extensive range of problems listed in Matthew 24, Mark 13 and Luke 21 which we shall consider in a later chapter. Those events are likely to be the prelude to the mighty battles described in Ezekiel 38 and 39 and Zechariah 14, which are the subject of this chapter.

Attitude to prophecy

Familiarity with key prophecies, at least in outline, is a feature of being a Christadelphian. In fact, a focus on God's purpose with Israel and the return of Christ is one of the defining points of the Christadelphian body of beliefs. That focus is perhaps now not as intense, partly because the 'spirit of the age' discourages extensive reading, and partly because alternative views on future prophecies in recent decades may have caused some to put the topic aside as 'too hard'. The former is a fact of life we have to battle against and the latter ought not to concern us, apart from where opinions are clearly fanciful.

A single, consistent opinion on how prophetical events will unfold may generate confidence about outcomes but it is not necessarily objective. We certainly need to hold firmly to the aspects of future prophecies that are 'absolute' but it is not a failure of faith to acknowledge that there are 'less certain' aspects. Indeed it may be preferable to accept that some level of variation is likely and keep a watchful eye on how world events develop whilst evaluating them against the prophetic word.

A fixed view on the 'less certain' aspects may have to be changed if events occur quite differently or if there are permanent changes in world situations. Such an outcome could adversely affect our faith. We all are likely to have a personal view on the precision of some events, but it is unreasonable to demand consensus in the absence of definitive scriptural statements.

Invasion of Israel

Ezekiel 38 and 39, and Zechariah 14 are chapters that provide extensive information on an invasion or invasions of Israel. Both prophecies contain parts that are 'absolute' and parts that are 'less certain'.

In the 'absolute' category we have:

1. Israel will be invaded.
2. The invasion takes place after Israel has been regathered from the nations.
3. The invasion occurs in "the latter years".
4. Ezekiel defines the invaders as being from "the north" whilst Zechariah describes those invaders, or possibly another group, as "all nations".
5. The northern invader is supported by several other nations.
6. Another group of nations questions the invaders about their intended purpose but apparently does not engage the invaders in battle.
7. The invading nations from the north are completely destroyed by God.
8. God's involvement in causing the destruction of

Russian military parade

Photo: Alexander Natruskin – Reuters

the northern invaders is apparent to all nations.

Even if we limit our consideration to this 'absolute' category we have, through belief in the word of God, an amazing understanding that escapes the attention of most people including those who wrestle with modern Middle Eastern issues. We know that no amount of Arab/Israeli peace talks or speeches in the General Assembly of the United Nations will prevent the conflict that is to occur in the region. We also know that the events described by Ezekiel and Zechariah will occur at or near the return of Jesus Christ.

This may be sufficient information for many believers but the prophecies contain observations on other aspects of latter time events that are worth considering. That information fits into the 'less certain' category and includes the following aspects that have long been debated:

1. Whether Ezekiel and Zechariah describe the same battle or two separate battles.
2. Whether all or only some of the events take place before Christ returns.
3. The current identity of the participating nations.

4. The reason for the split in the Arab bloc, with some supporting the invaders and others apparently aligned with the nations that question the invaders' intentions.

Those who like to consider such matters find it interesting to review military and political developments against the prophetic record. In so doing they are helped to see the active work of God in bringing to fulfilment His covenant with natural Israel and those who have been joined to it through belief and baptism. Nevertheless, no matter how interesting and how helpful a consideration of the 'less certain' aspects may be we cannot expect unanimity of opinion on them.

One battle or two?

The key features of each prophecy are encapsulated in a few verses:

"Thus says the Lord GOD: Behold, I am against you, O Gog, chief prince of Meshech and Tubal. And I will turn you about and put hooks into your jaws, and I will bring you out, and all your army, horses and horsemen, all of them clothed in full armour, a great host, all of them with buckler and shield, wielding swords. Persia, Cush, and Put are with them, all of them with shield and helmet; Gomer and all his hordes; Beth-togarmah from the uttermost parts of the north with all his hordes – many peoples are with you."

(Ezekiel 38:3-6)

"Behold, a day is coming for the LORD, when the spoil taken from you will be divided in your midst. For I will gather all the nations against Jerusalem to battle, and the city shall be taken and the houses plundered and the women raped. Half of the city shall go out into exile, but the rest of the people shall not be cut off from the city. Then the LORD will go out and fight against those nations as when he fights on a day of battle. On that day his feet shall stand on the Mount of Olives that lies before Jerusalem on the east, and the Mount of Olives shall be split in two from east to west by a very wide valley, so that one half of the Mount shall move northwards, and the other half southwards."

(Zechariah 14:1-4)

Some are convinced that the two prophets are describing the same battle but with certain variances in the details provided. Others consider that two distinctly different events are described. The key lines of reasoning applied to the differing views are set out in the following sections:

The case for one battle

Supporters of the single battle concept consider that Ezekiel and Zechariah are referring to the same event – an invasion of Israel from the north. A primary reasoning is that the events described by Ezekiel will occur in the order of the chapters in that section of his prophecy, other than the events in verses 22 to 28 of chapter 37, which will happen later.

The battle described in chapters 38 and 39 follows Ezekiel's vision of the restoration of Israel in chapter 37 and precedes his vision of the temple to be constructed in the kingdom age as described in chapter 40.

It is also considered that Ezekiel 39:25 establishes the battle as prior to Messiah's manifestation to Israel because in those verses God states that as a consequence of the destruction of the Gogian army "the fortunes of Jacob" will be restored. That is an outcome that would already have been achieved had Christ been revealed to them prior to the battle. Verses 26 and 27 refer to the godlessness of the returned Jews living in the land and to the punishment consequently brought

125

upon them, including exile into the lands of the invaders.

The Gogian invaders descend upon Israel for reasons stated in Ezekiel 38:10-12:

> "Thus says the Lord GOD: On that day, thoughts will come into your mind, and you will devise an evil scheme and say, 'I will go up against the land of unwalled villages. I will fall upon the quiet people who dwell securely, all of them dwelling without walls, and having no bars or gates,' to seize spoil and carry off plunder, to turn your hand against the waste places that are now inhabited, and the people who were gathered from the nations, who have acquired livestock and goods, who dwell at the centre of the earth."

This invasion against an "unwalled people" may be triggered by Israel and the surrounding Arab nations entering into a peace treaty which would be perceived as long-term and binding in contrast to all previous endeavours to negotiate a peace treaty. As a consequence of the period of peace generated by this treaty, Israel's economy would boom to the extent that the Gogian forces invade from the north to possess the "spoils" that have been produced. Israel's strategically placed location in the Middle East will also be an influence in Gog risking global warfare to secure control of the region. The peace treaty that places Israel in a position of "dwelling securely" would be broader than the existing treaties with Egypt and Jordan as, by necessity, it must encompass most, if not all, Arab nations.[1]

Alternatively, the concept of Israel dwelling securely may be a reflection of Israel's confidence in its military prowess and its ability to engage and defeat any foe that threatens the Jewish state.

1 John Allfree, *Ezekiel*, page 404.

A recently developed concept is that the "spoil" may be Israel's offshore gas fields. The Tamar and Leviathan gas fields, discovered in 2009 and 2010 respectively, are located in the Mediterranean Sea off the coast of Israel and are amongst the world's largest offshore gas discoveries. Production from these wells has the potential to threaten Russia's near monopoly of gas supply to Europe. As at 2013 the fields have not been put into production and this is another item for students of prophecy to add to their "watch" list.

Some efforts in past years to define the reason for the invasion have been incorrect and consequently quite unhelpful. However, searching for a definition of the "spoil" may be unnecessary as God could cause the northern nations to be brought down for any number of reasons. "And I will turn you about and put hooks into your jaws." (verse 4).

The invasion is initiated by a great army which descends from the "uttermost parts of the north" and is joined by certain European, Middle Eastern and African nations. A more extensive review of the nations involved in the attack on Israel is contained in the next chapter.

The case for two battles

Those who favour the two battles scenario consider that Zechariah describes an Arab invasion of Israel prior to the return of Christ, whilst Ezekiel describes an invasion from the north after the return. Specific reasoning for two quite separate battles is outlined below:

<u>Definition of the nations</u>. Zechariah refers to "all the nations", whereas Ezekiel specifically defines the individual nations that descend on Israel. This leaves open the question of what is intended by the expression "all the nations". Some consider that it may refer to a United Nations force representative of the majority of member countries. However, "all"

does not necessarily mean worldwide, and instead could be interpreted in the context of the time in which the message was given or the circumstances to which it relates. The nations described as "all" may be all those in the immediate vicinity of Israel.

Psalm 83 is a possible source of information for the identity of nations that come against Israel. The Psalm lists nations that object to Israel's existence, a situation that applied when the Psalm was written, and commenced again in earnest after the establishment of the state of Israel in 1948. That opposition continues to the present time, with statements from extremist Arab groups being remarkably similar to the outbursts against Israel recorded in the Psalm:

"O God, do not keep silence; do not hold your peace or be still, O God! For behold your enemies make an uproar; those who hate you have raised their heads. They lay crafty plans against your people; they consult together against your treasured ones. They say, 'Come, let us wipe them out as a nation; let the name of Israel be remembered no more!' For they conspire with one accord; against you they make a covenant – the tents of Edom and the Ishmaelites, Moab and the Hagrites, Gebal and Ammon and Amalek, Philistia with the inhabitants of Tyre; Asshur also has joined them; they are the strong arm of the children of Lot." (Psalm 83:1-8)

There is compelling logic in the concept that Israel's implacable enemies of old will be the nations that initially overrun Israel in the latter days. An invasion of armies from the north will subsequently descend upon Israel to oppose the Lord Jesus who will have revealed himself in saving Israel from the Arab nations. Nations endorsing false religion will be more inclined to oppose the declared rule of Christ than to attack the nation of Israel for ideological or economic reasons.

Outcomes of the battles. The Zechariah record is very explicit about the outcome of the first invasion and there is no good news in it for Israel:

"For I will gather all the nations against Jerusalem to battle, and the city shall be taken and the houses plundered and the women raped. Half of the city shall go out into exile, but the rest of the people shall not be cut off from the city." (Zechariah 14:2)

The period of exile is not stated but the word is usually only applied to a reasonably lengthy period of time. Israel's distress is therefore unlikely to last for only a few days. If the events of Ezekiel 39 are to take place in the order of the verses in the chapter, the invaders from the north will be destroyed by God before inflicting punishment on Israel:

"You shall fall on the mountains of Israel, you and all your hordes and the peoples who are with you. I will give you to birds of prey of every sort and to the beasts of the field to be devoured." (Ezekiel 39:4)

On this basis verses 23 to 29 are a concluding notation referring to exile and punishment over many centuries and not to punishment inflicted by the Gogian invasion. To make it otherwise requires Israel to be taken into exile to the countries of the Gogian army: "when I have brought them back from the peoples and gathered them from their enemies' lands …" (39:27).

Dwelling securely ("safely", KJV). Ezekiel in chapter 38:8 and 10 speaks of Israel "dwelling securely" but does not define the cause of the security. There is no indication that the expression refers to an Israeli/Arab peace treaty and the uprisings that commenced in 2011 to depose Arab leaders could lead to existing treaties being scrapped let alone a broader treaty being developed. Zechariah chapter 14 has only one occurrence of the word "securely", but the circumstances that bring about that security are clearly defined. After his description of the physical changes that occur in Jerusalem as Christ stands on the Mount of Olives, Zechariah states:

"And the LORD will be king over all the earth. On that day the LORD will be one and his name one. The whole land shall be turned into a plain from Geba to Rimmon south of Jerusalem. But Jerusalem shall remain aloft on its site from the Gate of Benjamin to the place of the former gate, to the Corner Gate, and from the Tower of Hananel to the king's wine presses. And it shall be inhabited, for there shall never again be a decree of utter destruction. Jerusalem *shall dwell in security*." (14:9-11)

There is a strong indicator here that Israel will not dwell in true security until Christ returns. Some other scriptures that point to the nation's security being contingent upon the return of Christ are:

"Behold, the days are coming, declares the LORD, when I will raise up for David a righteous Branch, and he shall reign as king and deal wisely, and shall execute justice and righteousness in the land. In his days Judah will be saved, and Israel *will dwell securely*." (Jeremiah 23:5,6)

"Thus says the Lord GOD: When I gather the house of Israel from the peoples among whom they are scattered, and manifest my holiness in them in the sight of the nations, then they shall dwell in their own land that I gave to my servant Jacob. And they shall dwell securely in it, and they shall build houses and plant vineyards. They *shall dwell securely*, when I execute judgments upon all their neighbours who have treated them with contempt. Then they will know that I am the LORD their God." (Ezekiel 28:25,26)

Interestingly, these verses speak of a time when God brings judgement upon Israel's neighbours,

possibly the Arab nations of Psalm 83, rather than upon invaders from the north. In Ezekiel 28 (quoted above) the prophet may be alluding to the battle of Zechariah 14 preceding the battle he describes in chapter 38.

Zechariah provides some interesting observations on villages without walls:

"... Jerusalem shall be inhabited as villages without walls, because of the multitude of people and livestock within it. And I will be to her a wall of fire all around, declares the LORD, and I will be the glory in her midst." (Zechariah 2:4,5)

All these passages suggest that Israel dwells securely and turns to God after the return of Christ. Israel's change of heart will, in all probability, be in response to the Lord Jesus delivering them from the parlous circumstances described in Zechariah 14. (Other passages with relevance to dwelling securely are Jeremiah 32:37,38 and 33:14-16.) If Israel is not to dwell securely until Christ has returned, it is reasonable to attribute Ezekiel's reference to "security" in chapters 38 and 39 to a period following the return of Christ.[2]

The changing fortunes of the Arabs

The nineteenth century was a time in which many books on latter-day prophecies were written by learned expositors, including our Christadelphian 'pioneer' writers. At that time, what now comprises the Arab states, was an area populated by poor Arab tribes. Britain and, to some extent, France were yet to draw the borders that now define many of the current nations of the Middle East and to

2 For an alternative approach to Israel dwelling securely under which it is seen to refer to the modern Israeli state's confidence in its own military strength, see an article entitled "Israel dwelling securely", by Brother Geoff Henstock, *The Christadelphian*, February 2003, page 49.

Old Dubai: pre-oil wealth

Photo: Sid Levett

Modern Dubai

Photo: Sid Levett

appoint the rulers who established dynasties, many of which continue to the present.

As the vast oil deposits had not yet been discovered, it was inconceivable that powerful nations holding incredible wealth would develop from these tribes. The oil, and the wealth it generates, has provided these nations with influence over the West as well as enabling them to maintain powerful military forces. Had those expositors been able to perceive what was to develop from the Arab tribes they may well have seen Zechariah 14 in a different light. The line of thought established by their writings may consequently have included the possibility of Arab/Islamic military action against Israel as a precursor or at least an accompaniment to the northern invasion.

Our reaction to prophetical knowledge

Debating the finer points of whether one or two battles take place can be interesting but it is not the key issue. The language of the two prophecies does not necessarily preclude one or the other option and the scenario we prefer will be a personal opinion based on an evaluation of the reasons for and against. However, totally disregarding the

potential for matters to develop in a manner not precisely in accord with our perception may be detrimental to our faith.

We have the privilege of knowing that very major events will take place in Israel prior to and surrounding the return of Christ. The world's statesmen may express opinions, the United Nations may pass resolutions, but nothing will thwart the purpose of God. We have an understanding of that purpose and should be humbled by the privilege and encouraged to lead lives appropriate to the knowledge we possess.

"But the day of the Lord will come like a thief, and then the heavens will pass away with a roar, and the heavenly bodies will be burned up and dissolved, and the earth and the works that are done on it will be exposed. Since all these things are thus to be dissolved, what sort of people ought you to be in lives of holiness and godliness, waiting for and hastening the coming of the day of God, because of which the heavens will be set on fire and dissolved, and the heavenly bodies will melt as they burn! But according to his promise we are waiting for new heavens and a new earth in which righteousness dwells." (2 Peter 3:10-13)

Further Reading

Brother John Thomas, *Elpis Israel,* pages 418-420, 14th edition.

Brother W H Boulton, *The Book of the Prophet Ezekiel.*

Brother John Allfree, *Ezekiel.*

Brother Harry Whittaker, *The Last Days.*

Karl Meyer & Shareen Brysac, *Kingmakers – The Invention of the Modern Middle East.*

14

INVADERS FROM THE NORTH

SEVERAL prophecies refer to an invasion of Israel in the latter days – Ezekiel 38, Joel 3 and Zechariah 14 in particular. Determining whether these chapters refer to the same or separate battles is an interesting exercise, but in this chapter we shall address the intriguing question of the identity of the nation that comes from "the uttermost parts of the north" (Ezekiel 38:15), together with the names of the other nations that join the invading force. This requires us to delve into the longstanding debate of whether in verses 2 and 3 of Ezekiel 38 the Hebrew word *Ros* should be translated as "Rosh" or as "*chief* prince". The debate is significant because some students of the Bible prefer versions in which "Rosh" is translated as a place name and from that declare it to be Russia because of linguistic similarity. That reasoning is severely weakened if "chief prince" is the correct translation.

Some scholars contend that in the context of Ezekiel 38 *Ros* is a noun and should be translated as the place name "Rosh". The opinion of other scholars is that the more common practice of translating *Ros* as an adjective should be maintained here and that "chief" in the expression "*chief* prince" is therefore correct.

Readers may question why a book intended as an introduction to latter-day prophecy is taking them into Hebrew grammar! Please bear with us as it is an important part of forming an objective opinion on this significant prophecy about a mighty battle and the revealing of God's power. However, readers with no interest in the translation debate can elect to avoid the boxed section on the next page.

Might it be Russia irrespective of translation?

The inconclusive debate described above does not, however, mean that an opinion cannot be formed on the names of the nations in Ezekiel 38 as other information is provided including historical records that can be used as indicators, if not actual proof. For example, some scholars consider that the Hebrew word *Ros* can be applied to a people from the far north and that the ancient name Magog refers to a people who inhabited the southern region of modern day Russia. Gesenius after declaring "Rosh" to be the correct translation, added:

> "… undoubtedly the Russians, who are mentioned by the Byzantine writers of the tenth century, under the name the Ros, dwelling to the north of Taurus."[1]

Because of this strongly expressed opinion Gesenius is often quoted in articles and websites of American evangelicals who are desperately keen to see Russia, their arch-enemy, named as the main protagonist of Israel and Jesus Christ. That might mean either that Gesenius is universally regarded as authoritative or that he is one of the very few sources of such statements. As with the grammatical debate, alternative views are held, with some scholars stating that *Ros*, irrespective

1 Gesenius, Hebrew Lexicon, page 752.

The debate over "Rosh" or "chief prince"

Enthusiasm to identify Russia as the main protagonist ought not to prevail over appropriate scriptural analysis. Searching for commentators who endorse an opinion we prefer and quoting them as proof does not lead to 'job done; Russia it is'. Wilhelm Gesenius (1786-1842) is often the commentator of choice and frequently quoted in Christadelphian writings and presentations. He was a renowned Hebrew scholar and certainly worth referencing as a supporter of the *Rosh/Russia* opinion. However, it is inappropriate scholarship to quote one expert as 'proof' but to ignore the complexities of the reasoning and the many experts who hold an alternative opinion.

The grammatical issue is complicated. Gesenius described it as "Contrary to English, which in lengthy enumerations uses *and* to connect only the last member of the series, in Hebrew *polysyndeton* is customary." In all honesty most of us would have to concede that we are not qualified to express an opinion on such a matter. Bible translators are also divided on the topic with the KJV, RSV, ESV and NIV using "chief prince" and the RV, NEB and NKJV preferring "Rosh" (with several offering the alternative translation in the margin).

The Septuagint (Greek translation from Hebrew around 300 BC) translates *Ros* as "Rosh" which might be taken as the definitive Hebrew understanding of *Ros* at that time but Jewish opinion, both ancient and modern, is divided. For example, the following Jewish scholars have utilised many Jewish writings in their research and all have opted for "chief prince" rather than "Rosh":

- Rabbi Dr. S Fisch, *Ezekiel Commentary*, 1972.
- Rabbis Scherman and Zlotowitz in their expansive work *Ezekiel – With Commentary Anthologized from Talmudic, Midrashic and Rabbinic Sources*, 1988.
- David H Stern in his 1998 work the *Complete Jewish Bible*.

Gesenius stated that "*Rosh*" is a proper name of a northern nation, mentioned with Meshech and Tubal."[1] However, other scholars, both Jewish and non-Jewish, disagree with reasons such as, "... in the absence of any satisfactory identification (of *Ros*) and in view of the frequent coupling of Meshech and Tubal, we must suppose *Ros* to be in apposition to, or even a gloss on, the word *prince*."[2] A resolution cannot be obtained by determining the number of Biblical scholars or secular historians who support a particular opinion and we shall have to accept that the jury is still out on which is the preferred translation.

---

1 Gesenius, *Hebrew Lexicon*, page 752.
2 John B Taylor, *Tyndale Old Testament Commentaries – Ezekiel*, page 244.

of how translated, is not representative of Russia, for example:

> "Rosh is impossible to identify. Of course any connexion between the name and Russia is to be rejected."[2]

We are, therefore, again faced with two schools of thought very positively expressed, but other indicators of a Russian connection, both secular and scriptural, over an extended period of time, are available.

The first century Jewish historian, Josephus, wrote:

> "Magog founded those that from him were named Magogites, but who by the Greeks are called Scythians."[3]

The Scythians occupied an area between the Black and Caspian Seas approximately equivalent to the boundaries of Moldova and Ukraine. They were mentioned by the Greek historian Herodotus (c. 485-425 BC) as a ferocious people and would have been known in Ezekiel's time from invasions during the reign of Josiah.

The French Protestant scholar, Samuel Bochart (1599–1667) was fluent in many languages and produced several major written works. His observations on *Ros* in his book *Geographica Sacra seu Phaleg et Canaan* were paraphrased by Brother John Thomas as "Ros, is the most ancient form under which history makes mention of the name of Russia ..."[4] Bochart's capacity to draw conclusions from similar words in different languages has been criticised by many, including the philosopher Voltaire, but whether or not the

linguistic similarity is valid his opinions serve to show that four centuries ago Russia was seen by some as the probable aggressor.

Matthew Henry in his Bible Commentary published in 1706 stated that he considered the prophecy was fulfilled in past invasions of Israel but he generously mentioned that others held alternative views: "Some think they find them (Gog and Magog) afar off, in Scythia, Tartary, and Russia."[5]

There are clearly variances in the underlying reasoning but these observations at least establish that for several centuries some scholars have believed that Ezekiel's prophecy refers primarily to the nation of Russia.

Could *Ros* be the Rus?

Another point of debate is whether the Hebrew word *Ros* is the source of the name of a tribe from the far north called the Rus. A people of that name have been identified from around the ninth century which is a very long gap from Ezekiel's writings but might be an indicator of a connection. Modern historians refer to these people, for example:

> "It was in this condition (i.e., tribes settled in small stone fortresses) that the 'Rus' found the Slavs as they came down from the north. In the past there was lively historical debate about the identity of the Rus, but today there does not seem much doubt that they were Scandinavian Vikings, or 'Varangians', as the Slavs called them, merchant warriors seeking to dominate the trade routes which traversed territory settled by Slavic, Baltic, and Finno-Ugrian peoples."[6]

> "The Vikings, the greatest of European adventurers, penetrated deep into the Slavic

---

2 A B Davidson, *Cambridge Bible Commentary*, page 300.
3 Flavius Josephus, *Antiquities*, 1:6.1.
4 Brother John Thomas, *Elpis Israel*, page 424, 14th edition.

5 Matthew Henry, *Commentary On The Whole Bible*, (Hendrickson Publishers 2008), page 1118.
6 Geoffrey Hosking, *Russia and the Russians*, page 30.

heartland, intent both on trading and on expanding their political influence. Viking settlements were important in crystallizing the situation, and they were instrumental in creating the first Russian state, Rus, which came into being during the 9th century."[7]

"The Vikings (sometimes called the Varangians were nicknamed the *Rus* (rowers); they gave their nickname to the whole people whom they ruled."[8]

Merril Unger, editor of the well regarded *Unger's Bible Dictionary*, wrote in another work that there were linguistic difficulties in relating *Ros* to the 'Rus' but added:

"However, when other evidence is considered, there can be little doubt that the reference is to the nation Russia. In fact, in the light of the end-time prophetic picture, there is no other reasonable alternative."[9]

None of these references provide proof that Ezekiel was referring to Russia, or that he understood that such a nation would one day exist, but they are indicators that Russia is the intended nation.

Meschech and Tubal

Some Bible students contend that Meschech and Tubal can be linked to Moscow and Tobolski. Linguistic scholars are, however, generally dismissive of this assertion on the grounds that word similarity in different languages is not a basis for declaring them to be the same. We will, therefore, put that contention to one side. Ancient writers such as Herodotus and Josephus consider that these two sons of Japheth (Genesis

7 Peter Waldron, *Russia Of The Tsars*, page 12.
8 Paul Crowson, *A History of the Russian People*, page 5.
9 Merril Unger, *Beyond the Crystal Ball* (Moody Bible Institute 1973), page 82.

10:2) occupied areas of land in the vicinity of the Black and Caspian Seas approximately equivalent to modern day Georgia and Armenia and possibly extending into Azerbaijan and Kazakhstan. Their descendants could, of course, have migrated north at some stage but there is no empirical data to establish if that occurred.

These countries were part of the Soviet Union prior to its collapse in 1991 and Islam is the majority religion in the latter two which has raised the question of whether Ezekiel was referring to an Islamic invasion of Israel from this region. It seems beyond doubt that these nations will form part of the invading force, but it is most improbable that they will be the main instigators or the major force to be destroyed. The context requires the destruction of a great military force to reveal the glory and power of God's name to the nations. That is not going to be achieved by the destruction of the armies of a few former republics of the Soviet Union, for God says of the destruction of Gog:

"With pestilence and bloodshed I will enter into judgment with him, and I will rain upon him and his hordes and the many peoples who are with him torrential rains and hailstones, fire and sulphur. So I will show my greatness and my holiness and make myself known in the eyes of many nations. Then they will know that I am the LORD."   (Ezekiel 38:22,23)

Persia, Cush and Put

We are on safer ground here as there is considerable agreement about the identity of these nations. Furthermore there is no surprise about their inclusion in a group of nations holding evil intent against Israel. Persia is modern day Iran, a nation that opposes Israel's right to exist and supports terrorist groups such as Hamas. The former Iranian leader, President Mahmoud Ahmadinejad, on

Photo: Daniella Zalcman – Wikimedia Commons

Former Iranian President Ahmadinejad

several occasions addressed the Annual General Assembly of the United Nations with a tirade of abuse against Israel in particular and the West in general. At the September, 2012 assembly he stated that "Israel has no roots in the Middle East and would be eliminated".

Cush was the eldest son of Ham and there is a reasonable degree of consensus amongst historians and Bible scholars that his descendants occupied the area now known as Ethiopia and Sudan and perhaps further south into east Africa. The current dire economic condition of Ethiopia and Sudan raises the question of what contribution they could make to the group of invading nations, but circumstances may change. It is possible, but conjectural, that Cush is representative of a broader group of African nations and it may be significant that the African Union with fifty-four member states is currently headquartered in Addis Ababa, the capital of Ethiopia.

There is considerable unanimity about Put being modern day Libya and the anti-Israeli attitude of

this nation, especially under the direction of former leader Gaddafi, is well known. A less commonly held opinion is that Put refers to the ancient Libyans whose descendants are conjectured to have migrated into Africa. This opinion is worthy of consideration as Put was also a son of Ham and it is unlikely that the descendants of the two sons would display the markedly different physical characteristics of present day Libyans and Ethiopians.

Gomer

Identification of the modern day descendants of Gomer presents some challenges. The contention that several nations of Central and Western Europe descend from Gomer and that they will invade Israel with the Gogian host is a significant claim and requires solid data in support. The evidence put forward is primarily from the oft quoted first century historian, Josephus, who stated:

"Gomer founded those whom the Greeks now call Galatians (Gauls) but were then called Gomerites."[10]

However, the weight of scholastic opinion is that Gomer founded the Cimmerians, a people who lived near the Black Sea until forced westwards by the Scythians. The opinion of Josephus may also be correct for it is possible that both nations descended from Gomer but through different sons. Herodotus and Gesenius refer to the Cimmerians, as does the respected nineteenth century British Assyriologist and linguist, Alexander Sayce, who stated:

"Gomer is the Ginirra of the Assyrian inscriptions, the Cimmerians of the Greek writers."[11]

10 Flavius Josephus, *Antiquities*, 1:6.1.
11 Alexander Sayce, *The Races of the Old Testament*, page 45.

Brother John Thomas related Gomer (Gaul) to France and Magog to Germany[12] but a broader application of the Gauls and Cimmerians to Western Europe in general is applied by Brother John Allfree.[13] This has some support from secular historians who generally relate ancient Gaul to France, Belgium, Switzerland, the Netherlands and Germany west of the Rhine. It is difficult, however, to establish categorical evidence that Gomer was the founder of Gaul but there are indicators additional to the opinion of Josephus.

Jerome (AD 347-420), son of Eusebius and translator of the Bible into Latin (Vulgate), wrote in *Comentarii in Epistolam ad Galatos* that the Galatians/Gauls of Ancyra in Turkey and the Treveri of Trier in what is now the German Rhineland spoke the same language. There is some Jewish opinion on a German connection with the 1906 Jewish Encyclopedia stating that Gomer stands for either Cimmerii or Germany, apparently based on Talmud writings from the third to fifth centuries AD. The reason for this is not stated and it may be a Rabbinical opinion that became a traditional view, but again it provides some support for a European connection. Barbara Tuchman writes in *Bible and Sword* about the desire of nations in ancient times to attribute their origins to someone famous from legend or scripture (a summation of those views follows but those seeking further information are referred to Tuchman's book). In ancient England debate centred around the founder being Brutus, grandson of the Trojan Aeneas or Gomer, grandson of Noah and by the seventh century one or both versions had taken hold as fact. A century later the Venerable Bede, known as the father of English history, cautiously offered suppositions that the

founders came from Scythia, the ancient name for the region around the Black Sea. To the contrary, the twelfth century chronicler Geoffrey of Monmouth positively declared the legendary Brutus to be the founder. During the Reformation period interest in Biblical origins was high and Gomer became the preferred elder Briton. The Elizabethan historian William Camden, attempting to finalise the question, also declared in favour of Gomer stating, "This is my judgement concerning the original of the Britons; or rather my conjecture."[14] Tuchman adds that tradition is not always superseded by science. We can conclude that no empirical evidence exists for the ancestry of England and Europe but there are indicators of connections back to Genesis.

Togarmah

"As an ultimate destination for the 'house of Togarmah,' Armenia – either its people or its culture – would seem to be the best candidate. Much earlier, however, elements of the 'house of Togarmah' may have been part of the great 2nd and 1st millennium BCE Japhetic movements far to the north, and assimilated into modern Russia and Turkey."[15]

This statement reflects general consensus that the descendants of Togarmah, a son of Gomer, occupied territories in modern day Armenia and Turkey. The participation of both these nations in an invasion of Israel is not surprising, particularly with Turkey's increasingly Islamist outlook. The present Turkish Prime Minister, Recep Erdogan, has reflected this by including anti-Israel rhetoric in addresses to the United Nations and other organisations. In an address to the Eurasian Islamic Council in Istanbul in November 2012 he stated that, "Those who

12 Brother John Thomas, *Elpis Israel*, pages 428 and 432, 14th edition.
13 Brother John Allfree, *Ezekiel*, page 398.

14 Barbara Tuchman, *Bible and Sword*, pages 1-12.
15 Jon Ruthven, *The Prophecy That Is Shaping History (2003)*, page 102.

associate Islam with terrorism close their eyes in the face of mass killing of Muslims, turning their heads from the massacre of children in Gaza."[16]

Sheba and Dedan

Again there is considerable unanimity amongst scholars on the whereabouts of these nations with most concurring that they were in the region now known as the Saudi peninsula. Well regarded publications such as *The Lion Atlas of Bible History*, the *Oxford Bible Atlas* and the *ESV Study Bible* record Sheba and Dedan in maps of Arabia.

They possibly represent Saudi Arabia, the Persian Gulf emirates, Muscat and Yemen, leaving us with the question, Why do these nations apparently stand apart from other Arab nations at the time of the end? It would be unwise to be categorical but it points to a split occurring at some time in the Arab bloc. Those who favour the concept of an Arab attack against Israel prior to the Gogian invasion will see it as evidence they have been defeated by God at an earlier stage. Others contend that most Arab nations will not be involved by virtue of having entered into peace treaties with Israel, a prospect that currently seems improbable but cannot be discounted. A third factor that may influence the alignment of Islamic states at the time of the end is tension between the Sunni and Shia factions within Islam. Arab nations closest to Israel, including those on the Arabian Peninsula, are dominated by Sunni Moslems while Iran (Persia) is dominated by the Shia sect.

The merchants of Tarshish

Of all the nations mentioned in Ezekiel 38 Tarshish is possibly the most difficult to identify firmly. Applying it to Britain requires using Tarshish as a representative title rather than searching for a

16 *The Examiner*, November 19, 2012.

literal location as is usually done with the other nations. As we have previously mentioned, there is a reasonable level of consensus amongst scholars on the identification of many of the listed nations, but the application of Gomer to Europe and Tarshish to Britain is predominately, although not exclusively, a Christadelphian viewpoint.

The most commonly held opinion of Bible scholars is that Tarshish was located in the vicinity of Spain. As this opinion is expressed in many sources we will constrain the amount of detail by not quoting from the references. However, placing Tarshish in Spain presents its own difficulties as, although it may fit with the trading practices of Ezekiel's time, it does not provide us with the identification of a nation, either then or now, with the credentials or the power to question the intention of the Gogian forces when they enter the land (verse 13).

Because of this difficulty it is apparent why a representative nation for Tarshish was sought. From a nineteenth century perspective Britain, with its trading and military might and widespread support in religious and political circles for Jewish restoration, was the prime candidate. Ezekiel's reference to "young lions" contributed to the concept with Britain having a lion as a symbol and the outposts of the British Empire often referred to as young lions.

Britain may be a correct interpretation but heraldic records establish that lions feature in the coats-of-arms of many nations. The identification of the lion with Britain appears to have had its beginnings with King Richard I in the twelfth century and evolved over several centuries into a national symbol. This would not have been known in Ezekiel's time and, if the key nations were to be identified by such symbols, the question remains, Why was Magog not identified as a bear?

Brother John Thomas identified Britain as the Daughter of Tyre, the Daughter of Tarshish.[17] He also considered that in the latter days there would be a Tarshish power to the east of Israel with whom the Jews who returned to the Holy Land would trade.[18] The only passage which suggests this is Ezekiel 38:13. In ancient times Israel traded with India, referred to as Tarshish (1 Kings 10:21,22). It is interesting that in recent decades commercial ties between Israel and India have become very strong and that trade in military technology is a hallmark of that trade.[19]

The hope that Britain would be the continuing protector of the Holy Land and supporter of Jewish restoration was dashed with the restrictive practices applied to immigration during the British Mandate administration of Palestine and the cessation of the Mandate in 1948. Unfortunately this did not lead to extensive review and the concept that Britain was Tarshish was tenaciously defended. For example, writers in *The Christadelphian* in the 1950s pointed to Britain maintaining military bases in the Middle East and, in the 1980s, mentioned the decline of the nation's power but were encouraged that the then Prime Minister, Margaret Thatcher, was meeting with the leaders of Arab states! Of course, Britain's decision in the 1960s to withdraw her troops from "East of Suez" was somewhat reversed when she again became militarily involved in the Middle East in the 1990s and early years of the twenty-first century. It may also be significant that key players in the British Commonwealth, including Australia and Canada, continue to take a strong interest in Israel and the Middle East in spite of their distance from the region.

The fact that initial expectations were not met is not cause to reject the concept that Tarshish has application to Britain, but debate on the matter in the light of current circumstances would be appropriate. Some evangelical groups identify the United States as Tarshish, based on it being the leading economic and military power of the past century and a major supporter of Israel, particularly since the Six-Day War of 1967. Others believe that initially it was Britain but that the mantle has been passed to the United States. Clearly the call to us is to watch political developments and compare them to the prophetical word. The future role of the United States warrants attention as there are indicators of a distancing, albeit small at this stage, from the previous close affinity with Israel.

Origins of the listed nations

A number of writers, including Brother John Allfree in his book *Ezekiel*, have observed that with the exception of Cush and Put, which descend from Ham, the nations comprising the Gogian forces descend from Japheth as described in the genealogies of Genesis 10, and that not one of the nations is Semitic in origin.[20] His explanation for this is that the Arab nations descended from Shem will have entered into a peace treaty with Israel. Alternative options are not explored by Brother Allfree but, as mentioned in the section on

---

17 For details of his reasoning and for other opinions, including the tin mining connection, the reader is referred to the informative commentary provided in *The Bible Magazine*, Vol. 20, Issue No. 3, July 2007. Some will find the information convincing but others may feel that more evidence is necessary to support the concept that Britain is Tarshish.

18 Brother John Thomas, *Elpis Israel*, page 441, 14th edition.

19 Readers interested in following up the Eastern Tarshish concept are referred to an article entitled, "India and Israel" in *The Testimony*, August 1997.

20 Brother John Allfree, *Ezekiel – An Exposition of Chapters 1-39*, pages 400,401.

Sheba and Dedan, some Bible students consider that the Semitic nations listed in Psalm 83 will have previously entered into battle with Israel and been defeated by the returned Christ.

The fact that the Gogian army primarily consists of the descendants of Japheth is endorsed in modern Jewish writings, one example being:

"Meschech and Tubal are names of Japheth's sons; Persia is identified with Japheth's son Teras, and Togarmah is a grandson of Japheth. From this it seems that when, finally, the forces of evil are to be pitted against Israel, the Japhetic tribes will be in the forefront of the battle."[21]

The reason for the majority of invading nations being from the descendants of Japheth has not been extensively discussed over the years and is a matter that warrants further consideration.

Nations not mentioned

Another intriguing question is what action will be taken by militaristic nations with cultures unlikely to accept the future role of Jesus Christ. In the current state of world affairs, this question could be asked of China and North Korea, followed closely by India.

One option is that the destruction of Gog will be so severe that other nations will offer allegiance to Christ; alternatively, nations such as these may be included in the "all nations" of Joel 3:2 and "the kings of the whole world" of Revelation 16:14 assembled for battle "on the great day of God the Almighty". India, as we have already seen, may have a supportive relationship with Israel at the time of the end and this may have an impact on her response to Christ.

21 Scherman and Zlotowitz, *Ezekiel – With Commentary Anthologized from Talmudic, Midrashic and Rabbinic Sources*, page 581.

A privilege to know

The purpose of prophecies such as we are considering is to inform us of events that will occur at the 'end of days'; events that are integrally related to the return of Christ. These events will shake the earth and will take place at or around the time when the members of the true household of God will meet their Lord. The prophecies are provided for warning and encouragement and it is a great privilege to know, at least in broad form, of things that will come upon the earth.

Bible students of previous centuries debated when this mighty battle would occur. Many thought it would be in their time, but the trigger-point for the occurrence of these prophecies had not been reached for Israel was not back in the land. That great sign of Christ's return, the re-establishment of the nation of Israel, has now taken place and therefore we live in a time when the Gogian invasion and the revealing of God's name to the nations could occur. The enormity of having that knowledge should fill us with awe at being a member of God's household.

As described in previous chapters, prophecies fulfilled over the past century did not take place with the precision anticipated by the interpreters within the time frames expected and it is therefore unreasonable to expect exactitude about future events. As Bible students we should find it profitable and stimulating to debate meanings and possible variations but unanimity of opinion on all aspects cannot be demanded. Unfortunately, many writings on prophecy have focused on defending a position rather than objectively analysing and debating options. No amount of positively declaring a matter to be so will actually make it so.

The renowned Rabbi, Elijah ben Solomon (1720-1797), known as "the genius from Vilnius" made the following prediction that became an oral tradition in some segments of European Jewry:

> "When the Russian navy passes through the Bosporus (that is, on the way to the Mediterranean through the Dardanelles) it will be time to put on Sabbath clothes in anticipation of the coming Messiah."[22]

His opinion may have been heavily influenced by the political position of the time but it will strike a chord with many Christadelphians. Whatever the background may have been, it is a helpful observation with its reminder that latter-day prophecies are not simply an academic matter but are connected with the return of our Lord and the fulfilment of the promises to the patriarchs.

Within our community views on prophecy range from those who consider that it has all been determined and no further consideration is necessary, to those whose understanding is limited to the fact that major events will occur in the Middle East, and others somewhere in between. As members of God's household, wherever we may sit in the spectrum of prophetical understanding, we ought to work on developing our knowledge of what is to occur, especially as we see events building up to the end of Gentile days.

> "And the LORD will be king over all the earth. On that day the LORD will be one and his name one." (Zechariah 14:9)

Further Reading

Brother John Thomas, *Elpis Israel,* pages 421-437, 14th edition.

Brother John Allfree, Ezekiel, pages 384-415.

Jon Ruthven, *The Prophecy That Is Shaping History (2003).*

---

22 *ibid*

15

OTHER LATTER-DAY PROPHECIES

IN earlier chapters we considered some of the key prophecies which relate to the latter days and the return of Christ. There are several other passages which also add to our understanding of the signs of the Lord's return and take us forward into the period after Christ returns and the process by which he re-establishes the throne of David in Jerusalem. We shall consider briefly a few of these.

Israel's God inhabits eternity (Isaiah 57:15). This is a concept beyond the capacity of time-bound mortal men and women fully to comprehend. We must take care not to impose our own limitations on God's inspired revelation through the prophets. We should not be surprised that much of what is revealed in the scriptures is timeless: this is as true of many of the prophecies as it is of the Law of Moses, the poetical books and the epistles which impart moral guidance to God's servants.

Daniel 11

Since the nineteenth century it has been fashionable for critics to declare that the book of Daniel was written at the time of the Maccabees (about 164 BC) rather than in the sixth century BC as the Bible suggests. There is only very flimsy circumstantial evidence for a late date for the book; the key trigger for this sceptical position was the remarkably detailed prophecy of Daniel 11 which outlines events which transpired in relation to the Holy Land and the Jews in the years between the time of Daniel and the revival of Jewish nationalism under the Maccabees.

Sceptical critics cannot conceive of a prophecy being fulfilled in such detail hundreds of years after the event. This is the consequence of a mindset which discounts the divine and has little regard for inspiration. The fact that the book appears in the Septuagint, which was translated in about 286 BC, proves not only that it existed at that time but also was already well received as part of the Hebrew canon of scripture. This is well in advance of many of the events predicted in such minute detail in verses 1 to 35.

The matters predicted in the first thirty-five verses were fulfilled exactly as recorded in the centuries between Daniel's time and the days of Christ. The interpretation of this passage is covered in a number of books to which readers may refer[1] and we shall not go over that fascinating history here. It does, however, confirm that God is in control of the affairs of the nations, but our particular interest is in how the concluding verses of Daniel 11 relate to events concerning Israel and Jerusalem at the time of the end.

It is evident that there is a break in the prophecy at verse 36: from verse 36 to 39 nothing is said of either the king of the north or the king of the south who have featured so prominently until then; in addition, verse 35 concludes with a reference

---

1 Books which outline the significance of Daniel 11:1-35 include Brother John Thomas, *Exposition of Daniel*, pages 48-55; *Elpis Israel* (14th edition), pages 398-405; and Brother Edmund Green, *The Prophecy of Daniel*, pages 112-124.

to "the time of the end, for it still awaits the appointed time". Verses 36 to 39 are parenthetical, and verse 40 opens by taking up the reference from verse 35 to "the time of the end". That we are justified in concluding that the end referred to is the end of the times of the Gentiles seems clear from the reference later in the prophecy to the intervention of Michael on behalf of Israel and the resurrection of the dead (Daniel 12:1,2).

Daniel 11:40-45 describes an invasion of the Holy Land by a mighty army from the north. After initial success the invading force establishes itself in Jerusalem (verse 45) after which it is divinely overthrown. There are obvious parallels between this passage and the invasion described in Ezekiel 38-39:

Daniel 11-12	Ezekiel 38-39
King of the north invades (11:40)	Gog comes from the north (38:15)
A massive military force (11:40)	A massive military force (38:4)
The prophecy personifies the invader as "he"	Gog is personally addressed (38:3; 39:1)
Libya and Ethiopia are allies (11:43)	Libya and Ethiopia are allies (38:5)
A challenge comes from the east (11:44)	Sheba and Dedan (to the east) challenge Gog (38:13)
Comes to an end on "the glorious holy mountain" (11:45)	Comes to an end on "the mountains of Israel" (39:4)
Unexpectedly encounters divine resistance (12:1)	Unexpectedly encounters divine resistance (38:19-23)

When this invasion takes place there will be "a time of trouble, such as never has been since there was a nation till that time" (Daniel 12:1). It is then that Michael (perhaps the Lord Jesus Christ himself) intervenes on behalf of Israel. The language the prophet uses is clearly intended to incorporate both natural and spiritual Israel, for the standing up of Michael is linked with the resurrection and deliverance of "everyone whose name shall be found written in the book". This serves to remind us that the fulfilment of God's promises to the patriarchs involves all who have embraced those promises through baptism into Christ.

Obadiah

Many Bible prophecies are remarkably precise in terms of application and timing, but there are others that reflect the timelessness of the God who inspired them. In his book, *Glimpses of Glory*, Brother Dudley Fifield draws attention to what he describes as "recurring fulfilments" of certain prophecies, citing as examples Deuteronomy 28:49,50, Psalm 2 and Psalm 83.[2]

Obadiah is another example of this in the way in which he speaks of the enmity of Edom towards Israel.[3] The prophet describes a hostility that had its roots in Genesis and the conflict between Jacob and Esau, and which is therefore linked to the promises to the patriarchs and their application. This conflict between Israel (Jacob) and Edom (Esau) is described in Ezekiel 35:5 as a "perpetual enmity" (KJV, "hatred").

2 Brother Dudley Fifield, *Glimpses of Glory*, chapter 20, "Interpreting Bible Prophecy".
3 *ibid*, chapter 38, "Obadiah".

While the early verses of Obadiah almost certainly refer to a specific incident or to specific incidents in which Edom afflicted Judah, there is a turning point in verse 11 to 14 where the verbs used by the prophet could apply either to past or future events. The KJV translates these verses as if they are describing historical acts. While the ESV also renders verse 11 as if the events were past, from verses 12 to 14 it brings out clearly the more timeless nature of the passage:

> "But do not gloat over the day of your brother in the day of his misfortune; do not rejoice over the people of Judah in the day of their ruin; do not boast in the day of distress. Do not enter the gate of my people in the day of their calamity; do not gloat over his disaster in the day of his calamity; do not loot his wealth in the day of his calamity. Do not stand at the crossroads to cut off his fugitives; do not hand over his survivors in the day of distress."

This is followed by verse 15 where the prophet ceases referring specifically to Edom and refers to "all the nations":

> "For the day of the LORD is near upon all the nations. As you have done, it shall be done to you; your deeds shall return on your own head."

This suggests that Edom in Obadiah stands for all those nations which afflict Israel, perhaps those listed in Psalm 83 as referenced in Chapter 13. In accordance with the promise of God to Abraham that "him who dishonours (KJV, "curseth") you I will curse" (Genesis 12:3), nations which like Edom oppress Israel will find themselves similarly oppressed.

The prophet goes on to speak of the glories of the kingdom age when Israel shall dwell securely and unthreatened in its own land, and shall even control the land of neighbouring hostile powers:

> "Those of the Negeb shall possess Mount Esau, and those of the Shephelah shall possess the land of the Philistines; they shall possess the land of Ephraim and the land of Samaria, and Benjamin shall possess Gilead. The exiles of this host of the people of Israel shall possess the land of the Canaanites as far as Zarephath, and the exiles of Jerusalem who are in Sepharad shall possess the cities of the Negeb."

(Obadiah 19,20)

Mount Esau is located in modern Jordan, while the Shephelah is the coastal plain toward the south of the land, and the land of the Philistines would equate to the modern Gaza Strip region. Ephraim and Samaria today is in large part the territory referred to as the West Bank, while Gilead is today northern Jordan and, perhaps, the Golan region. Zarephath is in southern Lebanon. All of these territories have since the rebirth of Israel been sources of harassment of the Jewish state; many of them have been a haven for Palestinian terrorists. Obadiah says that in the kingdom age this threat will be eliminated.

The prophet goes on to say that this will occur when "Saviours shall go up to Mount Zion to rule Mount Esau, and the kingdom shall be the LORD's" (verse 21). The plural word "saviours" in this verse almost certainly is a reference to the immortalised saints who at that time will reign with their Lord, having as mortal men and women embraced the promises to Abraham through Christ.

Olivet Prophecy

Immediately prior to our Lord's crucifixion he addressed his disciples as they gazed from the Mount of Olives upon the glory of Herod's Temple. The words he spoke on that occasion have become known as the Olivet Prophecy and they are recorded in Matthew 24, Mark 13 and Luke 21. A thrice-recorded message surely conveys important teaching for the disciples of every age.

Expositors have long debated the significance of this prophecy, with some ascribing its predictions to the events associated with the Roman campaign against Judea which led to the sacking of Jerusalem from AD 66 to AD 70, and others seeking to apply at least some of the imagery to the last days accompanying the return of Christ to earth. It is not our intention to attempt a detailed exposition of this interesting prophecy, but rather to comment on its relevance to those who today are yearning for the return of the Master and the establishment of God's kingdom on earth.

In every age the faithful have yearned for the Messiah to appear. The faithful remnant in first century Judea welcomed Jesus as their Messiah and since that day subsequent generations have anxiously looked for the signs that his return is near. It is clear from the record of the Olivet Prophecy that this is as it should be and indeed that the purpose of the prophecy is to generate such a spirit:

"But concerning that day or that hour, no one knows, not even the angels in heaven, nor the Son, but only the Father. Be on guard, *keep awake*. For you do not know when the time will come. It is like a man going on a journey, when he leaves home and puts his servants in charge, each with his work, and commands the doorkeeper to *stay awake*. Therefore *stay awake* – for you do not know when the master of the house will come, in the evening, or at midnight, or when the rooster crows, or in the morning – lest he come suddenly and find you asleep. And what I say to you I say to all: *Stay awake*."
(Mark 13:32-37)

The repeated exhortation to wakefulness impresses upon us the need to be alert to the signs around us. This is a command from our Master, one which we cannot obey if we take no interest in the prophecies that God has recorded for our encouragement and guidance.

Parts of the Olivet Prophecy clearly relate to events in the first century. For example, the following words obviously apply to the experience of the apostles as recorded in the book of Acts:

"But be on your guard. For they will deliver you over to councils, and you will be beaten in synagogues, and you will stand before governors and kings for my sake, to bear witness before them."
(Mark 13:9)

The following words also have a first century application, being a description of the siege of Jerusalem by the Romans which culminated in the sacking of the city in AD 70:

"But when you see Jerusalem surrounded by armies, then know that its desolation has come near. Then let those who are in Judea flee to the mountains, and let those who are inside the city depart, and let not those who are out in the country enter it, for these are days of vengeance, to fulfil all that is written. Alas for women who are pregnant and for those who are nursing infants in those days! For there will be great distress upon the earth and wrath against this people. They will fall by the edge of the sword and be led captive among all nations, and Jerusalem will be trampled underfoot by the Gentiles ..."
(Luke 21:20-24)

Whatever application the prophecy has to the first century, it would seem undeniable that it also has application to the time when our Lord returns to earth to restore David's throne in Jerusalem. As noted in Chapter 12, Luke 21:24 concludes with the words ... "until the times of the Gentiles are fulfilled", meaning that there is to be an end to the treading down of the Holy City. When will that be? It will be at the time described in the words which follow:

"There will be signs in sun and moon and stars, and on the earth distress of nations in perplexity because of the roaring of the sea and the waves, people fainting with fear and with foreboding of what is coming on the world. For the powers of the heavens will be shaken. And then they will see the Son of Man coming in a cloud with power and great glory."

(verses 25-27)

As with the book of Revelation, the language and imagery of the Olivet Prophecy draws heavily upon Old Testament sources. These verses are particularly heavy with allusions to Old Testament prophecies. It is significant that those prophecies relate to a range of nations which have openly challenged the purpose of God and persecuted God's chosen people since the time of Genesis, and look forward to a time when these haughty foes of Israel will be overcome and Zion exalted:

Babylon

"For the stars of the heavens and their constellations will not give their light; the sun will be dark at its rising, and the moon will not shed its light. I will punish the world for its evil, and the wicked for their iniquity; I will put an end to the pomp of the arrogant, and lay low the pompous pride of the ruthless."

(Isaiah 13:10,11)

Egypt

"When I blot you out, I will cover the heavens and make their stars dark; I will cover the sun with a cloud, and the moon shall not give its light. All the bright lights of heaven will I make dark over you, and put darkness on your land, declares the Lord GOD." (Ezekiel 32:7,8)

Edom

"All the host of heaven shall rot away, and the skies roll up like a scroll. All their host shall fall, as leaves fall from the vine, like leaves falling from the fig tree. For my sword has drunk its fill in the heavens; behold, it descends for judgment upon Edom, upon the people I have devoted to destruction ... For the LORD has a day of vengeance, a year of recompense for the cause of Zion." (Isaiah 34:4,5,8)

While this last passage specifically identifies Edom as a target, reference to "all the host of heaven", as in Obadiah, suggests that it has relevance to nations more generally. Together the subjects of these prophecies stand for the kingdom of men in its opposition to God and His purpose, and Jesus drew upon this imagery to speak of a period of upheaval, anxiety and turmoil; or to use the language of Daniel, "a time of trouble, such as never has been since there was a nation till that time" (Daniel 12:1).

As we have already seen, Daniel 12:1 in its context relates to the time when the Lord returns and the dead are resurrected for judgement. Yet in the Olivet Prophecy the Lord applied the language of Daniel 12:1 to the time when the Romans besieged Jerusalem:

"For in those days there will be such tribulation as has not been from the beginning of the creation that God created until now, and never will be." (Mark 13:19)

Does this suggest that we are meant to see in this prophecy another example of recurring fulfilment? Certainly in the past students of prophecy have interpreted the cessation of the treading down of Jerusalem as applying to events which were happening at that time, for example:

- in 1897 to the emergence of the Zionist movement;
- in 1917, to the capture of Jerusalem by the British immediately after the Balfour Declaration had been issued;
- in 1948 to the independence of Israel and its control of at least part of Jerusalem;
- in 1967 to Israeli capture of the Old City of Jerusalem;
- in 1980 to the declaration of Jerusalem as Israel's indivisible and eternal capital.

On the basis of what we suggested in Chapter 12, all of these interpretations to the ending of the times of the Gentiles were premature, but that does not mean we should demean the enthusiasm and earnestness which sought a more immediate application of the prophecy. The objective of the Olivet Prophecy is to encourage the faithful always to be watching for signs of the Lord's return. In this regard Brother L G Sargent observed about the Olivet Prophecy:

> "It revealed many signs, yet it left them as servants keeping the house in constant readiness for the Master's return at an unknown time. Because of this paradoxical character, down through the centuries the discourse has served its double aim of at once rousing expectation and counselling continued endurance."[4]

The complete ending of Jerusalem's treading down by the Gentiles will come only when a divine ruler is installed on the restored throne of David.

A time of great trouble

The three Gospels that contain the Olivet Prophecy refer to earthquakes, famines and pestilences. As mentioned above, Mark adds an observation about a period of tribulation not previously seen, from which it is apparent that the return of Christ will be preceded by a period of great difficulty. The context indicates a broad spread of problems ranging from wars to natural catastrophes and quite likely extending to economic and societal breakdown. Over the centuries believers searching for an indicator of the Lord's return have seen events in their times that they perceived as meeting the listed criteria. However, a key aspect of this prophecy is that it has application only after Israel is back in the land. That has occurred and thus we can evaluate if current issues and natural catastrophes might fit the description.

Many a presentation has been given on how wars, major natural catastrophes and declining moral standards of the time provide evidence of the nearness of Christ's return. This is a significant assertion, but is it valid? It is very useful that such things be brought to our attention to assist our 'watching' but we must be wary of declaring them to be 'evidence'. It is reasonable in the present time, however, to see signs of fulfilment in certain events. We do not need expert advice to inform us that major famines have been constant in recent years, especially in Africa, as they have been extensively publicised in the media. Moral standards have declined in a few decades to levels unimaginable to a previous generation, with practices once barely mentioned becoming regarded as quite acceptable.

The question about natural catastrophes is whether they are becoming more frequent and more intense, or is that simply an impression gained from the global media with its current ability to report almost instantly from every corner of the earth. Debate on global climate change contains many claims and counter-claims making it difficult to obtain objective and unbiased data. Objective data

4 Brother L G Sargent, *A Sound Mind*, page 72.

is available, however, from a relatively unknown and under-utilised source.

Much of the cost of natural catastrophes is met by the insurance industry, in particular by the major reinsurers in Europe who provide catastrophe cover to insurance companies. These companies undertake extensive research into the frequency, intensity and cost of natural and man-made catastrophes. The data is complex and voluminous and cannot be fully dealt with here but, in brief, it establishes that in the past few decades the frequency of events such as storms in Europe and hurricanes in the United States has not increased but the intensity has escalated. Earthquake frequency likewise does not appear to have increased but outcomes are becoming significantly worse because of the continuing escalation in urban living and the huge amount of accompanying infrastructure.

Responses to disasters are therefore much more challenging and the economic cost to affected countries has the potential to become unmanageable. Major earthquakes or hurricanes in areas of high population and extensive industrialisation such as parts of Japan and the west coast of the U.S. could produce huge economic difficulties for both countries.

In this context there is reasonable evidence that at least some of the natural events referred to in the Olivet Prophecy are now occurring and that an escalation in the effect is probable. Some Bible students have looked for reasons why the U.S. and other Western nations may remain on the sidelines during the northern host's invasion of Israel. The economic effect of major natural catastrophes might be that cause. Readers interested in further data from studies on natural catastrophes are referred to the addendum at the end of this chapter.

The sign of the Son of Man

The desperate times described by the Lord as accompanying the ending of the times of the Gentiles are the signal for a great sign:

"Immediately after the tribulation of those days the sun will be darkened, and the moon will not give its light, and the stars will fall from heaven, and the powers of the heavens will be shaken. *Then will appear in heaven the sign of the Son of Man*, and then all the tribes of the earth will mourn, and they will see the Son of Man coming on the clouds of heaven with power and great glory. And he will send out his angels with a loud trumpet call, and they will gather his elect from the four winds, from one end of heaven to the other." (Matthew 24:29-31)

Various suggestions have been made as to what might be the sign which shall appear in heaven. A star appeared when Jesus was born so perhaps the appearance of a literal star or comet will accompany his return. Many suggestions have been raised in the pages of *The Christadelphian* including that the sign will be natural phenomena such as the darkening of the sun and moon similar to the darkness at the giving of the law at Sinai and during the crucifixion[5] and, alternatively, the appearing of the nation of Israel "in the heavens" as a U.N. member state has been proposed.[6] The second option fits more appropriately with the sign of his coming (verse 3) rather than the immediate sign of his appearing (verse 30). Given the symbolic nature of the language in the immediate context, however, it may be unnecessary to look for a literal fulfilment in some astronomical phenomenon or other activity.

5 Brother A Winter-More, *The Christadelphian*, 1962, page 534.
6 Brother John Marshall, *The Christadelphian*, 1984, page 256.

The Lord drew the image from Daniel 7 and that passage helps us to determine his meaning:

"I saw in the night visions, and behold, with the clouds of heaven there came one like a son of man, and he came to the Ancient of Days and was presented before him. And to him was given dominion and glory and a kingdom, that all peoples, nations, and languages should serve him; his dominion is an everlasting dominion, which shall not pass away, and his kingdom one that shall not be destroyed." (Daniel 7:13,14)

Daniel 7:27 refers to "clouds of heaven" which accompany the Son of Man. This may be a reference to "the (immortalised) saints of the Most High" who shall reign with him. If this is so, we may conclude that the sign of the Son of Man is in fact the Lord Jesus Christ himself coming in power to restore David's throne.

"Then the moon will be confounded and the sun ashamed, for the LORD of hosts reigns on Mount Zion and in Jerusalem, and his glory will be before his elders." (Isaiah 24:23)

We can also consider in this context the advice of the Apostle Peter to pay attention "until the day dawns and the morning star rises in your hearts" (2 Peter 1:19) and Jesus' description of himself as "the bright morning star" (Revelation 22:16).

The fig tree

Reference to the sign of the coming of the Son of Man is followed immediately by the parable of the fig tree. This is no mere coincidence. The fact that in all three records of the Olivet Prophecy the parable of the fig tree follows immediately after the reference to the return of Christ is significant, and its significance comes out particularly clearly in the Luke record:

"'Now when these things begin to take place, straighten up and raise your heads, because your redemption is drawing near.' And he told them a parable: 'Look at the fig tree, and all the trees. As soon as they come out in leaf, you see for yourselves and know that the summer is already near. So also, when you see these things taking place, you know that the kingdom of God is near.'" (Luke 21:28-31)

Only a short time before the Lord uttered these words on the Mount of Olives his disciples had seen their Lord curse a fig tree which withered immediately (Matthew 21:19,20). The fig tree clearly represented the faithless nation of Israel which failed to bring forth the fruit of repentance. It is likely that this incident also took place on the Mount of Olives, for the Lord and the disciples were on their way from Bethany to Jerusalem at the time (verse 18). Perhaps the disciples could see the withered tree as Jesus now spoke of a time when a fig tree should shoot forth new growth.

Israel was in the process of rejecting its Messiah and so the nation would be rejected. But the parable of the fig tree confirmed that, just as Jerusalem's treading down by the Gentiles would not last forever, a day would come when Israel's independence would be restored. The fig tree would revive at the time appointed. So it was that in 1948 the fig tree sent forth new leaves, at a time when many other trees also were sprouting new growth. Perhaps the other trees represent the many other nations which in the middle of the twentieth century attained to independence at about the same time that Israel revived.

Israel's revival confirms that the Son of Man is near. As our Lord said: "When all this is beginning to take place, grieve no longer. Lift up your heads, because your deliverance is drawing near" (Weymouth). We must take heed of the parable of the fig tree and the message of the Olivet Prophecy and "watch". The record of the prophecy in Luke 21 concludes with words which must always have been relevant but which seem especially appropriate for those who seek to serve their Lord in the twenty-first century:

"But watch yourselves lest your hearts be weighed down with dissipation ('self-indulgence', Weymouth) and drunkenness and cares of this life, and that day come upon you suddenly like a trap. For it will come upon all who dwell on the face of the whole earth. But stay awake at all times, praying that you may have strength to escape all these things that are going to take place, and to stand before the Son of Man."

(Luke 21:34-36)

ADDENDUM ON NATURAL CATASTROPHES AT THE TIME OF THE END

The Swiss Reinsurance Company in Zurich maintains extensive data on natural catastrophes. Some of the data is available only to clients, but a summary of global events is published on its website. The increasing intensity of natural events reflects in the economic cost and, with the costs of past events adjusted to current values, 2011 was the most costly year to date for disasters.

"In terms of economic losses, natural catastrophes and man-made disasters cost society over US$370 billion in 2011, the highest amount ever recorded, versus US$226 billion in 2010. The historic earthquake in Japan alone caused at least US$210 billion in damage."[7]

The increasing intensity of storms and hurricanes was noted in 2005 and has been verified by subsequent events:

"For the first time ever [2005], three hurricanes attained category 5, the highest on the Saffir-Simpson scale ... The increase in hurricane losses is related to the warm phase of 'Atlantic multidecadal oscillation' (AMO) in the North Atlantic. This warm phase started in 1995 and is expected to last for another 10 to 30 years. Given such climatological conditions, propitious to windstorms, the above-average hurricane activity can be expected to continue, entailing more intense hurricanes."[8]

Several catastrophic earthquakes occurred in 2010 and 2011 with intensities described as:

"From a seismological point of view, the Haiti and New Zealand events [of 2010] were similar. Both had a moment magnitude (Mw) of 7.0, and each produced a similar amount of seismic energy, thought to be the equivalent of 475 kilotonnes of explosives. Both events also exposed roughly 1,000 km^2 of land to severe shaking for roughly one minute. By comparison, the Chile event released roughly 500 times the energy of the Haiti event. It was also 500 times more powerful than the New Zealand event, subjecting an area of roughly 100,000 km^2 to severe shaking for up to three minutes ... A significant trend has been noted on the exposure side: population growth and higher population density, especially in urban areas, exposes more people to a single damaging earthquake. Moreover, many of the rapidly growing urban areas with high population densities are located in seismically active areas (e.g., Istanbul, Mexico City, Jakarta, Manila, Tokyo). As a result, the probability of earthquakes with a high death toll continuously increases, although the seismic threat itself remains unchanged."[9]

---

7 *sigma* magazine No. 2/2012 of Swiss Reinsurance Company, www.swissre.com/sigma

8 *sigma* magazine No. 2/2006.
9 *sigma* magazine No..1/2011.

Photo: Gabriel Goh – Wikimedia Commons

Earthquake damage, Christchurch, NZ.

The 2011 earthquake in the city of Christchurch caused immense damage and the loss of many lives. The data above establishes that should an earthquake of even greater intensity, such as in Chile in 2010, occur in a densely populated or heavily industrialised area the damage and death-toll is likely to reach levels never seen in the world's history. Readers must reach their own conclusions on whether this data is sufficient for establishing a link with the Olivet Prophecy, but we consider that it is at least a strong indicator that we could be living in the time frame spoken of in the prophecy.

Another publication of Swiss Reinsurance, (described as a handbook but actually encyclopaedic in size and extent of information), includes data identifying that high seismic activity can occur in various regions after long periods of inactivity. The activity is attributed to the release of energy from up to 500 years of energy accumulation, but the timing of the phases cannot be predicted. High seismic activity is characterised by a large number of great earthquakes in all seismic regions. Allowing some margin for the inaccuracy of records, periods of high seismic activity occurred for several decades from AD 360, 740, 1031 and 1650 with the last

several-decade phase commencing around 1897. It remains to be seen if the activity in recent years is the beginning of a new phase of high activity.

Bible students are likely to be intrigued by the following observation about the phasing of activity in a region of particular interest:

"The eastern section of the Mediterranean appears to have been rather quiet for a long time. In particular there have been no reports of earthquakes which proved their great magnitude by tsunami or by destruction over a large area and perceptible over a considerable range. This was not always so. Even if historical reports require a very conservative approach, and not even the years given are to be trusted, it appears that the events recorded were substantially more severe than those witnessed during the last few centuries."[10]

The information provided here is a brief summation of an extensive amount of data and it would be unwise to draw definitive conclusions. However, it raises for consideration the possibility that the many years of minimal seismic activity in the eastern section of the Mediterranean may be a period of energy accumulation, the release of which will be revealed in the splitting of the Mount of Olives at the return of Christ (Zechariah 14:4).

Further Reading

Brother Tony Benson, *Stormy Wind Fulfilling His Word* (the place of weather, volcanoes and earthquakes in fulfilling Bible prophecy).

10 Swiss Reinsurance Company, *Earthquakes and Volcanic Eruptions* (1992), page 102.

16

ARMAGEDDON

ARMAGEDDON is one of those highly emotive names with which many people are very familiar but which often is misunderstood. We sometimes see Armageddon used in newspapers or in popular novels and movies, but many people who use the name have only a vague idea of what it means.

Armageddon refers to events in the future which will take place after the return of Christ and the judgement seat. Why, then, should the details relating to Armageddon matter to us? Is this all just an interesting theological bypath of no practical value to us? Certainly not! Principally there are two reasons why this subject is important to us as the servants of God:

1. It provides an insight as to God's estimation of the kingdom of men and that should warn us against being seduced by the world around us; and

2. The signs of the times give us every reason to expect that this day is near, and a clear picture of the judgements about to be unleashed will be a powerful stimulus to prepare for that great and terrible day before it is too late.

The name Armageddon occurs once only in the Bible, in Revelation 16, within the context of the sixth vial (ESV, "bowl"). The vials are a series of visions about events leading up to and including the return of Christ. Armageddon is part of the sixth vial. This is important because Christ returns while the sixth vial is being worked out.

Although the name Armageddon is used only once, the events to which it relates are discussed in many prophecies and there are remarkable similarities between those prophecies and the matters symbolised in the sixth vial.

"The sixth angel poured out his bowl on the great river Euphrates, and its water was dried up, to prepare the way for the kings from the east. And I saw, coming out of the mouth of the dragon and out of the mouth of the beast and out of the mouth of the false prophet, three unclean spirits like frogs. For they are demonic spirits, performing signs, who go abroad to the kings of the whole world, to assemble them for battle on the great day of God the Almighty. ('Behold, I am coming like a thief! Blessed is the one who stays awake, keeping his garments on, that he may not go about naked and be seen exposed!') And they assembled them at the place that in Hebrew is called Armageddon."
(Revelation 16:12-16)

God gathers the nations

God directs the work of the frog-like spirits to gather the nations to the "battle on that great day of God the Almighty" in verse 14. The nations gather at Armageddon in verse 16. But the verse in the middle is the most important one for us. What we are meant to understand from the way verse 15 is inserted into the text of the sixth vial is that while the events of that vial are being worked out, but before they culminate in that "battle on the great day of God the Almighty", the Lord Jesus Christ

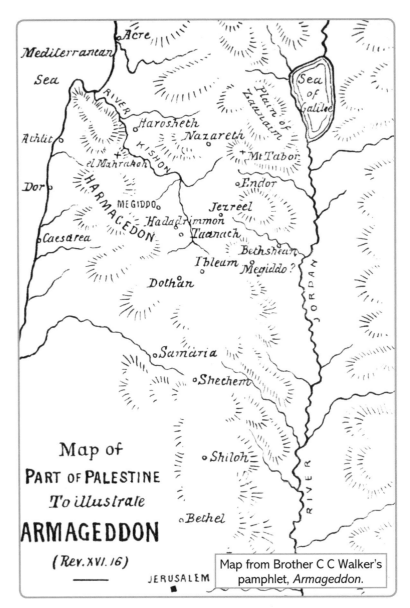

Map of
PART OF PALESTINE
To illustrate
ARMAGEDDON
(Rev. XVI. 16)

Map from Brother C C Walker's pamphlet, *Armageddon*.

returns to the earth. The frog-like spirits create the unstable environment that precedes the nations gathering together to invade Israel. It is then that God intervenes with Armageddon.

Armageddon a place

Verse 16 says Armageddon is a place, not an event. The battle of verse 14 is an event or perhaps even a campaign, but Armageddon is a place. Where is Armageddon?

All we know from verse 16 is that it is a Hebrew name. If we were told something were to occur at a place with a Russian name, you would automatically assume that it is likely to take place in Russia. In this case, the fact the name is Hebrew suggests it is in Israel. That, of course, should be no surprise. We have seen in the earlier chapters that Israel is the primary geographical focus of the promises which are at the heart of the Gospel and, therefore, of the events related to the return of Christ and the establishment of the kingdom of God.

Armageddon is not a place name easily located in Israel. In the RV, *Rotherham's Emphatic Translation*, and the *Bullinger Bible* margin, the name Armageddon is rendered as Har-Magedon. Brother C C Walker in his pamphlet entitled *Armageddon* supports that rendering.[1]

Brother John Thomas also supports this form of the name in his last writing on the subject. In *The Christadelphian*, volume 9 (1872), there appears the text of a partially completed Bible Dictionary, the project on which Brother Thomas had been engaged when he died. One of the entries he had completed was on Armageddon, and Brother Thomas noted that one early manuscript favoured the reading of Harmagedon[2] (he favoured this different spelling). Possibly this is a reference to the Codex Siniaticus that had recently been brought to light and which captured the interest of students at that time.

Whatever the facts about the manuscript, this version of the name has some support and it does suggest a solution to the question of Armageddon's location. Brother Walker suggests Har-Magedon in Hebrew would translate as the mountain of Megiddo.

In this map (see facing page) from Brother Walker's pamphlet he suggests Har-Magedon is the range of hills running south west from Mount Carmel and to the south of the Kishon river. The plain to the north of this range, the Valley of Jezreel, is an area that throughout history has been the site of many decisive battles. It includes the site of Megiddo.

The prophets present Jerusalem as the focus of conflict at the time of the end (e.g., Zechariah 12:1-3). It would seem appropriate, therefore, that Armageddon, associated as it is with "the battle on that great day of God the Almighty", should have some connection to Jerusalem. Having recognized the link between 'Harmagedon' and the area around Megiddo, Brother Thomas went on to describe the broader region the battle would involve:

> "Harmagedon, then, may be defined, as being bounded by the Mediterranean and the Sea of Chinnereth, or Tiberias, on the east and west; and extending to the mountain of the glory of the holy, which is Jerusalem; and therefore includes the Valley of Jezreel, and the Valley of Jehoshaphat ..."[3]

Armageddon rather than Har-Magedon

While Har-Magedon is preferred by a few translations, most support the rendering of the KJV and the ESV and adopt "Armageddon". That name, when translated from Hebrew, is thought by many to give a meaning suggestive of another line of thought altogether.

The interesting thing, however, is this second line of thought leads to similar conclusions as those which can be drawn from the alternative rendering, although they differ in terms of geography.

It is the view of many scholars that the name Armageddon signifies 'a heap of sheaves in a valley for judgement'. This view is supported by a range of Christadelphian authors, including Brother Thomas in *Eureka*,[4] and Brother Whittaker in his book on Revelation.[5] Under this approach, which recognises that Revelation is a book of symbol, Armageddon is viewed as a place of divine judgement, the place where God gathers the nations for judgement.

1 Brother C C Walker, *Armageddon* (published 1904), page 4.
2 *The Christadelphian*, Volume 9 (1872), pages 294-297.
3 *ibid*, page 295. A similar description is given in *Exposition of Daniel*, page 97.
4 Brother John Thomas, *Eureka*, Volume 3, pages 603,604.
5 Brother Harry Whittaker, *Revelation, A Biblical Approach*, page 202.

Armageddon in the Old Testament

Many of the figures and imagery in Revelation are drawn from the Old Testament. When we think of Armageddon as meaning 'a heap of sheaves in a valley for judgement', we can find in the Old Testament considerable support for this concept. In references sprinkled throughout the prophets there is imagery and language similar to that used in the sixth vial. The imagery used in Revelation has been drawn from these places. These include Isaiah 66:15-18, which is a clear statement that God will gather the nations to a terrible, divinely inflicted judgement, and Zephaniah 3:8, where the prophet uses similarly graphic language about God gathering the nations for judgement.

Daniel 2 contains an element of the imagery of Revelation 16 in a chapter which is the foundation stone for understanding God's prophetic plan with the nations. Even though the vision in Daniel 2 uses a different metaphor for its basis, there is a link to the imagery of Revelation 16:

> "Then the iron, the clay, the bronze, the silver, and the gold, all together were broken in pieces, and became like the chaff of the summer threshing floors; and the wind carried them away, so that not a trace of them could be found. But the stone that struck the image became a great mountain and filled the whole earth."
>
> (Daniel 2:35)

A metal image pulverised by a rock would be reduced to metal filings. But in a rare mixing of metaphors the dust of this ground-up metallic image is transformed into the chaff of the threshing floor, taking up the image of grain being threshed in judgement. The prophet Micah takes up this thought in more detail:

> "Now many nations are assembled against you, saying, 'Let her be defiled, and let our eyes gaze upon Zion.' But they do not know the thoughts of the LORD;[6] they do not understand his plan, that he has gathered them *as sheaves to the threshing floor*. Arise and *thresh*, O daughter of Zion, for I will make your horn iron, and I will make your hoofs bronze; you shall beat in pieces many peoples; and shall devote their gain to the LORD, their wealth to the Lord of the whole earth."
>
> (Micah 4:11-13)

A similar picture using the same imagery is presented in Isaiah 41 where God speaks of intervening to deliver His people, and using them as instruments for judgement of the nations:

> "Fear not, for I am with you; be not dismayed, for I am your God; I will strengthen you, I will help you, I will uphold you with my righteous right hand. Behold, all who are incensed against you shall be put to shame and confounded; those who strive against you shall be as nothing and shall perish. You shall seek those who contend with you, but you shall not find them; those who war against you shall be as nothing at all. For I, the LORD your God, hold your right hand; it is I who say to you, 'Fear not, I am the one who helps you.' Fear not, you worm Jacob, you men of Israel! I am the one who helps you, declares the LORD; your Redeemer is the Holy One of Israel. Behold, I make of you a threshing sledge, new, sharp, and having teeth; you shall thresh the mountains and crush them, and you shall make the hills like chaff; you shall winnow them, and the wind shall carry them away, and the tempest shall scatter them. And you shall rejoice in the LORD; in the Holy One of Israel you shall glory."
>
> (Isaiah 41:10-16)

6 Brother John Thomas, *Eureka*, Volume 3, page 603.

Armageddon and the Valley of Jehoshaphat

Concepts associated with the sixth vial are a recurring motif in the prophets, and this becomes especially obvious in Joel 3, a chapter laden with echoes of the sixth vial. Joel describes an invasion of the land of Israel in the last days. In verse 2 God gathers all nations to judgement:

> "I will *gather all the nations* and bring them down to the Valley of Jehoshaphat. And I will enter into judgment with them there, on behalf of my people and my heritage Israel, because they have scattered them among the nations and have divided up my land." (Joel 3:2)

So as in Ezekiel 38, Zephaniah 3, Isaiah 66 and Revelation 16, God brings the nations to the land of Israel for judgement. Joel has further words that echo the terms of the sixth vial:

> "Proclaim this among the nations: Consecrate for war; stir up the mighty men. Let all the men of war draw near; let them come up. Beat your plowshares into swords, and your pruning-hooks into spears; let the weak say, 'I am a warrior.' Hasten and come, all you surrounding nations, and gather yourselves there. Bring down your warriors, O LORD." (verses 9-11)

Here are words that speak of political instability arising from people asserting their independence. Even little, weak nations such as those that now abound in the area formerly occupied by the Ottoman Empire are seen to be arming themselves to the teeth to assert their authority. The prophet portrays a situation where war is imminent. In verse 1 it is Judah and Jerusalem that is at the heart of the conflict. And in verse 12 God intervenes to judge the nations:

> "Let the nations stir themselves up and come up to the Valley of Jehoshaphat; for there I will sit to judge all the surrounding nations."

As Israel's capital, and as the city that is at the heart of tensions in the Middle East, it is likely to be the focus of the invaders' attention. But curiously they are told to come up to a valley; normally you would come up to a hill and go down to a valley.

The valley to which they are summoned is the Valley of Jehoshaphat. Where is this valley? An ancient tradition dating from the time of Eusebius in about the fourth century identifies the Valley of Jehoshaphat as the Kidron Valley between Jerusalem and the Mount of Olives. Brother Thomas favoured that view, but the source of the theory is a thousand years after Joel wrote, and there are no contemporary records, in particular from within scripture, which provide support.

Perhaps Eusebius or his contemporaries linked the name with Jerusalem because of other prophecies such as Daniel 11 and Zechariah 14 that speak of a final conflict being centred on Jerusalem. While there is some logic in that assumption, there are several reasons for concluding that Joel did not intend to refer to a specific geographic spot. The name Jehoshaphat means 'the judgment of Yahweh'. Like the name Armageddon, almost certainly it is a symbolic place name. The prophet might well have used this form to remind his readers of Judah's remarkable deliverance from the invading armies of Ammon, Moab and Edom which occurred only about fifty years before in the days of King Jehoshaphat, as recorded in 2 Chronicles 20. In that chapter it is not clear where this deliverance was effected (although it might have been at Tekoa), so it is vain to try to pin it down to a specific valley such as Kidron.

The name Jeho-shaphat includes the word *shaphet* which also occurs in Joel 3:12 (Hebrew, 'to judge') and this supports the conclusion the name should be interpreted symbolically. Jehoshaphat is a play on words. Joel probably is referring to a general place of judgement rather than a specific valley. In any case, the vast host involved in this invasion would never fit into one valley in this region, and certainly not into the extremely tight Kidron Valley.

The parallels with the sixth vial are already quite strong, and they become stronger yet in verses 13 and 14:

> "Put in the sickle, for the harvest is ripe. Go in, tread, for the wine press is full. The vats overflow, for their evil is great. Multitudes, multitudes, in the valley of decision! For the day of the LORD is near in the valley of decision."

Verse 13 speaks of judgement of a vast multitude, and does so in terms of a harvest. In verse 14 the multitude is described as being in a valley of decision. The Hebrew word translated "decision" carries the idea of a sharp implement, a rasping tool used in the harvest. In Isaiah 28:27 this word is rendered as "threshing sledge" which was a structure with sharp stones embedded in its underside. It would be dragged across harvested grain to cut the grain from its stalk. While the word can mean 'decision', this is the only place where it is so translated in the KJV; probably the idea is more one of judgement or sentencing in this "day of the LORD". The multitude is being portrayed, in the terms of Armageddon, as sheaves gathered in a valley for threshing.

Olivet Prophecy

In our Lord's prophecy given on the Mount of Olives immediately prior to his arrest and crucifixion, Jesus drew attention to the return of Jews to the land as the great sign that his return to the earth would be imminent. Having prophesied of the impending destruction of Jerusalem (Luke 21:20-24), which was fulfilled when the Romans besieged and

View towards the Mount of Olives from Jerusalem

© NilsZ – fotolia.com

ultimately sacked the city in AD 70, he went on to speak of the restoration of the Jewish nation.

Using the parable of the fig tree, Jesus describes the rebirth of an independent Jewish state:

> "Look at the fig tree, and all the trees. As soon as they come out in leaf, you see for yourselves and know that the summer is already near. So also, when you see these things taking place, you know that the kingdom of God is near."
>
> (Luke 21:29-31)

The budding of the fig tree signifies the rebirth of Israel, a process which we have seen in early chapters took place over many decades and which in some senses is continuing to unfold. If we can see in the image of the fig tree a reference to Israel it may be valid to interpret the phrase, "and all the trees" as a reference to other non-Jewish nations which have appeared in the earth at about the same time (as suggested previously), especially in the Middle East following the drying up of the Euphrates. It may be significant that many of these new nations are exceptionally aggressive in their relationship with Israel, which is consistent with the picture presented in other prophecies that relate to this time.

Consistent with the warning of Revelation 16:15, the Lord's conclusion to this prophecy is one which applies to the saints in all ages:

> "But stay awake at all times, praying that you may have strength to escape all these things that are going to take place, and to stand before the Son of Man." (Luke 21:36)

So what is Armageddon?

Armageddon is a symbolic name for the place of judgement on the nations when Christ returns to establish God's throne. The centre of at least the initial conflict will be an Israel to which many Jews have returned from dispersion among the nations. The invader will cover the land, appear triumphant, but will meet his end through divine intervention. In that day of the battle of God Almighty the people will be delivered by God as they were in the days of Gideon and Deborah and Barak. The nations will be brought as sheaves into a valley for judgement and the chaff will be dispersed to the winds.

Recognising the certain and devastating judgements which are destined to be wrought upon the kingdom of men should encourage us to stand apart from a world which soon will perish forever. Let us have the wisdom to watch events as they unfold, encouraged that God is in control and that He will bring them to a climax soon when He intervenes to establish His kingdom. And as we watch, let us prepare for that great day by walking worthy of the calling wherewith we have been called.[7]

---

7 See Chapter 15 for more extensive commentary on the Olivet Prophecy.

17

WHERE IS THE PROMISE OF HIS COMING?

JEREMIAH prophesied to a world which, like our own, was on the eve of the outpouring of God's judgement. He warned the people of his day that there were those who would not remain faithful:

> "Thus says the LORD: 'Stand by the roads, and look, and ask for the ancient paths, where the good way is; and walk in it, and find rest for your souls. But they said, "We will not walk in it." I set watchmen over you, saying, "Pay attention to the sound of the trumpet!" But they said, "We will not pay attention".'" (Jeremiah 6:16,17)

It is significant that those who became ambivalent and even hostile towards the "ancient paths" also failed to heed the signs of the times and the warnings of the watchmen such as Jeremiah. The prophet went on to declare that those who disregarded the warnings would face disaster – a disaster which would in fact be the "fruit of their (own) devices (KJV, thoughts)":

> "Therefore hear, O nations, and know, O congregation, what will happen to them. Hear, O earth; behold, I am bringing disaster upon this people, the fruit of their devices, because they have not paid attention to my words; and as for my law, they have rejected it. What use to me is frankincense that comes from Sheba, or sweet cane from a distant land? Your burnt offerings are not acceptable, nor your sacrifices pleasing to me. Therefore thus says the LORD: 'Behold, I will lay before this people stumbling blocks against which they shall stumble; fathers

and sons together, neighbour and friend shall perish.'" (verses 18-21)

The call to walk in "ancient paths" does not mean that procedures should never be varied, and instead means that God's instructions are to be complied with and not changed through disbelief or compromise with the world. This is a challenge to all believers living in this present world that has essentially rejected belief in scriptural teachings. The root cause of the lack of respect for "the ancient paths" and disinterest in the signs of the times in Jeremiah's day was their failure to give attention to the word of God. They were engaged in elaborate religious activity but it was in vain because it was not in accord with God's word; worse still, it was dangerous because it distracted them from "the sound of the trumpet". We should heed Jeremiah's warning and ensure that we walk in the way of life with our ears alert to the trumpet call. There were forces which threatened to distract the faithful from the way of life in Jeremiah's day, and again in the first century. It is not surprising, therefore, that in the last days immediately prior to the return of Christ brothers and sisters should experience similar forces which threaten to undermine their faith in God's word.

A more sure word of prophecy

The Apostle Peter wrote to encourage brothers and sisters in the years immediately prior to the siege and fall of Jerusalem in AD 70. This was a tumultuous watershed for the brotherhood as it marked the final dissolution of the Mosaic system which, in the years since the crucifixion and resurrection of the Lord, had continued to operate side by side with the emerging Christian community.

In his second letter Peter appears to be addressing Gentile believers in particular because he refers to his readers as "those who have obtained a faith of equal standing with ours by the righteousness of our God and Saviour Jesus Christ" (2 Peter 1:1). He goes on in verse 4 to remind these Gentile believers that the great promises to the patriarchs are at the heart of the faith they had embraced: God "has granted to us his precious and very great promises, so that through them you may become partakers of the divine nature."

Having exhorted the believers to continue developing in the faith (verses 5-7), Peter encourages his readers to remember the key elements of their faith (verse 12). In fact remembrance is a key word in the letter. He reminds the brothers and sisters of the encouragement he had drawn as an eyewitness of the transfiguration (verses 16,17) and goes on to point out that this faith-sustaining manifestation was complemented by the prophetic word:

"And we have something more sure, the prophetic word, to which you will do well to pay attention as to a lamp shining in a dark place, until the day dawns and the morning star rises in your hearts." (verse 19)

Drawing upon Peter's words in this passage, in the opening section of *Elpis Israel*, Part Third, Brother John Thomas makes a clear statement about the value of prophecy in the life of the believer:

"This revelation (i.e., the prophetic word) is made that His people's faith may be confirmed and enlarged, and that in every generation they may know the times and seasons to which they stand related. Knowing the signs, they are enabled to discern the times; and while

consternation and dismay cause men's hearts to fail they are courageous, and rejoice in perceiving the approach of the Kingdom of God. This is the proper use of the prophetic word."[1]

Prophecy was never intended to make the saints political commentators nor make it possible for them accurately to predict the future machinations of the nations. God's intent was that it should shine in the darkness of a world that knows not God and help the saints to walk in the path of life, as Peter says:

"This is now the second letter that I am writing to you, beloved. In both of them I am stirring up your sincere mind by way of reminder, that you should remember the predictions of the holy prophets and the commandment of the Lord and Saviour through your apostles … You therefore, beloved, knowing this beforehand, take care that you are not carried away with the error of lawless people and lose your own stability."

(2 Peter 3:1,2,17)

In *Elpis Israel* Brother Thomas lists four benefits that flow from heeding Peter's advice in relation to the study of prophecy:

1. "that our faith may grow and be strengthened;

2. that our affections be detached from the fleeting present, and set more firmly on things to come;

3. that our minds may be fortified against error; and

4. that we may be prepared to meet the Lord as those who have kept their garments, and shall not be put to shame."[2]

These benefits have been available to students of prophecy in all ages. Daniel provides a case

1 Brother John Thomas, *Elpis Israel*, 14th edition, page 323.
2 *ibid*, page 324.

study of one faithful brother who benefited in the ways Peter describes from his study of prophecy:

> "In the first year of (Darius') reign, I, Daniel, perceived in the books the number of years that, according to the word of the LORD to Jeremiah the prophet, must pass before the end of the desolations of Jerusalem, namely, seventy years. Then I turned my face to the Lord God, seeking him by prayer and pleas for mercy with fasting and sackcloth and ashes."   (Daniel 9:2,3)

There can be no doubt that Daniel's faith was strengthened by his appreciation of prophecy and this must have helped him to resist the allurements available to him in Babylon. Those who follow Daniel's example today can be similarly strengthened in the face of modern forces which might otherwise prove destructive of their faith.

Where is the promise of his coming?

We live in a cynical age which is hostile to a simple faith in God's word. Although the words of Peter were written in the first instance to strengthen the faith of brothers and sisters living at the end of the Mosaic dispensation, their divine inspiration ensure that they are relevant to those who live at the end of the Christian dispensation (when the times of the Gentiles are being fulfilled):

> "... scoffers will come in the last days with scoffing, following their own sinful desires. They will say, 'Where is the promise of his coming? For ever since the fathers fell asleep, all things are continuing as they were from the beginning of creation.'"   (2 Peter 3:2-4)

The motivation of the scoffers is revealed in verse 3 – they are driven by sinful desires. Modern sceptics often link their rejection of the Bible as the inspired word of God with a rejection of its moral teaching. Such people are unable to conceive of divine intervention and are confident that the world will continue unaltered and unchallenged.

Peter goes on to show that "they deliberately overlook" the evidence of creation and also the judgement meted out in Noah's flood (verses 5,6). Rejection of these matters is the cornerstone of the sceptic's faith today. Modern "scoffers" do not just call into question God's prophetic plan, but also are dismissive of the evidence of creation. Instead they embrace a blind, irrational, barren commitment to evolution. They deride any who proclaim faith in creation as ill-educated, deluded and naive.

Faithful brothers and sisters should not allow their faith to be troubled by the arrogant assertions of modern scoffers. Yes, our Lord's return has been anticipated by the servants of the Lord in every age yet still we wait, but this will be seen as a problem only by those who fail to appreciate that an eternal God is not bound by the petty time frames against which men often judge events. There is a good reason why the Lord's return has been delayed, and we may be very grateful for that delay:

> "The Lord is not slow to fulfil his promise as some count slowness, but is patient towards you, not wishing that any should perish, but that all should reach repentance."   (verse 9)

The Lord's delay creates an opportunity for more to be called to the hope of Israel. And the Lord's delay also means that those who have been called have an opportunity to consider their ways and prepare for his coming:

> "But the day of the Lord will come like a thief, and then the heavens will pass away with a roar, and the heavenly bodies will be burned up and dissolved, and the earth and the works that are done on it will be exposed. Since all these things are thus to be dissolved, what sort of people ought you to be in lives of holiness

and godliness, waiting for and hastening the coming of the day of God, because of which the heavens will be set on fire and dissolved, and the heavenly bodies will melt as they burn! But according to his promise we are waiting for new heavens and a new earth in which righteousness dwells. Therefore, beloved, since you are waiting for these, be diligent to be found by him without spot or blemish, and at peace. And count the patience of our Lord as salvation …"

(verses 10-15)

We do not know the day or the hour when our Lord shall return, but we may be confident from the signs of the times, especially those relating to the natural seed of Abraham and the land of Israel, that we live in the era of his return. The Olivet Prophecy was intended to instil in us a commitment to watching both the signs of the times and our own way of life.

We were once "alienated from the commonwealth of Israel and strangers to the covenants of promise, having no hope and without God in the world" (Ephesians 2:12), but through the grace extended to us in Christ Jesus our Lord we have embraced the glorious hope of Israel. Let us not allow the scoffers of a godless age to distract us from these wonderful promises. Let us not be downcast by the taunts of men who are wise in the wisdom of this world, but ignorant (willingly so) of the hope that is revealed in the word of God and which is being worked out in the nations as we wait for the return of our Lord. Let us be alive to the wonder of God's unfolding plan and let us read it as if our life depends upon that reading – for in many ways it really does. Even so, Come, Lord Jesus!

Further Reading

Brother Islip Collyer, *Vox Dei – A Defence of Simple Faith*.
Brother Reg Carr, *A Goodly Heritage*, chapter 12.

APPENDIX

THE RELIGIOUS RIGHT

THE 'Religious Right'[1] is an informal coalition of religious groups that has grown into a major political force since the beginnings of the modern evangelical movement in the 1970s. In eighteenth century England those who questioned the doctrines and practices of the mainstream churches were called evangelicals, but its modern format developed primarily in the United States and spread throughout the Christian world. There are lessons for us in this growth and there are challenges.

The large numbers of people professing to be 'born again', the simple focus on 'Jesus saves' and an entertainment style of worship has had an impact on the majority of churches and we are not immune to this influence. When coupled with the fact that some evangelical groups have discovered, and are now profiling, prophecies relating to Israel, we can see why questions have been raised about the need for Christadelphians to retain our separateness from other churches. There may be merit in us reviewing practices that have been in place for many years but change solely because of an external influence that appears to be exciting needs careful thought. Reflection on background information about this new movement might assist in developing our thoughts on whether it is beneficial or detrimental to true faith and the method by which we worship our Heavenly Father.

1 This Appendix arises from the reference to the Religious Right in Chapter 11, "U.S. Presidents and Israel", on page 110.

Because of the political influence of the Religious Right a number of political commentators have analysed the growth of the movement and we can use these secular views to reduce potential bias from a religious perspective. In his review of the Bush family, the U.S. political and economic commentator, Kevin Phillips, states:

"Between 1960 and 2000, the membership of the evangelical Southern Baptist Convention jumped from ten million to seventeen million, while the Pentecostal churches soared from under two million to almost twelve million. On the more sedate side of the ledger, the mainline Episcopalians dropped from three-and-a-half million to two million, and the United Methodists slumped from more than ten million to under eight million ... Strict fundamentalist-type churches gained; doctrinally loose mainline churches – pillars of the old Protestant Republican establishment – shrank ... Abortion, pornography, and gay rights topped the concerns of the Pentecostal clergy. Presbyterian ministers, by contrast, prioritized hunger and poverty, civil rights, and the environment."[2]

While these observations tell us something about maintaining correct doctrines, or at least appropriate Christian morals, rather than engaging in social issues, the matter of the purported large number of members is perplexing. An interesting observation on this aspect is provided by the

2 Kevin Phillips, *American Dynasty*, page 216.

American journalist and author, Craig Unger, in his political review of George W Bush's presidency:

"According to a *Time*/CNN poll from 2002, 59 per cent of Americans believe the events in the Book of Revelation will take place. In addition, a January 2007 study by the Barna Group, a Christian research firm, found that there are as many as 84 million adult evangelicals in the United States – about 38 per cent of the population.

"Exactly what such surveys mean, however, is a different story. The same Barna Group poll, for example, found that when a 'theological filter' of nine rigorous questions was used to find out if respondents were *really* 'evangelical,' only 8 per cent of the adult population – 18 million people rather than 84 million – passed the test. Consequently, the actual number of evangelicals varies widely from one survey to another, and terms such as 'evangelical,' 'fundamentalist,' and 'born-again Christian' are open to a variety of interpretations. Perhaps most important, many millions of evangelicals belong to more than 200,000 churches, most of which are run by pastors who belong to conservative political organizations that make sure their flocks vote as a hard-right Republican bloc."[3]

The alleged numbers of evangelicals, even at the lower range, is still quite high and has caused some in the brotherhood to see merit in their ways. Again the observations of Craig Unger may help us to see what drives the movement.

"Between 1976 and 1998, the number of Americans who defined themselves as born-again evangelicals went from 34 to 47 per cent. The United States was defying the widely held assumption that societies become more secular as they become more modern. Astoundingly, postwar baby boomers, the generation ... dominated by the sixties counterculture, were more likely than any other demographic group to be born-again Christians. Moreover, throughout the seventies and eighties, evangelicalism, which had been largely a middle and lower-middle class phenomenon, became increasingly acceptable among the more affluent social classes. None of which would have happened unless the evangelical church was able to fill real or perceived needs for tens of millions of Americans ... In a world of bland suburban and exurban outposts and cookie-cutter shopping malls filled with fast-food outlets and faceless chain stores, the old fashioned, homespun, small-town *Leave it to Beaver* American culture had given way to the anonymity of the mass market. In a landscape ravaged by such alienation and isolation, the evangelical church increasingly provided both grand spectacles and a desperately needed source of community.

Millions of long-haired youths attended services each Sunday because church officials created an elaborate, fully developed evangelical counterculture that utilized all the marketing tools of the modern world they abhorred. In effect, they were acting like MTV marketing execs for Jesus, creating Jesus Nation. Christian rockers brought evangelical lyrics to secular tunes."[4]

These observations are based on the American scene where the movement began and, although that culture has not transmitted in full, the general style and influence is now worldwide. We can be thankful that there are such people for they can, to some extent, ameliorate the excesses of a

---

3 Unger, page 19.

4 *ibid*, page 85.

secular world but we must also see the shortfalls in their belief systems. Many evangelicals now acknowledge the role of Israel in God's plan and look to a Second Coming, but such beliefs are overlaid upon conventional doctrines such as heaven-going, the devil, the trinity and, especially in the U.S., the rapture. The emphasis on entertainment-style worship has had wide ramifications and, whilst there are no absolute scriptural directives on worship styles, the concept of mimicking an entertainment-driven world is contrary to the directive "to be sober-minded, dignified, self-controlled, sound in faith, in love, and in steadfastness" (Titus 2:2).

Of particular concern is the political, nationalistic and militaristic outlook that is integral to the movement. Doctrinal correctness is most important, but ultimately it is God who determines the purity of doctrine needed for a relationship with Him. There is, however, no debating that we are called to step aside from this world and to refrain from engagement in politics and military action, either as a participant or a supporter of the concept. There is a huge gulf between those, like Christadelphians, who look to Jesus Christ to deal with God's enemies and those who believe they are entitled to destroy men and women perceived to be 'evil'. One needs, therefore, to think very carefully about the influence of aspects of the evangelical movement in our brotherhood.

The movement is heavily influenced by 'neoconservatives', an expression applied to those, of either a secular or religious persuasion, who believe that the Western world faces a cultural crisis and that action needs to be taken to stem the downwards trend. Neoconservatives do not all share precisely the same opinion but commonly will oppose extensive government welfare, support free markets and assertively promote democracy and engagement in international affairs for the benefit of the West including by military means.

The *Encyclopedia Britannica* entry on the neoconservative ideology states that some supporters consider that the decline in values and religion can be traced to the eighteenth century European Enlightenment, whilst others see the counterculture of the 1960s as a key cause. The commentary continues with observations on causes of the rejection of previously held values:

"Neoconservatives agree with religious conservatives that the current crisis is due in part to the declining influence of religion in people's lives. People without a sense of something larger than themselves, something transcendent and eternal, are apt to turn to mindless entertainment – including drugs and alcohol – and to act selfishly and irresponsibly."[5]

Neoconservative ideology is generally contrary to Christadelphian belief but readers will, in all probability, concur with the observation above which highlights to us the pressing need to maintain pure doctrine and pure lifestyles in a world intent on removing itself further and further from the ways of God. A continuing awareness of the greatness of the covenant relationship we have with our Heavenly Father and the nearness of the return of His Son will help us in keeping separate from the world.

Further Reading

Brother Alfred Nicholls, *The Evangelical Revival*, The Christadelphian, 1983.

---

5 www.britannica.com/neoconservatism

SCRIPTURE INDEX